Praise for **thepurplebook**®

"Move over, Yellow Pages!" —*Time*

"A roadmap for shopping the Internet"
—*O Magazine*

"The Bible of Online Shopping Guides"
—*Kirkus Reviews*

"Shopaholics, rejoice! Like the Yellow
Pages—but, well, purple—this book is witty
and comprehensive." —*Boston Herald*

"Think of it as a Google for shoppers…The
sleekly designed book brims with helpful
cross-references and hints for getting the
most out of an online shopping experience."
—*Publishers Weekly*

"A well-planned guidebook, much like the
popular dining directories compiled by
Zagat—only bigger." —*Los Angeles Times*

"A consumer haven."—Bookreporter.com

thepurplebook®
green

an eco-friendly online shopping guide

GREEN EDITION

Hillary Mendelsohn
and Ian Anderson

thepurplebook
green edition

Editor-in-chief & Founder
Hillary Mendelsohn

Co-Founder
Lawrence Butler

Co-Author
Ian Anderson

Art Director
Jerome Curchod

Technology Director
Christian Giangreco

Copyright © 2008 by thepurplebook LLC
All rights reserved.

thepurplebook is a registered trademark of thepurplebook LLC

First Edition: January 2008
10 9 8 7 6 5 4 3 2 1

ISBN-10: 0-9799266-1-0
ISBN-13: 978-0-9799266-1-7
LCCN: 2007906858

Cover design by Jerome Curchod
Interior design by Jerome Curchod
Printed in Canada

This book is dedicated to my children, Max and Gabriella, who are my inspiration for change. Looking at them, I see wonder, promise and hope. It is my wish, and this book's mission, that we all embrace our responsibility as a member of the community, Earth, and set forth a wonderful example for the generations to follow. Their future depends on us.

*

Small change adds up!

acknowledgments

There is no greater source of alternative energy than the amazing team that makes each edition of **thepurplebook** possible. Together, we have turned a good idea into a great business! Thank you for all you do and who you are.

Ian, it has been an honor to work with you all of these years, and I have never seen your talent shine brighter or greener than it does with this book! May our friendship be evergreen.

Larry, your support, friendship and belief in me and our vision is the tree that shelters and nurtures my spirit.

Jerome, your creativity continues to delight and inspire. You make us look good.

Christian, we depend on your technical genius and loyalty.

Jeffrey, you always find a way to help us to make it work.

Larry, I love having you represent thepurplebook! You have always been a mentor, confidant and dear friend.

None of this would be possible without each of you, nor would it be any fun. I count on your talent, your gifts and most of all your friendship, and I am truly grateful to have you all in my world.

foreword

Nearly forty years ago, Kermit the Frog famously sang the lyrics, "It's not that easy, bein' green." Who would have thought this catchy little song would now provide the inspiration for this latest edition of thepurplebook: the definitive guide to exceptional online shopping?

At first glance, internet technology and environmental-ism might not seem to go together. But in our past seven years of research, we have noticed a growing trend of web shops embracing the green lifestyle. Increasingly, the worlds of fashion, home construction, health, beauty and manufacturing have shown an interest in presenting eco-friendly alternatives to all the products we buy, and they are almost universally available online—if you know where to look.

thepurplebook has searched far and wide to find the internet's best Earth-friendly shops, and what we've found fills us with optimism, pride and wonder. Listed within this edition are the amazing results, a great variety of sites that prove saving the planet is something we can all do, without sacrificing quality, durability or style.

Today, with **thepurplebook** green edition showing the way, it is easy being green!

Sincerely,

Hillary

thepurplebook®
green

CONTENTS

Introduction

Unless you've been living in a cave for the past thirty years, you have been hearing about the perils of pollution and climate change, and how, if we don't change our ways, humankind's impact on the Earth could threaten our very existence. If you *have* been living in a cave, you probably aren't a big a part of the problem, so you don't really need to worry about it.

As for the rest of us, there's never been a better time than right now to go green. If you're reading this book, we're going to assume you've decided to do just that. Fantastic! We won't barrage you with catastrophic statistics, or fearful tales of our planet's imminent demise— even if scare tactics might sell more books. Instead, we've put this *Green Edition* together with three simple goals:

1) Explore the ways we can reduce our environmental impact
2) Find the best places to shop for eco-friendly products
3) Share this information in as palatable a way as possible

Ultimately, we want to show that a greener lifestyle is not so complicated. You don't have to be rich or famous, antimaterialistic or militant with your beliefs, and there's no need to move into that cave just yet. All it takes is a little awareness and a slight adjustment to your shopping routine. Whether you realize it or not, you've probably already gotten started.

Furthermore, deciding to go green doesn't mean you should get rid of everything you own and replace it with something more envirofriendly. In fact, the greenest thing you can do is extend the lifespan of the products you already own, either through simple upkeep, maintenance and repair, or by donating them to organizations dedicated to second-hand distribution. When a product has outlived its original purpose and essentially falls apart, you may often be able to recycle at least part of it, if not the whole.

When it comes to shopping, it's usually a matter of buying eco-friendly versions of the same products you already use—in most cases you can simply switch out one brand for another. All it really takes is the most basic understanding of which ingredients and materials to watch for, and which to avoid.

Fortunately, basic understandings happen to be our specialty! If environmentalism is a new concept for you, start with our section on *The Green Lifestyle*, then move on to *Eco-Shopping 101*. If you're already familiar with the ins and outs of natural ingredients, recycled materials, renewable energy and sustainable agriculture, you may want to head straight to our *Green Shops* directory to find a wealth of terrific socially conscious web sites. But you'll miss out on a few surprising points of interest, and plenty of jokes. Either way, we hope **thepurplebook** can help in your efforts to save the world.

the green lifestyle

When you take a look at the sheer magnitude of the planet we're trying to save, you almost want to give up, crank the air conditioner to high and open all the windows. But consider the challenges faced by one of the first environmentalists on record: Noah. He was tasked to build an ark from scratch *and* track down a pair of every animal in *his* struggles against climate change. By comparison, we really have it pretty easy!

Still, that doesn't mean trying to go green all at once won't seem overwhelming. The most fitting way to make a smooth transition to the eco-friendly lifestyle may be to take it step-by-step, beginning with a few minor tweaks to your daily routine, then working up to some of the bigger adjustments.

But before you can start haranguing your friends and family to go green, you'll want to be familiar with the basic tenents of modern-day environmentalism. Here, we've laid out the key concepts addressed by earth-friendly online retailers and their products. Once you've gotten your head around these guidelines, it's up to you to decide whether you want to take action with Biblical, or merely human proportions.

Simply put: as you read through the following Pillars of the Green Lifestyle, ask yourself: "What am I willing to do?" We'll show you how to do it in the next chapter: *Eco-Shopping 101*.

>> Sustainability

The concept of sustainability may be summed up as: meeting the needs of the present without compromising the ability of future generations to meet their own needs. In other words, leaving behind fertile soil to cultivate, clean air to breathe, safe water to drink, fish to eat and plenty more trees to chop down (as needed). It's all about using the planet's natural resources without destroying nature in the process.

How to Practice Sustainability

When we speak of sustainable practices, we are usually referring to the actions of those who provide us with food, clothes and other products we need or want. After all, most of us aren't likely to chop down a tree or spray the earth with chemicals for the heck of it. The primary way we can promote the sustainability ethic is to patronize those farmers, fishers and manufacturers who do practice it. This will send a signal to the rest that we don't want to buy their merchandise it if comes at too high a cost for the earth.

Buy Organic

While use of the word *organic* is widespread, the term is often misused or misunderstood. Basically, it means farming the way humans did for thousands of years: without manmade chemicals or genetic manipulation that may do irrevocable harm to the soil's ability to nurture life. Debate continues over whether organic ingredients offer any particular nutritional benefits to people, but no one can argue that we're actually better off if we expose our bodies to the toxins and growth hormones of conventional agriculture. Bottom line: organic growing today significantly improves our chances of growing the same crops tomorrow, and lowers the odds we'll start growing superfluous body parts.

The good news is organic farms are flourishing across the United States, and as more people recognize the value of nonpolluting, nontoxic agriculture, certified-organic foods are becoming easier to find across the board. You can almost smell the soil replenishing itself (just don't breathe too deeply when the fertilizer's out).

Learn more about the benefits of organics at the following sites:

OTA.com
Organic-Nature-News.com

Support Managed Forests

Deforestation is another well-known term in Save-the-Planet circles, and with good enough reason. Surprisingly large areas of forest have been razed for reasons having nothing to do with publishing internet shopping guides (we print on recycled paper). However, wood and paper industries have decimated their fair share of treelines, so the concept of sustainable forestry has come along in an attempt to reverse the trend.

The thing is, wood products are still relatively sound choices from an ecological perspective. But in a best-case scenario, we'd only use wood cut from managed forests. *Managed Forestry* is the process of harvesting trees in such a way that the forest may regrow naturally, or with a little helpful planting. It sounds like a no-brainer, but there's a science to it that's not regularly practiced—yet.

Of course, you can't tell just by looking at wood where it's come from, but most eco-friendly manufacturers will fall over themselves to tell you about their green practices. By rule of thumb, if a product's description doesn't tell you outright that it's made from sustainable wood, it's probably not.

Learn more about sustainable lumber here: **FSCUS.org**

Support Responsible Fishing Practices

If you've ever applied for a fishing license, you know there is a system in place to keep you from emptying a lake or river over the course of a weekend, so that the fish population has a chance to reproduce and continue to thrive in its natural habitat.

The same principle is theoretically applied on a much larger scale to keep our oceans swimming with the fish that land on our dinner plates. Unfortunately, since oceans don't tend to fall under any national rules, responsible fishing policies are tougher to enforce than jury duty. This means it's up to the consumer to avoid supporting those who fish without regard for the future of the catch, which usually means taking the fishmongers at their word. This book will direct you to some trustworthy sources.

Learn more about sustainable fishing here: **MSC.org**

>> Conservation

If sustainability prevents us from abusing the resources we use, conservation makes sure there are still resources left over to use at all.   This means cutting down on the waste and extravagant overuse America has become famous for worldwide—not necessarily living like monks, but just being aware that a little nonchalance on our parts can lead to such dire unintended consequences as paper towel shortages in public restrooms, and global climate change.

How to Practice Conservation

Conservation promotes efficient use of water, preservation of the planet's biological diversity and protection of our atmosphere by stemming pollution. Does any of that sound good? We hope so, because a great deal of conservation is in the hands of individuals. That means it's up to us all to do things like take shorter showers, turn off the lights when we leave a room and to not throw away items that will kill animals that weren't smart enough to invent plastic.

For more info on conservation practices: **OneTonCO2.com**

Conserve Paper

Using wood from a sustainable source will save some forests, but it won't stop the endless mountains of paper clutter that build up around us. Minimizing paper use is a great way to save trees, as well as keep your home and office tidy.

PAPER CONSERVATION TIPS

- Use cloth napkins instead of paper
- Request electronic delivery for your bills
- Direct deposit your paycheck
- Start online banking
- File your taxes online
- Book ticketless travel
- Cancel phone book delivery and use:
  YellowPages.com
- Cancel newspaper subscriptions and find online versions at:
  OnlineNewspapers.com
- Stop junk mail, insurance and credit card offers:
  DMAConsumers.org
  OptoutPrescreen.com

WATER CONSERVATION TIPS

- Shut off the water while you brush your teeth; a running faucet can release gallons of water per minute.
- Water your lawn briefly in the early morning or late evening with drip sprinklers to prevent water loss to wind and sun.
- Maximize your washing machine's efficiency by doing larger loads, less frequently.

Find more tips at: **H2oUse.org**

Conserve Water

Knowing that nearly three-quarters of the planet's surface consists of water, it hardly stands to reason to think we're facing a shortage any time soon—after all, it does fall from the sky. But when you consider that all but a nominal percentage of this H2O is salt water, the issue of fresh water supply suddenly looms large on the horizon. As the population continues to grow, potable water will be increasingly unavailable to more and more parts of the world, until you can't even find plastic bottles of it at the gas station.

Water conservation is less about denying ourselves access to the essential, life-giving liquid than it is about not letting it go to waste. Simply fixing a leaky faucet can save immense quantities of water, while a few well-considered plumbing decisions will allow you to drastically reduce your water consumption on a daily basis without even thinking about it.

Conserve Electricity

If your father ever walked from room to room in the house, turning off lights and complaining that he wasn't made of money, you've probably already formed an energy-saving habit. Well, it turns out the old man was right: but conserving electricity doesn't just lower your utility bill, it also reduces your household carbon emissions.

The US uses more petroleum and electricity than any other nation. In fact, most of our energy is still derived from petroleum power, meaning the electricity we collectively use contributes to air pollution just as our cars do. Cutting your household electricity consumption helps reduce community demand, meaning less pollution overall. And, yes, it will save you money, so it pays to learn what you can do to minimize your home's power usage.

ELECTRICITY SAVING TIPS

- Unplug your cell phone charger when it's not in use; anytime it's plugged in it's drawing current.
- Set your thermostat down two degrees in the winter, up two degrees in the summer.
- Turn off computer monitors and TVs when not in use
- Regularly clean the filters of your dryer, air conditioner, furnace, vacuum and other appliances. Dirty filters force the appliance to use up to a third more energy.
- Turn off the lights, particularly in the daytime.

Avoid Littering

Our culture spends a lot of time talking about bigger issues such as carbon emissions, the greenhouse effect and depletion of the ozone layer. Though global warming offers evidence that humans are having a bigger effect on the planet than most of us thought possible, we should take care to remember that some of our smaller indiscretions still have a very real impact on the world around us.

Littering doesn't just anger neighbors who want to keep the neighborhood looking nice; it can do some real damage to our local ecosystems. Sure, much of our trash may drift harmlessly along until the elements break it down, but we can rarely anticipate the effect our waste is going to have on the animals and plants that subsist on the delicate balance of nature. You never know which carelessly discarded object is going to disrupt that balance.

Properly disposing of your trash, or even making the effort to pick up litter at your local park, playground and beach, will set a good example for children. Heck, it might even make you a role model for a few grown-ups who could use one.

>> Nontoxic & Biodegradable Goods

Although rainbow-colored water sounds beautiful on paper, we've all been around long enough to know that the puddle under your car has been contaminated by petroleum-based chemicals. The truth is, it's not always so easy tell when potentially harmful chemicals have been released into the environment. Every day there are toxins flushing down our drains when we do laundry, running down our driveways when we wash our cars and pouring from every orifice of local factories, sometimes without so much as a sud to let us know it. Even wiping down the kitchen counter with a chemical cleaner can corrupt the air we breathe indoors, adding to the list of invisible poisons that plague every creature on the planet.

Easier to see is the solid waste that builds up around our neighborhoods and in our landfills. The twentieth-century brought about a proliferation of marvelous new materials designed to make our lives easier, but many of these synthetic products do not decompose rapidly, if at all. When these materials are trashed, all we can do is stash them somewhere out of the way and hope they don't spawn some disgusting ooze that will one day creep its way back to us. Plastic six-pack rings, disposable diapers and grocery bags are just some of the things that will still be around long after we are dead, slowly contaminating the earth.

Switching to Nontoxic & Biodegradable Goods

It's probably naïve to say all synthetic products are bad; we wouldn't want to do without advanced medicines that save lives or computer chips that allow us to do a world of good.

But for every chemical or plastic product we encounter, we can ask ourselves: "Does the benefit of using this outweigh the environmental harm?" In many cases, a natural option will function as well as or better than its synthetic alternative, and will invariably prove better for the earth and your health.

Avoid Volatile Organic Compounds

One thing to watch out for is a class of chemicals called Volatile Organic Compounds (and yes, we *are* going to have to wax scientific for a moment; many apologies). Despite the word *organic* floating in the middle there, these chemicals are neither naturally occuring nor eco-friendly. Known as VOCs, they continually release toxins into the air in a process called *off-gassing*. This means tiny particles break off the surface of the compound, mixing into the oxygen we breathe.

Commonly found in paints, carpets and household cleaners, VOCs may offgas for years, usually inside our homes. In fact, the EPA attests that indoor pollution is up to five times greater than the outdoors in most parts of the United States, probably due to a preponderance of VOCs in commonly-used products. It can be difficult to identify and avoid VOCs, but the site **DiEnviro.com** should help, along with our shopping directory.

Avoid Petroleum-Based Products

When we talk about reducing petroleum use, gas-powered engines almost always dominate the discussion, perhaps rightfully so. But petroleum has literally thousands of uses in manufacture and production, and it can be surprising just how many products we use every day that have been manufactured using oil and oil derivatives.

Petrochemicals find their way into such innocuous seeming products as candles, makeup and skin care, carpets, furniture, medicines, soaps, toothpaste and clothes. We rarely notice their effect, positive or negative, on our health, and their cumulative effect on the environment isn't always evident. But if there's anything we've learned as a nation from the last several years, it's that weaning ourselves from all the glamour of petroleum is a very, very good thing.

Here are just a few familiar products that are usually made using petrochemicals or petroleum processes:
- Beauty & bath products
- Cleaning products
- Paraffin wax
- Inks and dyes
- Polyester, Nylon & Spandex
- Fertilizers
- Food preservatives
- Paints
- Insect repellent
- Glue (adhesives)
- Rubbing alcohol
- Upholstered furniture
- Crayons
- Floor tiles
- Candy
- Faux leather
- All plastics

WAYS TO USE LESS PLASTIC

- Buy reusable grocery and produce bags
- Use organic feminine products
- Use biodegradable pet poop bags
- Use cloth or biodegradable diapers
- Buy only recycled or biodegradable picnic ware
- Download movies and music rather than purchase CD/DVD

Reducing Your Household Waste

If you've never visited your local dump, you probably have good reason: it's not the most pleasant of places. Between the flies, the unidentifiable sludge, rats the size of dogs and of course the horrendous smells, you could pretty much consider it the earth's worst microclimate. What you may not realize is that this is not necessarily the end of it. Mountains of garbage are regularly moved from cities to the countryside, big holes in the ground and even onto boats. Rubbish can be easier to find than a parking space. And the more we throw away, the more likely we are to stumble onto a landfill when we're supposed to be exploring a nature reserve.

Minimize Packaging

There are several ways to reduce the amount of garbage our households produce. Chief among them is to reduce the amount of materials used to package the products we purchase. Since packaging usually just gets thrown away, it's the primary contributor to all the plastics, styrofoams and other synthetic materials that will presumably marvel landfill archeologists of the distant future.

Different companies opt for a variety of packaging designs and materials, some more eco-friendly than others. While packaging seems to be a necessary evil when it comes to marketing consumer goods, it's usually pretty easy to figure out when a product uses excessive or otherwise irresponsible packaging. If you avoid such products while shopping, you will help send a message to manufacturers that they should also consider minimizing packaging on their end. Refer to our *Recycling Guide* to weigh the pros and cons of common packaging materials, especially whether they can be recycled in your community, and buy in bulk whenever it's reasonable to do so.

Reuse Products When Possible

Disposable is a dirty word. Basically, anything designed to be disposable is destined for the landfill, so look for reuseable alternatives. This could mean canvas grocery bags, a stainless steel water bottle or cloth napkins. Look at the sort of objects you throw away often and see if you can find a more permanent alternative.

Compost

Composting your organic waste will also reduce the number of garbage bags you send to the curb each week. The inedible parts of fruits and vegetables, such as peels, stalks, stems pits and cores will naturally decompose into a soil-like substance that makes a terrific fertilizer (with no BS!). Learn more at **CompostGuide.com**.

>> Recycling

Of course, recycling is one of the best ways to send out your trash without contributing to landfill overflow. Paper, aluminum and glass are the most popularly recycled materials, with well-established programs in place in most parts of the country. You may even recycle some plastics, though figuring out which ones is a more difficult process (see page 24).

Across the US, recycling programs set in motion decades ago have been an overwhelming success. As generations of schoolkids have learned the merits of separating papers, metals and plastics, households have made recycling routine, and both public and private waste management systems have incorporated the pickup of recyclables into their schedules. This proves society can change its ways if we really want to.

Buy Recycled Goods

We are now faced with the realization that recycling is only part of the equation. As consumers, it's naïve to think we can just send out used newspapers, bottles and cans, and wash our hands of the problem. In order for the "cycle" part of recycling to work, we also need to *purchase* products made from these recycled materials. In some parts of the US, mountains of glass and aluminum still sit in landfills as post-consumer waste, waiting to be refashioned into new consumer goods. And these are the most popularly recycled commodities we have.

Many companies have seen the benefits of using recycled materials, and you may already unknowingly purchase products that use post-consumer waste. However, by seeking out products that reuse raw or manufactured materials, we encourage more companies to find ways to turn existing goods from potential trash into something great.

An example of this may be seen with synthetic fabrics such as polyester. Made using petroleum, polyester does not naturally decompose, meaning those Disco-era leisure suits stand to embarrass us for generations to come. But if a designer reuses the fabric of that suit to make a new dress or a track suit, all evidence of bad taste is destroyed, the fabric's life cycle is extended, and we get to enjoy the benefits of polyester without betraying our eco-friendly intentions. Everybody wins!

Find out more about buying recycled good here: **EPA.gov/cpg**

TPB RECYCLING GUIDE

Recycling programs vary by city and state, but chances are if you don't have a home pickup service you will find a recycling facility somewhere in your vicinity. These web sites should help you find one:

Earth911.org
NRC-Recycle.org
ThrowPlace.com

Along with glass, your local recycling program may accept one or all of the following: aluminum, mixed paper, plastic and tetra brik (a combination of the three). This means you'll want to get in the habit of recycling:

Aluminum cans and foil
Glass bottles and jars
Cardboard and tetra brik packaging
Newspapers and magazines
Plastic bottles

Facilities may accept these elements mixed together or ask you sort them. Regardless of which service is available to you, there are things you can do to make the recycling process more efficient:

• Collect newspapers in paper bags or tie them in bundles with twine or string.
• Remove the unrecyclable tops from plastic bottles.
• Rinse containers before recycling.

Recycling is not limited to these materials, though. In fact, it's unbelievably important to recycle potentially hazardous goods, including all electronics devices, fluorescent light bulbs, CDs and batteries. These sites will help you recycle these items:

BatteryRecycling.com:	Batteries
Bulbs.com:	Light bulbs
Eco-Cell.com:	Cell phones
FreeRecycling.com:	Cell phones
InterconRecycling.com:	Electronics
LampRecycle.org:	Light bulbs
RipMobile.com:	Cell phones
TechRecycle.com:	Electronics
WirelessRecycling.com:	Cell phones

TPB RECYCLING GUIDE

COMMON PACKAGING MATERIALS

Some products are packaged to extend the life of a perishable good, some for consumer convenience, and some merely for presentation. Consider the environmental impact of these common materials as you shop, and whether you will be able to safely dispose of them.

Metal: It actually costs less to recycle metal than it does to extract it from the earth, so reclaimed aluminum, steel and tin is remarkably common. This means cans and foils are are still among the best packaging options.
Accepted by nearly all recycling programs.

Glass: Its obvious environmental benefits include reusability, recyclability and biodegradability. However, the energy required to ship heavy and fragile bottles is a factor worth noting, when given alternatives.
Accepted by nearly all recycling programs.

Paper: Paper and cardboard packaging proves lightweight, fairly sustainable and easily recyclable. However, as it tears easily, a lot of paper packaging is strengthened with a coat of synthetic material. Be wary of coated bags and pouches that won't recycle.
Untreated paper accepted by nearly all recycling programs.

Laminates and Composites: Made using plastics in combination with other materials, these convenient packages are prevalent, but problematic ecologically. Examples include potato chip bags, milk cartons, toothpaste tubes and disposable microwave dinner trays. Basically, if it seems to share qualities of paper, plastic and/or metal, it's one of these compound materials.
Cannot be recycled.

Tetra Brik: Associated with rectangular soy milk and juice boxes, tetra brik includes layers of plastic, paper and metal foil. The rectangular containers ship efficiently and may sometimes be recycled. However, many programs still don't accept tetra brik, so check with your local recycler before embrracing it.
Occasionally accepted by recycling programs.

TPB RECYCLING GUIDE

Plastics: There are several types of plastic, and most plastic containers feature a three-arrow symbol and number to identify the plastic. Here's an explanation of each plastic and its uses. Check with your local recycling facility to see which plastics it will accept.

 PETE: Used to make bottles, trays and tubs. *Bottles accepted by most plastic recycling facilities, but usually not trays or tubs.*

 HDPE: A durable plastic usually used in thinner milk and detergent bottles. Also used to make some food containers. *Accepted by most plastic recycling facilities.*

 PVC: Also known as vinyl, this is most commonly found in plastic wrap, oil bottles, bubble wrap and plastic grocery bags. *Not typically accepted by local facilities, but bags may be recycled by local grocery stores.*

 LDPE: Flexible and virtually indestructible plastic found in thin produce bags and shrink wrap as well as computers, containers and six-pack rings. *Not typically accepted by local facilities, but bags may be recycled by local grocery stores.*

 PP: A rigid plastic used to make bottle caps and other hard plastic packaging, but also found in softer format as yogurt containers and diapers. *Occasionally accepted by local facilities.*

 PS: Also known as styrofoam, used to make take-out containers and packaging. A compressed form is also used as plastic utensils. *Packaging may be recycled for some uses, but any food utensils or containers go to a landfill.*

 MISC: Refers to mixed materials, laminates or less commonly used plastics. *Cannot be recycled.*

Learn more at: **RecycleNow.com**
EcoCycle.org

>> Renewable Energy

Based on the idea that we can use limitless natural resources such as the sun and wind to generate power, the concept of renewable energy has been at the forefront of the environmental discussion for almost as long as people have been talking around the campfire. Yet even as we wade deeper into the 21st century, the bulk of American electricity is produced by burning fossil fuels, releasing dozens of harmful substances into the air as well as high levels of carbon dioxide. While even the most cagey politicians agree there is a need for cleaner power than petroleum provides, finding any agreement on which alternative energy source will power our green homes of the future has been tantamount to impossible.

One reason for this may be that we don't yet have a feasible solution that is right for the entire planet. When it comes to reversing the trends of global climate change, the best answers might be found by adapting to the traits of our local climates.

However, production and distribution of power for a large market is complicated and costly, and though most utility companies have earnestly started pursuing green energy programs, it could be decades before the switch is close to complete. This means that relying on the traditional power-grid system may not be the greatest way to get our green on. A better answer could be a return to self-sufficiency. Increasingly, individual households are discovering that home energy production has long-term savings that exceed the short-term costs. And even those initial costs are going down, especially if you qualify for tax-deductions and other government incentive programs.

Obviously, converting your house to clean power is easier for homeowners than renters. However, the true measure of how successfully you can produce electricity depends on your local weather, and access to usable space. It will save you money in the long run, and it's probably a lot easier than you think! Check out these sites for more info:

CurrentEnergy.com
EERE.Energy.gov
Green-e.org
HomePower.com
NREL.gov
RenewableEnergyAccess.com

Solar Power

If you don't live somewhere the sun shines, now is probably a good time to move. If, on the other hand, there's a roof over you head that could capitalize on the sun's rays, you're probably a good candidate for solar power. There are two ways to harness the sun's rays:

Passive Solar: The simple method of conducting the sun's warmth to heat water or other materials. Sometimes coupled with photovoltaic cells on a massive scale to generate electricity.

Photovoltaic: The most-frequently discussed modern method, which uses hi-tech photovoltaic cells to directly convert sunlight into electricity.

There's nothing new about solar energy, except that the photovoltaic cells have gotten smaller, more efficient and cheaper. So why haven't more of us embraced the indefatigable resource? It could be cosmetic considerations, concerns over reliability or maybe just the plain old intimidation of science.

Fortunately, there are some user-friendly web sites to help you determine if solar panels are the right call for your household:

AbsolutelySolar.com
ASES.org
GoSolarCalifornia.ca.gov
PowerFilmSolar.com
Renu.Citizenre.com
SolarExpert.com

Wind Power

If solar energy is old news, harnessing the power of the wind is ancient history. While most of us don't currently have any need or inclination to grind our own grains, converting a recurring breeze into electricity is fast-becoming a viable option. While today's streamlined turbines little resemble the wood-thatched farm windmills of yore, the concept behind the windmill hasn't changed much, and you will consistently need strong winds to make it work. That said, residential wind generators have hit the market, so if your home is big enough to house one, and receives more than its fair share of gusty weather, you might be interested.

Check out this site to learn more: **AWEA.org**

Hydroelectric Power

Like windmills, waterwheels have long been used to power simple machinery, and similarly the concept has been implemented on a grander scale, with dams widely contributing power to grids worldwide. But these days, more sophisticated means of channeling river currents and waves are changing the way we can produce hydroelectric power on a smaller scale for personal use. With only a small potential customer base, the market for residential hydroelectric power is still fairly limited, but you may find some interesting resources at the following site: **Hydropower.inel.gov**

IS YOUR POWER ALREADY GREEN?

Your local utilities company is probably already exploring clean energy solutions. Energy producers in many parts of the country allow consumers to partake in green electricity programs. Contact your local utility provider to find out what you can do as a customer to support renewable concepts.

>> Fair Trade

Supporting a family halfway around the world by simply purchasing a fair trade product may seem to be a far cry from preventing climate change or turning the tide against pollution. But it doesn't sound bad, right? And in several ways our planet's long-term survival depends on alleviating poverty, famine and disease in developing nations.

When you're attempting to preserve the planet's resources, it's easy to see why preventing waste, prohibiting pollution, reducing carbon emissions, and conserving resources are important. The concept of fair trade is a bit trickier. Granted, there is a moral imperative to protect both human and workers' rights, to endorse safe working conditions, promote health benefits and prevent the exploitation of children, women and the impoverished.

For one, environmental stewardship is a luxury of those of us with economic stability. By supporting fair wages we will steadily enable citizens of poorer regions to stimulate their own economic growth, which will promote political stability and lead to more efficient use of resources. Both are of increasing importance as the population of the planet rises exponentially, putting an increasing strain on our finite supply of potable water and arable land. The fact is, most of the fastest growing populations exist in the poorest nations. Sadly, in today's world, civil unrest may too easily lead to use of weapons of mass destruction, most of which take a hefty toll on the earth as well as human life.

Lastly, although fair trade certification does not require organic growing methods, they are generally encouraged with premium prices offered as incentive. It stands to reason that, over time, successful fair trade agriculture will develop into widespread sustainable farming.

Learn more on this site: **TransFairUSA.org**

>> Education

There is plenty to learn about the environment, and new information and developments happen all the time. Keeping track of it all would seem to require some sort of sophisticated world wide network of constantly evolving news and reference materials... a web, if you will. The following sites should keep you knowledgeable, up-to-date and in-the-know.

Eco News
Check the latest green technology, business and legislation:

EcoFriend.org
EcoWorld.com
ENN.com
Grist.org

Eco Tips & Reference
Find lots of facts and tips on how to go green:

Climate.org
DiEnviro.com
EarthEasy.com
EPA.gov
EWG.org
FoodRoutes.org
GlobalStewards.org
OpenEcoSource.com
Organic-Nature-News.com
TheOrganicReport.com
WHFoods.com

Eco Blogs

What are other people talking about? Check out this sampling of environmental blogs to tap in to the e-community:

AGreenIdea.com
EcoFabulous.Blogs.com
EcoStreet.com
EcoTalkBlog.com
FabGreen.com
GreenThinkers.org
IdealBite.com
InHabitat.com
LazyEnvironmentalist.com
TheActionBlog.com

Eco-Friendly Consumer Reviews

Find out just how green a purported eco-product is, or which of the green options is best for you:

Ethiscore.org
GreatGreenGoods.com
PristinePlanet.com
ReallyNatural.com
SustainLane.com
TheDailyGreen.com
TreeHugger.com

WAYS IT PAYS TO GO GREEN

Go green and you might get some greenbacks back. The following sites will turn you on to some financial incentives to support environmentalism.

These sites will guide you to state and federal tax incentives for switching to renewable energy sources:

DSIREUSA.org
Energy.gov

These will guide you to eco-friendly mutual funds:

SocialInvest.org
SociallyResponsible.org

UNDERSTANDING GREEN LABELS

Gain a better understanding of the most common ecological claims that pop up on labels and packaging, direct from the organizations who issue them:

Certified Biodegradable
Indicates: A product is biodegradable according to federal standards.
Issued by: Scientific Certification Systems
SCSCertified.com

Certified Organic
Indicates: Meat or produce has been farmed without artificial pesticides, fertilizers, hormones or antibiotics.
Issued by: US Department of Agriculture
USDA.gov

Energy Star
Indicates: Appliances and electronics meet current energy efficiency standards.
Issued by: The Environmental Protection Agency
EnergyStar.gov

Fair Trade Certified
Indicates: A product has been grown and/or produced using fair labor and market practices.
Issued by: Trans Fair
TransFairUSA.org

FSC Certified
Indicates: Wood has been sustainably harvested.
Issued by: The Forest Stewardship Council
FSC.org

Green Seal Certified
Indicates: A wide range of products are environmentally-friendly based on a strict set of standards.
Issued by: Green Seal
GreenSeal.org

Marine Stewardship Council Certified
Indicates: Fish has been responsibly fished or farmed.
Issued by: The Marine Stewardship Council
MSC.org

UNDERSTANDING GREEN LABELS

For information on other manufacturers' claims, check out the following sites:

Eco-Labels.org: This consumer resource evaluates the usage and validity of hundreds of eco labels.

FTC.gov: The Federal Trade Commission's mandate is "to prevent fraud, deception, and unfair business practices in the marketplace."

FDA.gov: The Food & Drug Administration oversees ingredients labels for food, drugs and beauty products.

Green Web Directories

Find more information and more online resources with the help of these green specialty web portals and link aggregators:

AllianceForSustainability.net
EcoIQ.com
EcologyCenter.org
Envirolink.org
GreenMaven.com
Hugg.com
TheOrganicPages.com

Green Lifestyle Sites

These online magazines and communities will keep you appraised of new developments in green living, including features on people, places and trends:

Care2.com
CoOpAmerica.org
EcoRazzi.com
EMagazine.com
Green.Yahoo.com
GreenLightMag.com
Lime.com
PlentyMag.com
TheGreenGuide.com
WorldChanging.com

>> Charity

The main purpose of this book is to show how you can do right for the planet with the purchases you make from home, but that doesn't mean the world can't use a little additional help. The following environmental charity sites accept donations:

CleanAir-CoolPlanet.org: Global warming solutions

Conservation.org: Worldwide conservation programs

EarthJustice.org: Legal advocacy for environmental causes

EarthShare.org: Network of environmental charities

EnvironmentalDefense.org: Supports scientific research into environmental solutions

FOE.org: Environmental watchdog group

GreenPeace.org: Global conservation organization

LCV.org: Environmental political advocacy group

LNT.org: Promotes stewardship of the natural areas

NewDream.org: Advocates conservation and green production

NoHarm.org: Advocates eco-sensitive health care

NRDC.org: Environmental protection organization

NWF.org: Wildlife conservation and protection

OceanConservancy.org: Ocean conservation

OrganicConsumers.org: Organic consumer advocacy

Rainforest-Alliance.com: Saving the rain forests

SeafoodChoices.org: Helping seafood industry switch to sustainability

SevenGenerationsAhead.org: Conservation & sustainability

SierraClub.org: Supports a variety of environmental causes

SurfRider.org: Cleans and protects the ocean and coastlines

StopGlobalWarming.org: Global warming awareness

TheSustainableVillage.com: Promotes sustainable fair trade

TreesFTF.org: Tree-planting organization

UCSUSA.org: Scientists advocating environmental solutions

VolunteerMatch.org: Local volunteer opportunities

WWF.org: Protects the globe's wildlife

SWAP, SELL OR DONATE

Some recycling methods are more direct, offering valuable, profitable or gratifying results. Basically, if you have something you no longer want or need, chances are there is somebody else out there who will appreciate it. When you trade, sell or donate an item, you extend its life cycle and keep it out of a landfill.

Some common items to consider making second-hand:
Electronics
Sporting goods
Clothing and accessories
Books, music, movies, games
Furniture
Toys

Here are a few sites that will come in handy:

CraigsList.org	Sell, swap, donate
FreeCycle.com	Donate goods
IShareStuff.org	Swap and share
PaperbackSwap.com	Swap books
PeerFlix.com	Swap DVDs
Spun.com	Trade, sell books, movies, music and games
TitleTrader.com	Swap music, movies, games and books

>> Shop Local

You might wonder why an internet shopping guide would turn around and tell you to shop locally. Well, for one thing, patronizing locally-owned businesses, farmers and restaurants supports your community, which means your neighbors will be able to afford nicer green products.

But, moreso, shipping products cross-country increases carbon emissions. If you can find the eco-friendly merchandise you desire close to home, go for it. It's the green thing to do.

Unfortunately, a wide selection of earth-friendly goods are not yet available in brick-and-mortar stores, even in a lot of big cities. So, for the time being, the web is still the best place to find what you need, and to support a growing list of eco-conscious manufacturers. In the meantime, here are some handy local directories that will clue you in to green retailers in your hometown.

GreenPages.org: Directory of local eco-retailers
GreenPeople.org: Directory of local eco-retailers
HempStores.com: Local hemp retailer directory
CertifiedHumane.com: Locate sustainable, humanely raised beef
EatWellGuide.org: Locate sustainable foods in your area
LocalHarvest.org: Guide to local farmer's markets
FleaMarketGuide.com: Locate flea markets all over the country
GreenPeople.com: Locate a sustainable retailer

Or, check out these local eco-services:

BeyondPesticides.org: Locate nontoxic exterminators
NancysNatural.info: Natural cleaning service

MEET SOMEONE GREEN

Meeting people can be hard enough without having a clash of values. Check out these sites to meet others who are friendly to the environment:

GreenSingles.com
Care2.com

NOTES:

_____

_____

_____

_____

_____

_____

_____

_____

_____

_____

_____

_____

_____

_____

_____

_____

_____

_____

_____

_____

_____

eco-shopping
101

The difficulty in deciding how best to shop in an environmentally conscious way can be summed up by a single question we hear on a weekly basis: paper or plastic? Choosing paper can mean contributing to deforestation. Plastic production, on the other hand, consumes more energy and creates pollution. Depending on whichever problem has been the latest focus of the news media, the right answer might change before you've made it to the parking lot.

A third answer is to bring your own reusable hemp or cotton grocery bags to the store, so you may haul away your purchases without adding to your trash or recycling bins. This option perfectly illustrates how shopping your conscience sometimes means approaching your shopping decisions with a different mindset.

With very few exceptions you can find sustainably produced, recyclable, nontoxic and/or energy efficient alternatives to any household item, cleaning agent, outfit or foodstuff. Even without changing any facet of your lifestyle you can help stem the tide in the pollution of our planet. Go out of your way just a smidgen, and we might all just turn things around.

In this section we'll begin by exploring the easy, immediate shopping decisions we can regularly make to go green, then slowly work up to the big stuff. However far you're willing to go, we hope these steps will show just how easy it is to have a positive impact.

>> Food & Drink

The shelves of your local grocery store probably offer more choices of more food than you ever thought you'd need. But if you take a closer look, those long, well-lit aisles may reveal something less-appetizing—wasteful packaging, artificial ingredients and pollutant agricultural practices. Obviously, your daily nourishment is more important than just about everything on the planet except the water you drink and the air you breath—but there's the rub! With a few simple adjustments to your food shopping habits you may protect the planet without altering much of your diet at all.

The Problem: Irresponsible farming and fishing practices cause irreparable damage to our natural resources that will make it difficult for us to provide food for a growing world population.

The Culprits: Chemical pesticides and fertilizers that pollute our air, land and water.

The Solution: Purchasing organic and sustainable foods.

Ready-Made & Processed Organic Foods

When the term *organic* is applied to such things as frozen meals or cake mixes, different labels leave a lot of room for confusion. Here's the story: the USDA offers several different levels of certification, depending on what percentage of the ingredients are organic. In theory, foods labeled with the following terms are free of artificial, genetically modified or irradiated ingredients. They may contain manipulated ingredients like hydrogenated oils or high fructose corn syrup, but only if they're trying to pull one over on you.

100% Organic: As obvious as it may sound, to be certified 100% Organic, every individual ingredient must be certified organic.

Organic: Processed foods that bear the Certified Organic label must be made from at least 95% certified organic ingredients.

Made With Organic Ingredients: In order to claim a product was made using organic ingredients, at least 70% of the ingredients must be certified organic. This may be used as a marketing ploy.

Natural: Intended to mean a product was minimally processed and contains no artificial ingredients. However, there is no formal verification, so the word is often misused.

Produce

If your diet is rich with whole vegetables, fruits, nuts, herbs, spices fungi and grains, you're already eating in a water-efficient way, and you're probably healthier than half the people you know. Of course, you can always do a little extra to promote sustainability. Here are some shopping options that will keep your greens green.

Organic Produce

Certified Organic produce is raised without use of chemical pesticides or fertilizers, and without genetic modification, on land that has been free of chemicals for at least three years. You may sometimes hear claims that *Organic* is merely a marketing term used to offer the same products at a higher price. But the point of organics is to offer food that is free of any amount of potential toxins, harvested in a way that will preserve the fertility of the earth for future crops.

Since organic produce costs a little more than conventionally-raised goods, you may want to pick and choose which fruits, vegetables and grains you are willing to splurge on. Prioritize these ten, as they retain the highest levels of pesticides, even after washing:

- Peaches/Nectarines
- Strawberries
- Bananas
- Rice
- Oats
- Green Beans
- Apples
- Bell Peppers
- Grapes/Raisins
- Raspberries

For a full list of which agricultural items are your best organic bets, check out: **FoodNews.org**

Biodynamically Grown

Biodynamic agriculture is essentially the same as Organic, using no chemical or synthetic means to grow. Interestingly, this term dates back to the 1920s, in response to the first widespread use of chemicals in farming. The practice of natural agriculture had, of course, had already been in use for millennia.

Wildcrafted Ingredients

In food, health and beauty products you may come across the term, "wildcrafted," which means the plant in question grew naturally in the wild and was harvested in a responsible fashion (in other words, the entire plant has not been stripped bare).

Locally Grown & Farmers' Markets

Buying produce that has been grown locally reduces the pollution associated with both packaging and transport, but that's not the only benefit. In many cases, the in-season produce will be fresher and more affordable since you are dealing directly with the farmers who picked it. You'll find few more effective opportunities to support sustainable agriculture with your purchases.

Meat & Poultry

A common misconception is that in order to eat in an eco-friendly manner you have to adopt a vegetarian, vegan, macrobiotic or otherwise "health food" diet. Certainly, while eating green usually mean eating healthier, it doesn't necessarily mean giving up any particular kind of food, even meat. To wit—though your doctor might not want you to eat a bacon cheeseburger topped by fried egg, our planet will not be saved or lost by putting an end to the domestication of livestock. Go ahead and eat your green eggs and ham.

That said, raising animals does consume a great deal of natural resources, so limiting how often you eat meat and/or reducing portion sizes will contribute to a more sustainable food cycle. This is particularly true as our population grows, and increases demand at incalculable rates. It's well known that millions of acres in South America have been deforested, and the truth is many of these trees were razed to create grazing ground for cattle. There is a limit to how much livestock can be bred on this planet before we start to run out of other vital needs such as potable water and breathable air.

This means that the source of your routine intake of meat is of the utmost importance. As with fruits and vegetables, the key principles behind being an eco-conscious carnivore involve sustainable agriculture. What the animals eat, how they are raised and how natural their growth cycles are have an impact on the planet, and no less so upon your health. Here's what to look for.

Organic Meats

In the United States, Certified Organic meats have been raised without the use of chemical pesticides, antibiotics, growth hormones, inorganic foods or animal byproducts. Additionally they are required to spend a portion of their lives out in the open air.

Conventionally raised beef, in particular, retains more trace chemicals than other nonorganic meats. If you can only afford to buy one kind of organic meat, make beef a priority.

Free Range & Certified Humane

Neither confined to a stable or cage, these types of livestock are allowed to wander and eat in a relatively natural environment, roaming in the open and experiencing a life pretty similar to what they might have led in the wild (but with more humane predators).

Grass-Fed

This term usually applies to beef or lamb, but may be found in general dairy products and even eggs.   Like Free Range, it refers to a more natural feeding process. Specifically, the cattle grazes openly on grass rather than being fed grains. Proponents of grass-fed meats and eggs cite health advantages such as anti-carcinogenic properties, lower fat content and a high concentration of Omega-3 fatty acids, which will all likely add up to difference in taste. We'd recommend organic, partially grass-fed beef.

For more information about grass-fed meat, see: **EatWild.com**

Seafood

It is difficult to determine whether one fish may be considered more environmentally friendly than another. After all, most do swim free in oceans and rivers, and are therefore not subject to the same issues seen in domestic livestock. However, sadly, those oceans and rivers have already been polluted, meaning it's quite difficult to find fish that haven't been exposed to one contaminant or another, such as mercury, PCBs (industrial coolants) or pesticide runoff.

Fish farms often implement parasiticides and antibiotics, and in some incidents, accidentally release nonnative fish into the wild, where they may prove disruptive to local food chain, endangering the survival of other marine species.

Over-fishing is another issue that becomes more critical each year as the world's growing population consumes unprecedented quantities of seafood. Still, many parts of the ocean have already been depleted, with fishing fleets representing various nations moving on to threaten waters far from home.

Some destructive fishing techniques irrevocably damage ecosystems, whether it's a heavy net dredging the ocean floor or an unintentional catch being killed in the fishing process and thrown away. The most famous example of this "bycatch" occurs when feeding dolphins are caught, injured or killed in tuna nets. Although arguably the cutest of ocean creatures, dolphins are not the only animals suffering this fate!

Fortunately, there are examples of responsible aquaculture and open sea fishing. Online, you may find detailed lists of which fish species are most likely to be sustainably raised or caught, as well as which sources to look for. Additionally, the Marine Stewardship Council has recently begun to certify Fisheries and Fish Farms based on responsible management and environmental impact. Look for the MSC-Certified label and check out their site: **MSC.org.**

Bear in mind that responsible fishing policies do not intend to stop consumption of our favorite seafoods; rather to preserve existing populations so we will still be able to enjoy eating fish for years to come! Some fish, like the bluefin tuna and Chilean seabass have been overfished to the point they risk extinction. Others, like Atlantic salmon is raised on farms using environmentally irresponsible practices.

To see the full list of environmentally safe and unsafe seafood choices, check out: **OceansAlive.org**

Wine

Wine is big business, appropriating a lot of land and resources for what some might call a luxury crop (not that we *ever* would!). These terms give new meaning to the notion of drinking responsibly.

Organic & Biodynamic Wine

Enthusiasts will be loathe to limit their wine selections to Organic and Biodynamic varietals, but with an increasing number of vineyards embracing chemical-free production worldwide, earth-friendly bottles are gaining higher and higher marks, so even the strictest of connoisseurs will be sampling green wines in the years to come. For the casual drinker, Organic wine specialists like these will guide you to bottles covering a full range of budgets and tastes:

WineSpectator.com
WineMag.com

NSA Wine

The winemaking process results in the natural occurrence of sulfites. They act as a preservative, preventing microbial growth and contributing to the way a wine matures. Every wine contains sulfites, white typically more than red, but it is also a common practice to add synthetic sulfites to wine to make it age quicker. An NSA label indicates that no additional sulfites have been added, of course. That's a good thing.

Coffee

One way to stop the green movement in its tracks would be to ask coffee drinkers to give up their daily cup of joe. Fortunately, this is far from being the case, as eco-friendly coffees have long enjoyed widespread availability. As it happens, ethical coffee is thriving to such an extent that it can be considered a great victory for the environmental movement and a sure sign things can change for the better, once we decide it matters.

There are three terms to watch out for when shopping for coffee, and it's not at all difficult to find triple-certified beans.

Organic Coffee

As with all produce, coffee cultivation must be free of chemical pesticides, synthetic fertilizers and genetic modification to qualify as organic. And lest you think sustainable growing is region-specific, organic coffee is currently exported by no fewer than thiry-five nations on nearly every continent (Antarctica has not yet offered a worthy bean).

Shade Grown (or Bird Friendly) Coffee

A lot of coffee is grown in the sun because the beans mature quicker in the light. However, shade grown coffee has numerous benefits, number one being that it is grown without deforestation, preserving rain forest trees (the habitats for many birds). One of the best arguments, however, might be that the slower maturing process when beans are grown in the shade allows them to develop richer, more complex flavors, resulting in better coffee. Bird Friendly certification indicates a coffee is both Shade Grown and Organic.

Fair Trade Coffee

The global coffee market has been historically volatile, often at the expense of the farmer, and to the benefit of the importer or middleman. The fair trade movement establishes a steady market value and promotes direct trade between the coffee producers and importers or even roasters, reducing the number of hands beans pass through en route to the consumer, and ensuring farmers in all parts of the world may receive a just portion of the profit, providing grass roots economic sustainability, often in impoverished areas.

Other fair trade and organic items to look for include:

Chocolate
Tea
Sugar

>> Preparation & Service

Once your food is all greened up, it hardly seems rational to cook and serve it using environmentally irresponsible products. Fortunately, these aren't the type of products you throw away every day, so there are only a few things to consider in this category.

The Problem: Multiply the waste produced by one meal by 300 billion, and you can imagine how much we produce as a nation in just one year.

The Culprits: Disposable cookware, serviceware and take out packaging at restaurants and at home.

The Solution: Reusable, biodegradable and recycled service ware and storage containers.

Pots & Pans

Technology has only offered a few advances when it comes to pots and pans, and most of them may be summed up in the term *nonstick*. Unfortunately, synthetic pan surfaces have a tendency to scrape off with time, and may otherwise contaminate your foods before their short life cycles have passed. Going back to the classics, like cast iron, may actually do you better for cooking and health.

Service

Having a family dinner can save the planet. Well, not really, but it might do wonders for your feeling of togetherness. On the other hand, there are ways to make your mealtimes a little more eco-sensitive, and here they are.

Recycled Glass & Dinnerware

When it's time to buy new dishes and glasses, check around for some intriguing recycled options. Primarily made of glass, these sets are rarely less than beautiful. Better yet, if and when they eventually break, you'll know just where to toss them; the recycling bin.

Nontoxic Ceramics

Actually hewn from the earth, it's hard not to like ceramics. However, pottery production actually consumes a surprisingly large amount of resources per object. Fortunately they are sturdy enough to make it worthwhile, provided they are made with nontoxic glazes. Finding such products gets more likely with each passing year, but still is not an easy prospect. Keep your eyes open for it.

Linens

Obviously, when it comes to table linens, using sustainable fabrics, such as those discussed in the Apparel & Accessories section (see page 51), is preferable. But wait! We're not just talking about table cloths, but napkins too. Using cloth napkins and kitchen towels will greatly reduce the amount of trash produced by paper napkins and towels, especially if we're talking about big spills.

Party Supply

However we may try to avoid using disposable products, there are some occasions where it's not plausible, such as a large gathering. Bringing reusable cups and dinnerware for everyone who shows up to a large picnic, barbecue or other food-oriented party is more than a challenge, and trying to transport dirty dishes more than a chore.

Biodegradable Dinnerware

That's why biodegradable plastic is such a boon to green entertaining. Known as PLA, the corn and sugar-based material differs from regular plastic in that it's not petroleum-based and will naturally decompose, even in a compost heap. PLA foam and plastic cups, plates, bowls and cutlery may be disposed of relatively conscience-free, food-stains and all.

Recycled Dinnerware

A lot of plastic dinnerware is difficult to recycle at best, and when your plates, cups and cutlery happens to be made of polystyrene, recycling them is not deemed economically viable, so they will always be sent to a landfill. However, if you look close, you'll see that there are some plastic service products made from recycled materials, which probably indicates they can be recycled again. Biodegradable or recycled dinnerware and utensils may be tough to find in your local market, but that's why you have **thepurplebook**.

Eat Out and Take-Out

Cooking at home is doubtlessly the easiest way to ensure the food you eat is whole, natural and organic, but you're also quite likely to find eco-friendly restaurants in your area, especially using this site: **DineGreen.com.**

Whatever restaurant you settle on, bear in mind that take-out packaging is often non-recyclable and/or non-biodegradable. The convenience of home delivery will be tough to pass on (there are such things as green couch potatoes), but may work in a pinch if you can convince your favorite restaurants to use recyclable packaging.

Most reputable sit-down restaurants will prepare food using whole, rather than processed, colored, flavored and artificially preserved foods. Fast food restaurants, however, do not usually adhere to these principles, and usually use disposable packaging even when you do dine in. Adding to these issues would be the ubiquitous Drive-Thru window. Who among us haven't spent several minutes at a time with our car engines idling, waiting for greasy meals wrapped in paper and cardboard to be eaten with plastic utensils?

>> Household

If you look at your home as a microcosm of the planet and its atmosphere, you'll see that many of the same principles we use to preserve our planet's resources may be applied to keeping house. After all, you want your plants to flourish, you don't want gunk to gather in the corners, you like the air to stay fresh and you hate to see clutter pile up to congest your open spaces. And let's not forget that you try not to waste water or electricity, if only to keep those utilities bills down.

Basically, you want a neat, clean and healthy household. The problem is, some of the functional household products you use on a regular basis could be causing some problems.

The Problem: Common housekeeping and maintanance routines contribute heavily to local and global pollution.

The Culprits: Chemical household cleaners and energy wasting lighting.

The Solution: Using only nontoxic cleaning supplies and energy-efficient light bulbs.

Nontoxic Cleaners

Somewhere along the line, people were tricked into thinking that no surface could be absolutely clean unless it was bathed in bleaches and covered in chemicals. Granted, these chemicals do kill any microbes that might concern us, but what else are they killing? When you smell fumes, those are the potential toxins being released into the atmosphere. When you wash the suds down the drain, they will eventually make their way to a natural waterway.

Dienviro.com: Info about ingredients found in cleaning products
NancysNatural.info: Locate natural housecleaning services

Biodegradable Garbage Bags

Almost by definition, your garbage bags are heading for the landfill, where they and their contents will slowly decompose year after year at the bottom of a pile of other garbage bags. Conventional plastic garbage bags will not only take years to degrade, they will also slow down the decomposition of much of the garbage inside. Switching to biodegradable bags won't stop the landfill from overflowing, but it may shorten the time it takes for that landfill to be useful again.

Recycled Paper Goods (Paper Towels, etc.)

There's bound to be at least one disposable paper product in your home that you refuse to do without, but that's not to say you can't find more responsible ways to go about your daily business. We're referring to recycled-content paper goods, which will save trees without sacrificing function in the slightest. And in case you consider yourself a sensitive, um, soul, bear in mind that all recycled toilet paper is not as scratchy as you might think.

Lighting

How many environmentalists does it take to change a light bulb? The world is finding out, as the proliferation of energy efficient bulbs is a shining beacon of success in the eco-movement. In fact, the future of traditional incandescent bulbs is dim, and will soon burn out. If you're not yet tired of light bulb jokes, here are some bright ideas to help make your household lighting more earth-friendly!

CFL Bulbs (Compact Fluorescent Lights)

Perhaps the best, at least the best-advertised, alternative to the inefficient bulbs we grew up with, CFLs are making serious headway on flat-out replacing incandescents altogether. It's not surprising, given the amount of money we stand to save on electricity by using CFLs, and especially considering the fact they will last anywhere from eight to fifteen times longer than hot-burning filament bulbs.

Find out more about CFL bulbs at: **18seconds.org**.

LED Bulbs (Light Emitting Diodes)

Probably best known as the colored lighting responsible for Exit signs, traffic lights and novelty toys, science has only recently discovered ways to produce radiant white light using LED technology. But the incredibly efficient, virtually unbreakable and extraordinarily long-lasting bulbs have been quick to hit the market, and though early models do not match the luminosity of high-watt CFL or incandescent bulbs, progress is occurring at a rapid pace, so that most household lighting needs will soon best be met by LEDs.

Also, amber LED bulbs won't attract insects, making them great options for patio lighting.

Solar Powered Outdoor/Security Lighting

Using the sun to power light bulbs sounds like the setup to a joke; but solar-charging our outdoor lights is an increasingly practical way to keep your property securely lit without drawing power from your home. Aside from the obvious benefits of energy conservation, using outdoor lights with built-in photovoltaic cells allows you to shed light on any part of your property without the messy hassle of tapping into your home's electrical wiring. You may even find this technology used in concert with motion-sensors to give your home security a sun-powered assist.

Recycling Light Bulbs

The choice in light bulbs is shadowed by another environmental issue: disposal. Hard as you might look, you will not likely find any recycling options for incandescent light bulbs, and so most of us have no choice but to throw them away when they burn out.

Since CFLs last longer, you won't often have to worry about disposing of them. The problem is, they contain small amounts of mercury, so if they wind up in landfills or incinerators, the toxic metal is released into the environment. This means recycling CFL bulbs is especially important. Unfortunately, it's also rare to find a convenient recycling program. These links will help:

LampRecycle.org
Bulbs.com

Laundry

Laundry is a sensitive issue for environmentalists, as evidenced by each successive generation of unwashed hippie. The problem is trifold: water consumption, energy consumption and water pollution. Using a nontoxic, biodegradable laundry detergent will prevent chemical pollution from seeping into the public water system, but the first two require a bit more investment.

Water conservation is particularly tough, as every non-chemical clothes washing method requires water. When shopping for a machine, look at Energy Star rated appliances, and bear in mind that front-loading washers usually consume less water. While washing, make sure the water usage settings are accurately set so you don't use more than you need, and that high-temperature settings are used only when necessary to conserve energy. Washing less frequently and with larger loads will optimize your use of resources.

Drying your clothes with a machine uses a lot of electricity. Check your dryer for energy efficient or air dry settings, and make sure the filter is clean. Better yet, on a slow or sunny day, try drying your wash the old fashion way—on a clothesline. Call it the original use of solar power if it makes you feel better; either way, it costs you nothing and reduces energy consumption.

GREEN DRY CLEANING

Conventional dry cleaning is not your only option; in fact, the best eco-alternative to toxic dry cleaning may be *wet cleaning*, which uses computer technology to safely clean "dry clean only" garments. Look for it, or convince your dry cleaner to switch.

Also, ask your dry cleaner to switch to biodegradable "EcoHangers," which are available at:

HangerNetwork.com

>> Health & Beauty

In many ways, our personal beauty regimens may be the aspects of our lifestyles we're least willing to change for the environment's sake. It's easy enough to switch to organic tomatoes, to avoid wearing synthetic fibers or even to take shorter showers. But to give up the shampoo, conditioner, moisturizer, cleanser and makeup brands we've spend so many painstaking years matching to our personal body chemistry? That's tough to ask.

The good news is that these products don't have quite the enormous impact on the planet as other industries do. However, some of the commonly found synthetic materials might be detrimental to your own health! And you may be surprised to learn that some of these dubious substances aren't even the product's active ingredients!

The Problem: Our health and beauty regimens may expose our bodies and the environment to hazardous chemicals.

The Culprits: Personal care products that use questionable ingredients.

The Solution: Learning more about which ingredients to avoid and sticking to all-natural products.

INGREDIENTS TO AVOID

There are a number of potentially hazardous and unnatural chemicals that are commonly used in beauty products as colorants, preservatives, foaming agents and more, and often these ingredients have little or nothing to do with the product's intended purpose.

While a final conclusion has not yet been reached by the scientific community on how dangerous certain chemicals may or may not be, there are some known or suspected to potentially cause asthma, dermatological reactions, genetic damage, biological mutations or even cancer. Since the FDA has been historically slow to recognize certain chemicals as toxic, dozens of chemicals that are banned in other nations are perfectly acceptable in American ingredients lists.

These lists are supposed to allow consumers to make educated decisions about what we ingest or apply. But somewhere along the line these lists got longer, and scientific names made most of them incomprehensible, and we stopped looking.

Here is a short list of words to watch out for:

Parabens
Stearics
Pthlalates
Benzoates
Sodium Laurel Sulfates
Diethanolamine (DEA)
Triethanolamine (TEA)

Note that the terms "fragrances" and "aromas" may be used without listing the actual ingredients of the scent, and that "fragrance-free" may refer to the fact chemicals have been added to mask the product's odors

Learn more about common ingredients at these sites:

LivingNature.com
SukisNaturals.com
LifeKind.com
CosmeticsDatabase.com
TerrEssentials.com

Natural & Organic Products

Our skin absorbs 60% of everything we put on it. Many components of our daily beauty regimens contain carcinogens, petrochemicals and other hazardous toxins. There are lots of great natural and organic choices out there that provide healthier options that don't compromise on quality or cost more. They are better for you and the environment. Learn more about alternatives at these sites:

DiEnviro.com
NaturalHealthMag.com

Mineral Cosmetics

Most of the lipstick, foundation and blush you've ever used contained synthetic colorings, but that needn't be the case in the future. Safer mineral cosmetics are now readily available in terrific, rich colors.

Feminine Products

Any disposable monthly product is a cause for environmental concern, and a variety of feminine hygiene products may be just that. There are greener options available, ranging from nondisposable to biodegradable products.

Reusable Containers

Once you've settled into your regular green beauty regimen, consider what happens to the various shampoo, cleanser and lotion containers. Reusable containers may be a better option, whether you refill them with bulk beauty purchases, or opt for travel-size containers you can take with you for the rest of your life.

THE AEROSOL QUESTION

Some of us may be too young to remember the role aerosol sprays once played in depletion of the ozone layer. For most of us, though, aerosol hairsprays and deodorants will always be associated with the greenhouse effect, despite years of hearing that aerosol sprays are safe again.

The good news is that CFC's, the destructive elements in aerosol sprays, have indeed been out of use for decades. However, the pressurized cans are almost never recyclable, so using aerosols still lay a heavy burden on the planet, just in a different way.

>> Apparel & Accessories

When it comes to absolute life necessities, clothes and accessories rank somewhere down the list of priorities behind air, water, food and shelter, grouped just ahead of medicine and caffeinated beverages. But fashion somehow feels more important, maybe for reasons of self-expression or perhaps simple vanity. Regardless, the way we dress is important both personally and professionally, so balancing the need to look good with the urge to do right by the planet means walking a fine line. Which makes sense, because it often boils down to your choice of thread—natural or synthetic.

The Problem: The fashion industry is responsible for unleashing massive amounts of chemicals directly into the environment.

The Culprits: Synthetic fabrics, chemical dyes and even natural fabrics made using nonsustainable methods.

The Solution: Only buying clothes and accessories that use organic, recycled and sustainable fibers, and low-impact dyes.

Buying Clothes With Sustainable Fabrics

Today's market offers a great variety of fabric options that allow you to dress well while reducing your impact on the planet. Unfortunately, doing so often requires cutting down on impulse buys and, if you devote yourself to eco-friendly materials and manufacturing processes, you will likely leave a lot of great looking clothes and accessories on the rack. The good news is that each year more clothing labels are making the switch to sustainable fabrics and production, and so any effort you make will contribute to the demand for a finer array of earth-friendly fashions next season.

Wardrobe basics, such as jeans, t-shirts and underwear, make for an good place to start the switch to sustainable materials as without sacrificing personal tastes, you may support the clothing industry's gradual reformation. However, don't think for a minute that stylish garb cannot be found in the eco skein! If you specifically narrow your search to green attire, you are going to find casual, contemporary and up-to-the-minute designer fashions for most occasions, and these clothes may soon become the favorites in your wardrobe. How do we know? Because we've seen what's out there and taken special care to include the best of it in this book, naturally.

Here is a list of fabrics that look and feel good to wear, along with some of their desirable qualities:

Organic Cotton

On the face of it, cotton itself seems plenty natural and not the slightest bit perilous to our planet. However, as you may have heard, conventionally raised cotton accounts for as much as a quarter of chemical pesticide and fertilizer use worldwide, making cotton one of the most pollutant industries around. Though the relative toxicity of these substances is always up for debate, several of the "safe" chemicals used in the past have since been found to be quite dangerous to both humans and the ecosystem. Irrigation runoff releases these toxins into waterways, where a long list of plants and animals are unintentionally exposed to them. Additionally, some of the chemicals even linger on the fabric right up to the moment we put it against our skin. Heard enough? Organic cotton usually costs a bit more, but it offers the same level of comfort and fashion, without the mess.

Colorgrown Cotton

Since chemical bleaches and dyes are usually as, or more, damaging to the ecosystem as synthetic pesticides, even some processed organic cotton attire can be trouble. While you may sidestep this by only supporting manufacturers that use low-impact and vegetable dyes, another terrific option is colorgrown cotton. This comes from plants that have been bred to produce naturally tinted cotton, usually green or brown.

Benefits of Organic Cotton
- Comfortable
- Durable
- Breathable
- Versatile, and can be woven into a variety of thicknesses and textures, including jersey, terry cloth, velvet, chenille, flannel, canvas, sateen, denim and twill

Hemp

Almost synonymous with earth-friendly clothing, hemp is seen by many as a great panacea to the world's environmental woes. Of course, that's overstating the situation, but the highly versatile crop definitely has a place in ecologically sound manufacturing and agriculture. Hemp requires relatively little water to grow, and a natural resilience to insects means it's generally cultivated without pesticides, making it sort of de facto organic (obtaining organic certification is a costly bureaucratic process, so hemp growers rarely seek it).

Although it cannot be used as a drug, misconceptions surrounding hemp's relation to marijuana unfortunately prevent it from being grown legally in this country. However, it is still widely available as an import, and may be legally sold, so you will find no shortage of hemp goods distributed online. The fabric itself is sturdy but can also be quite coarse, so you will often find it blended with other textiles such as cotton, bamboo and soy to improve comfort and drape. Conversely, you will often find 100% hemp fabrics applied to accessories like backpacks, toiletry cases and reusable grocery bags, making for a great alternative to plastic.

Benefits of Hemp
- Biodegradable
- Antibiotic
- UV Protectant
- Highly Durable
- Cool in warm weather (breathable)
- Warm in cool weather

Wool, Cashmere and Alpaca

When it comes to using animal fibers, it's always nice to know that no animals have been harmed in the production of your sweater. Sheared or combed, the sheep, goats and alpaca providing these yarns are left in no different a state than before giving up their coats, except they're maybe a little cooler. Consequently, each woolly animal may be seen as a renewable resource. So is it green?

Like cotton, it usually depends on the source. A lot of livestock are fed grass and grains grown using chemical pesticides and fertilizers. They may also be administered antibiotics and growth hormones. You will come across organic wool on occasion, which makes it easy to know the sheep were raised naturally. However, certification for cashmere or alpaca is much less common. This doesn't necessarily mean the fabric in question was raised irresponsibly—many sustainable ranchers simply don't seek the organic label—but it does mean the yarn's origin matters. If you want to avoid doubts, dedicated eco-retailers usually only sell ethically-sourced wool.

Benefits of Wools
- Insulating
- Soft and comfortable (especially cashmere and alpaca)
- Moisture absorbent
- Breathable

Silk

Seeing as silk has been cultivated in China for nearly five-thousand years, it would seem pretty tough to argue its sustainability. Silkworms feed exclusively on mulberry leaves, which grow continually over the tree's lifespan. So, even though one mulberry tree's worth of leaves produce little silk, relatively speaking the process is not super detrimental to the planet.

Still, there isn't yet any standard process to certify organic silk, so it's virtually impossible to know whether artificial means have been used to raise the trees or control the growth of the silkworms. Vigilant shoppers might on occasion find silk culled from producers proud to assert their sustainable practices, which is ideal. Additionally, some animal activists have qualms with the treatment of the silkworms, which are actually caterpillars who create silk when weaving their cocoons. To preserve the integrity of the silk threads (which are secreted in long, continuous strands), the caterpillars are killed before they can damage the cocoons to emerge as moths.

Some silks are designated as "Peace" or "Vegetarian" silk, which means the caterpillars haven't been killed in the process. However, because the strands have been broken by the moth, these silk fibers must be spun into yarns (like wool, linen or cashmere), creating a weaker but arguably softer fabric.

Benefits of Silk
◎ Soft, smooth and light
◎ Cool in warm, warm in cool weather
◎ Hypoallergenic

KEEP UP WITH GREEN FASHION

Style doesn't stop just because you're dressing yourself with the planet in mind. These sites will dish the newest developments in green fashions:

Eco-Chick.com
EcoLuxe.co.uk
ThisIsMyLab.com
InHabitat.com
MissMalaprop.com
Sprig.com
SustainableStyle.org

Linen

Linen is derived from the fibers of the flax, aka linseed, plant. Like hemp, flax grows with minimal resources and can thrive with little or no pesticides. It also grows rather quickly and, in most cases, a natural process is still used to extract the fibers. Also like hemp, it's rare to find certified organic linen, but when you consider that most parts of the plant are used for different purposes (such as natural wood finish and linoleum), linen turns out to be a pretty sustainable textile. As residents of a tropical climate will tell you, it's a terrific fabric for hot, humid weather, as it feels cool against the skin. It also wicks and absorbs moisture rather well, yet dries quickly.

Benefits of Linen
◎ Cool in warm weather
◎ Wicks moisture and dries quickly

Rayon (aka Tencel, Modal or Viscose)

Probably because of its name, rayon is commonly miscategorized as synthetic, but technically speaking it's derived from a natural source, i.e. cellulose wood pulp. The chemical process of extracting the cellulose fibers is not ideal. However, the biodegradable fabric is often made from recycled or remnant wood, and can emulate the properties of wool, cotton, linen or silk.

Benefits of Rayon
◎ Cool in warm weather
◎ Absorbent
◎ Soft and smooth

Bamboo Fabric

Widely celebrated as a boon to environmentalism, bamboo had myriad uses in the production of wood furniture and servicewares. But it's a less-obvious use of the stiff grass that has the fashion-world buzzing: as a textile. When converted into fabric, bamboo takes some of the benefits of silk, linen and polyester.

Benefits of Bamboo
◎ Soft, smooth and light
◎ Cool in warm, warm in cool weather
◎ Wicks moisture and dries quickly
◎ Blocks UV rays
◎ Antibacterial
◎ Hypoallergenic

To learn more visit: **BambooClothes.com**

GREEN FABRICS AND COLD WATER WASH

Naturally antibiotic materials, such as bamboo, hemp, soy and rayon, offer additional eco benefits: they may be washed less frequently, and in cold water. This can greatly reduce your water and energy bills.

They also tend to dry quickly, which makes them ideal candidates to air dry. In fact, high heat is not condusive to a long lifespan for these fabrics, so if you do put them in the dryer, adjust your settings accordingly. Either way, the energy savings for a single load of green laundry is astounding!

Soy Fabric

Another fairly surprising addition to the garment landscape is fabric spun from soy beans. The soy in question may or may not be organic (usually not), but the good news is that soy is considered a fairly renewable crop, and though genetic modification is common, heavy use of pesticides is not the norm. Better still, the fabric is made from the parts left over once the bean has been used to make tofu or soymilk, so spinning it into thread creates a brilliant use of a common manufacturing byproduct.

Benefits of Soy
- Soft and comfortable (like silk or cashmere)
- Made from byproduct of soymilk and tofu production
- Antibiotic
- Blocks UV rays

PLA Fibers (Polylactide Acid)

Relatively new to the eco-fiber landscape, PLA is essentially polyester, but with one key difference: it's biodegradable. Derived from corn or sugarcane, the vegetable-based polymer contains no petrochemicals, nor are any used in its manufacture. Of course, the actual production process would be too complex to be explained here even if we could. What we do know is that various chemicals are involved, but the end result should decompose within a couple of months—in a landfill, not while you're wearing it.

Benefits of PLA
- Biodegradable
- Antibiotic
- Same properties as polyester

Vegetable-Tanned Leather

Obviously, leather is not the most popular fashion choice of animal advocates, but it can be sustainably produced, even if the results are hard to find. To begin with, organic leather is slowly turning up on the eco-market, which makes sense when you consider the growing popularity of organically-raised beef. However, the most earth-friendly option is vegetable-tanned leather. Conventional tanning and washing techniques involve heavy use of chemicals and dyes, which notoriously pollute bodies of water. Vegetable-based tans don't do the same result in the same damaging pollution, but still produce beautiful leather.

Benefits of Leather
- Highly durable
- Warm
- Protective against harsh weather and winds

Recycled & Reclaimed Fabrics

The recycling bug hasn't been limited to newspapers and beer cans—a slew of emerging fashion labels have taken to repurposing used fabrics to create beautiful new designs. We've seen vintage silk scarves turned into classy tops, boring old sweaters turned into funky new sweaters and even used trucking tarps turned into slick designer handbags. Incorporating reclaimed materials into fashion items can be expressive and trendy as well as green, and there are plenty of other potential benefits depending on which fabric is used. Really the only limit is the availability of materials and ingenuity of the producer.

Used & Vintage Attire

You might not have realized it, but the last time you went thrift store shopping you were practicing sound conservation principles. Keeping functional items in action keeps them out of the landfill, extending the life cycle of the product and in some small way reducing the need for manufacture of new goods. And you thought you were just saving money.

Of course, the term "vintage" usually applies to especially well-preserved clothes or to used garments with a pedigree. Such attire may in fact cost as much as comparable new garb, or even more if the item is rare. But the concept remains the same: buying vintage is green, even if the outfit in question is a troubling early experiment in polyester.

Accessories

Accessories pretty much follow the same eco-standards as apparel, with a few exceptions. For one thing, you are much more likely to find accessories made from recycled materials, particularly when it comes to handbags. There are a few special considerations worth addressing.

Conflict-Free Jewelry

As if avoiding products that pollute the earth wasn't serious enough, the world must now face up to the knowledge that the cost of precious stones may run way higher than their pricetags would indicate.

Copious human rights abuses have been reported in the mining of gemstones worldwide, including child labor, forced labor, and perilous working conditions. Such practices often fund militias, guerilla groups and other civil instability, and nearly always involve environmentally detrimental mining practices. If you want a diamond to be forever guiltless, look for the Conflict Free certification. Otherwise, you may find jewelry created with alternative materials.

Shoes

Finding eco-friendly shoes might have been one of our biggest challenges, but it can be done, and we found several lines of fashionable, functional, planet-friendly footwear. These shoes, sandals and boots may include recycled materials, natural rubber, vegetable-tanned leather, hemp and other canvases. Note that we have not included petroleum-based vegan leather in this group; although it's better for the longevity of cows, vegetable-tanned genuine leathe remains the best eco option.

Functional Accessories

These may not be the most appealing ways to accessorize, but they can do a lot to reduce your dependence on disposable items. Buying these items right now will drastically lower your environmental impact in the coming year.

Reusable Grocery Bags

Plastic grocery bags in particular have been creating pollution problems around the world, as the flimsy but slow-to-degrade bags are easily caught up in a breeze and wind up landing in every nook and cranny of the landscape, as well as in bodies of water. A great way to avoid the paper-or-plastic issue is to bring your own reusable hemp or cotton canvas bags to the store. Every single time you shop with your own bag, you are reducing waste.

Reusable Water Bottles

The ubiquitous plastic water bottle may be convenient, and even a bit of a status symbol, but as its popularity has skyrocketed, so has the number of bottles winding up in landfills. Buying a metal or even heavy plastic water container to travel with you from home to the workplace and abroad will save you money but still allow you to quench that thirst wherever you go—without the waste!

Reusable Food Containers

Packing a lunch can save you money, but if you're packing a brown bag with several plastic baggies five times a week you can create a lot of waste. If your whole family is doing it, the amount multiplies. Even in a single month, this can add up. By using reusable containers such as lunch bags, lunch boxes, tupperware, thermoses or bento boxes, you can reduce that garbage output to almost nothing. And that's not even talking about household leftovers.

Avoid Toxic Bleaches, Washes and Dyes

The garment industry is massive, encompassing most nations on the planet and responsible for incalculable production each year. Still, although it's easy to imagine pollution coming out of the sort of factories that produce cars, plastics or computers, the idea that the shirts on our backs may be responsible for untold contamination of the environment is tougher to envision. But it's true.

Most clothing manufacturers use toxic bleaches and petrochemical dyes to achieve bright colors and perfectly rendered patterns. Many use chemical-based garment washes to control the texture and sheen of the fabrics. However natural a material might be to begin with, when it's put through a conventional manufacturing process it's exposed to a variety of unnatural substances. The damaging part is that many of the factories where this takes place do not regulate the disposal of these chemicals, and the runoff usually winds up finding its way into the nearest body of water.

There are alternatives, including a growing number of nontoxic vegetable, soy-based and low-impact dyes. You'll even find unbleached and undyed clothes that don't look half-bad (assuming you're into earth tones).

TAKE POLITICAL ACTION

Reducing demand for goods made without regard for our environment helps, but letting your elected officials know what you think is more important than ever. Send a message to the right people at: **Congress.org**

>> Babies & Children

A good litmus test for whether you think a product is friendly to the earth is to ask yourself whether you think it's friendly enough for your baby: if a product is too toxic for an infant, it's probably too toxic for the planet. But the flipside may be more important to remember: if it's not good for the earth, you definitely don't want to expose your newborn to it.

The Problem: Babies and children are more vulnerable to the dangerous chemicals used in agriculture and manufacturing.

The Culprits: Potentially toxic plastics and chemically-treated products including food, clothes, bath products and toys.

The Solution: Avoiding plastics, toxic finishes, nonorganic fabrics and chemical ingredients.

While miniscule quantities of hazardous chemicals may not have immediate, adverse health effects on adults, with babies it can be a different matter. Their tiny developing bodies are especially vulnerable to the toxins released by irresponsible manufacturing and disposal, whether it gets to them through the air, water or direct contact with their mouths, hands and skin.

Unfortunately, when it comes to toys and other baby products, there is no universal mandate for companies to disclose which chemicals are used during manufacturing, meaning there's the potential for any plastic toy, and even some natural ones, to contain toxins that are potentially harmful and/or disruptive to development.

Which isn't to say the plastic toy your parents buy their grandchild is a ticking time bomb. Obviously, it's easy to succumb to fearfulness when you try to establish a safe environment for your child—a parent's greatest natural anxiety is failing to do something right—but in most cases a toy, blanket, booty or shampoo intended for children is going to be safe for children. The surest way to look out for your child's future is to shop responsibly and go green.

Baby Clothes & Accessories

Shopping for green baby clothes doesn't prove very different from doing so for adults: you'll find organic cotton, bamboo, soy and silks. You may notice one huge difference though: a much bigger selection. It seems that the aforementioned parental anxiety has really expanded the eco-friendly baby market in the past decade, and you will find no shortage of excellent merchandise that is both earth- and baby-friendly. In particular, you may see a lot of organic colorgrown cotton and other natural fabrics that use no chemicals or bleaches whatsoever.

Diapers

Arguably the most important baby garment, the diaper, sort of has its own way of protecting the environment. Of course, you don't have to be a parent to understand how much waste a tot can produce.

Cloth Diapers

It feels odd to suggest our society collectively switch to reusable cloth diapers, since it was only a few decades ago we really switched away from them. In that time, though, we have seen the disposable plastic diaper become the poster-villain for overflowing landfills. Considering how many diapers a baby goes through a day, for how many years, that every single one of us was a baby once and that the majority of us wore disposables in the late-twentieth century, it's little wonder.

Today's cloth diapers and diaper covers have definitely updated the concept, with cute patterns and more, let's call them aerodynamic, designs. Or, you may opt to go for undyed organic cotton or hemp designs. But the real question remains whether you feel comfortable handing them down to a younger sibling.

However pure you decide to shop, simply reusing the end product will have an impact. The reemerging cloth diaper trend won't change the fact that every disposable diaper ever worn will outlive us all, but it might reverse the trend and help make our future landfills better—or at least fewer—places.

Learn more about cloth diapering at these sites:

DiaperJungle.com
DiaperNet.org

Biodegradable Disposable Diapers

If the mess of cleaning cloth diapers is too much to bear, or the convenience of disposable diapers too tempting to stand, you might be in the market for a new breed of biodegradable disposables. Made from a variety of materials (some even use recycled parts) there are several different types, ranging from inside liners that you flush down the toilet to fully decomposable fabrics that you may toss out with the trash with relatively little remorse.

Bath & Skin Care

As with adult beauty products, there is the potential that some pretty unappealing ingredients will show up in baby bath products. Labels like *Extra Sensitive* and *Gentle* that are typically found on baby skin products might be seen as a concession that the adult versions are a little harsh, but even with these labels, check to see what sort of chemicals a product might contain before committing to it. Since a baby's skin is about as naturally pure as it gets, there's really no reason to put anything but natural ingredients on it.

Toys

When your kid wants a particular toy, explaining that its plastic construction, styrofoam packaging and chemical dyes are harmful to the planet will rarely change his or her mind; such are the perils of advertising. Nevertheless, it *is* possible to find some great green toys for them to enjoy as well, even if you have to sneak them in to your child's life with bright, colorful wrapping, ribbons and fanfare.

Finding natural toys is not an overwhelming task; even the large toy chains will offer wood toys, plush animals and other plastic-free options. However, for the purposes of this book we've raised the bar a little bit, looking for toys made with sustainable materials and natural finishes. In short, nothing that could release toxins when, for example, a baby decides to see what it tastes like.

BACK TO SCHOOL GUIDE

Students of any age can start the school year off on the right foot with these greener options:
- Purchase used textbooks
- Use a laptop instead of a desktop
- Purchase recycled paper and pencils
- Create "no idle" zones in school carpool pickup lines
- Eat trash free lunches: bring a reusable lunch box, reusable containers, cloth napkin, and silverware
- Look into healthy school lunch options at:

FarmToSchool.org

>> Pets

If you're trying to switch to a greener lifestyle you're probably not going to leave your pets behind: after all, left to their own devices they would have little more impact on the planet than the occasional mess on the lawn and some chewed up sticks.

The earth-friendly pet market is slightly behind the human one, so you won't find a whole lot of sustainable-fabric dog sweaters. However, when it comes to basic pet care, you will find a lot of all-natural products, and on occasion some using sustainable and organic principles.

The Problem: Pet products are even more likely than human products to damage the planet.

The Culprits: Any pet product made using nonsustainable practices.

The Solution: Shopping for your pet as green as you would shop for yourself.

Natural Foods, Treats & Supplements

Making your animal's diet eco-friendly may not seem like a big deal, but it's actually easy enough to accomplish that it's pointless not to. Although a recent movement to introduce only human-grade ingredients into dog and cat food usually produces good results, if you stick to searching for foods with all-natural ingredients your pet will surely be healthier and happier. Finding certified organic pet food is also possible and, though it won't necessarily win you any points with the furrier members of your household, it will certainly help support sustainable agriculture.

Sustainable Accessories

When it comes to dressing and accessorizing your pets, collars, leashes, beds, toys and apparel comprise a massive industry with endless options. Just like people products, these will often be made with synthetic or chemical-laden fibers. Considering your pet doesn't care too much about design, texture or fit, you might as well stick to easy-to-come-by sustainable fabrics such as organic cotton or the inexpensive hemp. In some cases, enterprising manufacturers have even incorporated recycled materials, such as reclaimed polystyrene fill for pet beds.

Nontoxic Grooming & Health Products

Whether it's shampoo or flea dip, the products you use to keep your pets clean don't require chemicals in order to work. You will find a great number of natural, nontoxic alternatives that won't pollute the environment or your animal's coat.

Biodegradable Poop Bags

Picking up after your dog doesn't have to be such a dirty job. Although replacing plastic bags with biodegradable ones won't make the act of scooping any less unsavory, at least your pooch's daily output won't take up space in a landfill while the bag takes years and years to decompose.

Biodegradable Kitty Litter

Your cat may not go on the lawn, but that doesn't mean its waste is friendly to the planet. Some cat litter varieties release chemicals into the environment. There's little need for this, as a variety of cat litters are made from natural or recycled ingredients that are just as biodegradable as that which they're designed to hide.

>> Stationery, Office & Gifts

Viewed one way, personal, professional and social obligations might seem to offer us little choice but to shirk our environmental endeavors. But we prefer to see them as giving us a new range of opportunities to go green. More than that, these transactions allow us to share eco-values with friends, family and associates. A gift, in particular, can show someone just how good green can get.

The Problem: Paper production is often pollutant, while paper waste contributes heavily to deforestation.

The Culprits: Nonsustainable paper and other wasteful packaging.

The Solution: Tree-free, reusable and recycled paper and packaging products.

Paper Products

Even in our new e-world, paper continues to hold an important place in daily life, whether it's used for a legal document, symbolic gesture, mass publication or a good, old-fashioned letter. It's impossible to count just how many trees have been cut down since the advent of paper, but it's a safe bet to assume that more have been felled than replanted.

It's not realistic to simply stop consuming paper altogether—it accomplishes too many essential functions. But there are ways to lessen the number of new trees used to produce it. Sustainable paper is currently used to make a variety of products, and the number is growing every day. Which, of course, leaves more trees to grow every day as well.

Recycled Paper

Of course, the number one way to buy paper without contributing to deforestation is to find items made using recycled content. When you see the word *Recycled* on the label, it means that its production used a high enough percentage of recycled materials to meet guidelines set by the EPA, usually at least 70%. There are two kinds of recycled paper content to watch out for:

Post-consumer: The better use of recycled materials, taken from the paper you put in your recycling bins.

Post-industrial, or Recovered: The leftover scraps from wood manufacturing have been collected and used.

The availability of recycled paper has grown considerably across a wide range of consumer products:

Printer paper
Paper towels
Toilet paper
Personal stationery

Tree-Free Paper

Stop the presses! As it turns out, paper doesn't need to come from trees. In fact, a number of companies are now producing paper from a variety of renewable resources including hemp, bananas and lokta (a bush found in southeast Asia). Not only do the results live up to the standards of traditional wood-based paper (such as the ability to absorb ink), but they often look and feel terrific as well. Thanks to their aesthetically appealing qualities, tree-free papers are most often used to make journals, invitations or personal stationeries.

Wrapping Paper & Gift Bags

Wrapping gifts may not be the most vital use of paper, but the practice is not likely to go anywhere anytime soon. Fortunately, the ardent environmentalist need not resort to wrapping gifts in the Sunday comics. A burgeoning industry makes giftwrap available in a beautiful assortment of recycled prints.

Another eco-friendly option is to offer your gift in a reusable gift bag. Made from materials like cotton and hemp, not only do these lovely bags conserve trees, they also encourage the giftee to pass a giftbag along to the next recipient, beginning a life-cycle that will help keep glossy wrapping paper out of the landfills.

Personal Checks
Especially in this age of electronic transfers and online banking, your checkbook's not the most obvious place to affect environmental progress. However, there are shops that specialize in printing checks on sustainable paper with nontoxic inks, as green as cash itself.

Packaging & Delivery
Boxes and packing materials are no exceptions to the environmental movement. Fact is, these are prime candidates for the most direct form of recycling: reusing. If you buy them new, look for recycled cardboard and biodegradable packing materials. Otherwise, when you receive an incoming shipment, say from an online order, turn around and use the same stuff for your outgoing mail.

Candles
If you already realize that many conventional candles are made with petrochemical-based paraffin, even though many perfectly natural alternatives are available, we like to assume you've already switched over to vegetable, palm, soy, beeswax or other green options.

While you're at it, don't forget that essential oils make for great, clean burning scents much more reliable than other "fragrances" or "aromatics," which are typically just code for "chemicals."

Office Supplies
Most of your green household practices may also be applied to your green workplace. Whether your office is in or outside the home, here are ways to be ecologically sound as well as productive:

- Recycle all used glass, paper and plastic products
- Print using both sides of a piece of paper
- Reuse paper clips
- Use recycled products such as paper file folders, plastic binders and refurbished printer cartridges
- Look for the Energy Star rating when buying computers, printers, copiers, fax machines and phones
- Turn off inactive office equipment, and turn out the lights when you leave
- Unplug PDA, phone and battery chargers

Check these sites to find out more about keeping a green office:

CartridgeWorldUSA.com
ConservaTree.org
TheGreenOffice.com

SUSTAINABLE BUSINESS

Making money doesn't have to mean forgetting about your eco-values. Check out these sites for some recommended green business practices:

GreenBiz.com
SustainableBusiness.com

>> Furnishings

When shopping for green furniture and home accents, the same rules apply: look for sustainable and nontoxic materials. This will not always be easy, because there are thousands of furniture manufacturers out there and most of them have not caught on to socially-responsible methods.

The Problem: Most furniture production uses toxic methods and depletes natural resources.

The Culprits: Plastics, irresponsibly harvested woods, chemical dyes and toxic upholstery.

The Solution: Search for furniture and accents using only sustainable materials and production, or buy used/vintage/antique products.

We've found several sites offering plenty of great options, though. Here are some things to look for.

Sustainable Woods

Opting for wood furniture may be the easiest way to green up your interior design motif, but, as usual you'll want to stick to wood from sustainable sources. Bamboo, FSC Certified and reclaimed lumber will usually be the best ways to go, along with the occasional cork components.

Nontoxic Finishes

More proof that shopping for eco-friendly furniture requires a lot of attention to detail, a lot of wood pieces may be finished with chemicals that will off-gas, releasing toxins into the air you breathe indoors. Whether or not a wood is sustainably sourced, you may wish to seek out vegetable-based stains for your furniture.

Nontoxic Upholstery

One of the bigger surprises when you seek out environmentally safe furniture is that upholstery usually doesn't fit the bill. The problem is that most conventional upholstery uses nonbiodegradable materials for the cushioning, and, for reasons we cannot fathom, formaldehyde during construction. Like toxic finishes, these cushions may off-gas regardless of whether they're couched in eco-safe fabrics like hemp, wool or vegetable-tanned leather. Keep an eye out for nontoxic upholstery in local and online furniture shops, and don't be afraid to ask questions.

Bed & Bath

As it turns out, when it comes to sustainability, the easiest home furnishing components to replace are also the easiest to find. Green bed linens and towels make up a huge market, and there are so many stores offering them it's a wonder we don't trip over any on the way out of the house. Between organic fabrics, hemp blends, bamboo, linen and silk, all your bases are covered, meaning you may turn your attention to seeking out a good organic mattress.

Recycled Materials

When shopping for your home's decorative and functional furnishings, recycled materials can be a great way to go. Whether it's plastic, glass or ingeniously constructed pieces made from somebody else's discarded trash, you won't have any trouble tracking down hip and modern designs that show off your envirofriendly taste.

Antiques

If it's not contemporary looks you're into, why buy newly manufactured products in the first place? Millions of finely crafted pieces have been constructed over the past few centuries, and many have long outlived their original owners. Heck, the passage of time being what it is, you may even find some brilliant antique modern furniture. Basically, any time you buy something second-, third- or twelfth-hand, you're being kind to the planet.

>> Gardening & Landscaping

Most of your local gardening stores doubtlessly carry a wide variety of fertilizers, plant foods and pesticides that promise superior growth. However, many contain chemicals that can be toxic to the atmosphere and to your own health. Some may actually be detrimental to the soil itself, meaning you'll be able to grow less the next time around.

The Problem: Nonorganic and genetically-manipulated agriculture is gradually depleting our soil of nutrients.

The Culprits: Genetically modified seeds, along with chemical pesticides and fertilizers.

The Solution: Use compost and mulch, beneficial insects and open-pollinated, organic and heirloom seeds.

Sticking to natural and organic gardening products reduces the risk of exposing yourself and your local environment to toxins. These sites will help you get started:

One-Garden.org
OrganicGardening.com

Nontoxic Pesticides & Fertilizers

Of course, the biggest hurdles to overcome when you want to garden organically are insects and nutrient-poor soil. But since any gardening site you find in this book will offer chemical-free choices, switching to natural methods proves no great leap. These sites will help:

BeyondPesticides.org
Panna.org

Beneficial Insects

While pesticides were clearly developed to wage war against aphids, grasshoppers and other insects that might ruin your garden or crop, a more natural effective method is to introduce predatory insects like ladybugs, beetles and praying mantis, which will devour the pests while leaving your plants relatively unscathed. You may actually buy these bugs from a nursery, but you will probably want to be certain exactly which pest you want eaten first.

This great beneficial insect guide can help: **PlanetNatural.com**

Composting & Mulching

When it comes to natural fertilizers, a sure way to keep your lawn and garden lush and green is to turn fallen leaves, dead plants, wood chips, shredded newspapers and leftover foods into compost or mulch. In both processes you essentially allow a mixture of organic matter to decompose into a nourishing soil-like substance. The difference between the two really lies in the application.

Compost

Composting involves putting your organic materials into a pile or bin and letting worms and microbes do the work of breaking them down until such time you are ready to distribute the matter to your soil.

Mulch

Mulching is used to help soil retain moisture and preserve it against weeds, insects and erosion. You simply spread out your organic materials over the top of the soil and they will naturally decompose, feeding your plants as they begin to grow. You may also use recycled natural rubber for this, or buy organic sheet mulch.

COMPOSTING GUIDE

One of the great benefits of composting and mulching is the chance to make use of some of the waste produced by your household and the plants around your property.

Whatever your dietary habits at home, you are bound to wind up with inedible scraps after preparing a meal. Rather than throwing them away to a landfill or sending them down the garbage disposal where they will help clog your local water treatment plant, these leftovers may be composted and used as an excellent fertilizer. Meat and dairy products should not be composted, but most of your unused whole foods will greatly help your lawn and garden. Here are some examples:

Melon rinds
Carrot stems
Apple cores
Any fruit peels
Coffee grounds (and filters)
Tea bags
Crushed egg shells

Check this site for more info: **CompostGuide.com**

Seeds

The seeds you use won't make a huge impact on the Earth—after all, if you're gardening with sustainable methods you are already doing your part. Nevertheless, here are some terms to watch out for when seed shopping that may increase your efforts.

Open-Pollinated Seeds

Many conventional seeds produce a non-seeding plant, meaning that once you grow your flower, fruit, herb or vegetable, you will need to procure more seeds to continue growing. Open pollination allows plants to grow and reproduce naturally, promoting biodiversity.

Organic Seeds

Certified organic seeds are taken, of course, from certified organic plants, which means you can be sure to avoid genetic modification or unforeseen effects of chemicals. The resulting plants will also produce seeds you may use for the next generation.

Heirloom Seeds

The rising popularity of heirloom plants may be seen as a response to the industrialization of agriculture. It's essentially a way to preserve smaller, successful strains of flowers and vegetables that might otherwise be lost in the wake of large farms. By nurturing heirlooms, you will be furthering the line in a natural way, in most cases with especially beautiful and/or delicious results.

Irrigation

When it comes to watering your lawn and garden, you want the means to justify the ends—trying to water a tropical oasis in a desert makes about as much sense as trying to plant a redwood in a skyrise apartment. In other words, responsible irrigation is largely about growing plants suitable to your region's climate.

That said, there are a couple of ways to conserve your water usage that will still provide your plants with the H2O they need.

Rain Barrels

In the rainy season, your lawn and garden will get more wet than they probably need; it's the dry times that force you to turn to the hose. However, it's a simple matter to gather rain in barrels during the wet season, then siphon your future irrigation need from them later. Obviously, if you're paying a high water bill each month, the relatively small one-time cost of a rain barrel is almost enough to sing and dance about.

Soaker Hoses
Use soaker hoses in flower/plant beds for drip irrigation and you'll use less than half the water your sprinklers use for the same soaking. Water early in the morning or in the evening.

Electric & Push Mowers

Fans of gas engines will tell you that you just can't get the same power and acceleration driving with an electric engine, and they may have a point. However, how much torque do you need when the same type of engine is being used to cut something as flimsy as grass? Electric mowers will certainly do the trick, and they won't run any differently if you charge them with solar power. Push mowers require a bit more physical exertion on your part, but there may be no cleaner power source on the planet than a fit environmentalist.

>> Electronics & Appliances

In the face of rising pollution and dwindling resources, a lot of us are counting on technology to save us—never mind that technology has played a huge role in getting us where we are today. Since the vast majority of electricity we use is derived from fossil fuels, the more electricity we use, the more pollution we create. In other words, our cars aren't the only culprits in this global warming mess; look around and you'll find a household buzzing with electricity guzzling products. Fortunately, you have many options to help minimize your consumption—and your energy bill.

The Problem: Using gadgets and appliances consumes a lot of water and energy.

The Culprits: Disposable batteries and any powered devices that use electricity and water inefficiently.

The Solution: Use rechargeable batteries, keep powered equipment properly maintained and only buy new devices that qualify for the Environmental Protection Agency's Energy Star rating.

Energy Star Rated Appliances

The Energy Star rating system is the Environmental Protection Agency's way of telling you that a particular appliance or electronics device operates more efficiently than the average such machine did prior to 1994. Using Energy Star designated products can severely reduce your energy use, increasing your ability to run your entire household on renewable power source!

As an added plus, in the cases of those appliances that use water, Energy Star ratings also indicate a significant reduction in gallons per use.

Learn about efficient appliances at: **EnergyStar.gov**

Energy Star Rated Electronics

The Energy Star rating doesn't just apply to appliances. Many home and personal electronics items such as computers, televisions, phones, monitors, printers and DVD players have also earned the high efficiency rating. Given the huge variety of products and manufacturers in this field, opting for an energy saving model requires little sacrifice. In fact, chances are you may have bought Energy Star products without realizing it. Check your computer's system controls to see if such settings are available and turned on!

Learn about efficient appliances at: **MyGreenElectronics.com**

Solar Appliances

Supporting renewable energy is still possible, even if you don't have enough space to set up solar panels to power your home. Various solar appliances are turning up, including water heaters, fan and ventilation systems, outdoor lighting and even some refrigerators.

Portable Solar Chargers

Solar power also isn't something you can only get at home. A great range of small-charge, portable photovoltaic cell panels are available to capture sunlight wherever it shines. You'll be able to charge personal electronics devices such as cell phones, digital cameras and MP3 players without an outlet, even while camping. We've even come across dozens of backpacks designed with built-in solar generators, so you can literally charge as you go!

Rechargeable Batteries

Batteries have long been the lifeblood of the personal electronics industry, and though most modern portable devices are packaged with proprietary batteries and chargers, a good number of products still require the old AA, AAA, C, D and 9-Volt varieties the majority of us grew up using. Probably out of habit, most of us are still buying the popular and well-advertised disposable battery brands. Although these may be recycled, if you know where to send them, an obvious, more direct and cheaper way to go about it has been available for decades: rechargeable versions.

Rechargeable versions of just about every battery size and strength can be found, often with a longer lifespan than popular brands. Although the initial purchase of batteries and charger will cost a little bit more than disposable alternatives, it's actually surprising how affordable they can be. And since you can recharge them hundreds of times, you won't have to spend money on new ones for years. You may even find solar battery chargers that will further lessen your carbon footprint.

GREENER COMMUNICATIONS

Whether you're speaking on the phone or logging on for an internet shopping session, there's no reason your communications can't support the greater good. Check out the following service providers, which make supporting a sustainable future a priority:

BetterWorldTelecom.com
EarthTones.com
EcoISP.com
LocomotiveMedia.com
WorkingAssets.com

Heating & Cooling

Particularly in the summer and winter, we expend a huge amount of energy each year on climate control. This is tough to get around, especially in extreme weather regions. But there are some ways to use this energy more efficiently, as complicated as installing a new ventilation system and as simple as putting in a ceiling fan. We'll explore some of the simpler ones, but you may learn more in general at the following sites:

HomeEnergy.org
RehabAdvisor.pathnet.org

Sealants & Insulation

It's not a new concept—make it harder for hot or cool air to escape through the cracks, seams and even walls of your home, and you improve the energy efficiency of your climate control devices. Obviously, some insulates are better than others, and though you won't find any asbestos on the market anymore (we hope), several existing options have the potential to do more harm than necessary. Likewise, chemical sealants are the standard, but we've found plenty of sites that feature eco-friendly alternatives to both.

Programmable Thermostats

A programmable thermostat will keep track of your home's temperature, and also make sure it's not still running when nobody's home. You can even find some smart thermostats that you can control remotely. An added benefit of these is that you may time it so that you walk into a cool home in the summer, and a warm one in the winter, without needlessly driving up your energy bill. If you really want to have an impact, merely setting your household temperature two degrees lower in the winter and higher in the summer will comfortably save a surprising amount of energy.

Planting Trees

Planting a tree has obvious benefits, but if you landscape cleverly, trees can provide shade to parts of your home exposed to the sun, and/or moderate protection from the wind when it gets cold. Did we say this was clever? Humans and animals have both been using trees as basic heating and cooling systems since prehistoric times.

Cleaner Air & Water

We tend to spend so much of our environmental effort on improving conditions for the outside world that it's easy to forget about the quality of our household air and water. It's not just about better tastes and smells—we could be breathing and ingesting chemicals we'd universally prefer to do without.

Water Filters

Filtering the water going into your home is generally more about personal health than the environment, but if you have good filtration methods in place you may use alternate water sources to meet your household needs, avoiding the dreaded plastic water bottle. There's no single 100% reliable method to making water free of toxins or parasites, so knowing a little bit about your local water source will help you decide whether you'll require charcoal or sand filters, reverse osmosis membranes or something more sophisticated.

Air Filters

Although you may not be aware of it, the exposed surfaces of your home may be off-gassing, which means they are releasing potentially toxic chemicals into the air. The paint on your walls, the upholstery of your sofa, even the fibers of your carpet might be contributing to a decline of air quality, not just of the earth's atmosphere, but directly into your living room. Air filters will consume electricity, but they will also wipe these toxins from the air you breathe and, placed properly, may even trap some of these noxious gases before they get outside.

>> Building Green

A popular talking point for both activists and the media is green building, and certainly the idea of converting your home to a more earth-friendly structure has its appeal. However, while incremental upgrades, as needed, may help make your abode more sustainable and self-sufficient, tearing up your floorboards and replacing your heating system all at once isn't just costly, it can be wasteful itself. Many of the principles behind green construction can only be implemented from the ground up, requiring detailed planning before a house is even built.

The Problem: Many conventional construction practices result in homes that are environmentally hazardous, wasteful of resources and energy inefficient.

The Culprits: Nonsustainable lumber, toxic insulation and paint and poor climate control considerations.

The Solution: When building, search for green contractors, source renewable or recycled materials, design the space for passive heating and cooling and install a geographically appropriate renewable energy generator.

LEED Certification

The US Green Building Council has established a system of benchmarks for establishing what makes a green building. The LEED ratings (Leadership in Energy and Environmental Design), seek to improve building and planning techniques in the hope that future construction will consider the environment as a matter of routine.

LEED endorses the following green building principles:
- Passive heating/cooling design
- Renewable energy sources
- Water collection/use
- Local-climate-appropriate insulation
- Sustainable materials, i.e. FSC-certified or reclaimed lumber
- Low-VOC paints and sealants

Your geography will have a great impact on the techniques used to build. For example, if you live in a very sunny area, solar energy might work, whereas if you live somewhere more volatile, wind power might make more sense. Passive heating and cooling considerations will take into account your home's altitude and exposure to the sun.

A sustainable, low impact home is a beautiful thing to behold, but if we all went out to build one we'd have to destroy a lot of nature or tear down a lot of perfectly sound structures. For most of us, this is currently just something to think about, and we can learn more at the US Green Building Council web site: **USGBC.org**

Contractors & Materials

Even if you are ready to build, finding engineers, architects and contractors qualified or willing to build green is difficult; sustainable materials are another problem altogether.

These sites should help you find green building professionals:

BuildingGreen.com
GreenBuilder.com
GreenBuildingBlocks.com
GreenBuildingPages.com
GreenHomeBuilding.com
GreenHomeGuide.com
Oikos.com
StrawBale.com

And these sites can lead you to green building materials:

Builder2Builder.com:	Salvaged materials
SalvageWeb.com:	Salvaged materials
AltuWood.com:	Reclaimed lumber
Bamboo2000.com:	Bamboo flooring
CeilingsPlus.com:	Eco-friendly ceilings
FSCUS.org:	Sustainable lumber

GREEN REAL ESTATE

Maybe your current home isn't green, but your future home can be. If you're on the market for a new pad, check out these green real estate listings:

EcoBroker.com
GreenHomesForSale.com
ListedGreen.com

>> Home Improvement

The good news is making an existing space safer and more efficient can be done. Of course, as with any home improvement project, it can prove a costly and time-consuming process. Here, we'll discuss just a few of the household upgrades you can pursue to make your living space greener.

The Problem: Most of our homes are water and energy inefficient, and potentially toxic.

The Culprits: Chemically treated floors, carpets and paints, outdated plumbing, wasteful climate control design.

The Solution: Water-conserving faucets and fixtures, nontoxic insulation and paints, sustainable flooring materials.

Low VOC Paints

VOC's, or Volatile Organic Compounds, are commonly found toxins that off-gas, meaning they evaporate off of solid surfaces to pollute the air. Conventional paints are particularly notorious sources of these gases, which have been linked to a variety of health issues. And it's not just the fumes you experience when the paint is still drying—the VOC's continue to off-gas for years. Fortunately, there are a growing variety of alternative solutions, including milk paints and other formulations which promise as little as zero-VOC's (which are actually just extremely small amounts). With such alternatives now available, there's really little sacrifice here.

Water-Saving Fixtures

Aerator faucets provide a very cheap way to conserve water. These simple devices mix air into the water flow so that it remains pressurized while reducing consumption. The most popular application of this idea is the water-efficient showerhead. The dreaded drizzle of the "low-flow" showerhead is fast becoming history as savvier design technologies are making it possible to wash your hair and rinse it too.

Flooring & Carpeting

Mankind has found dozens of ways to improve upon the dirt floor, but some of them have been less than ideal. However, these days it's possible to install floors without contributing to deforestation.

FSC-Certified Lumber
Hardwood floors may be the most-appealing option, but if it means cutting down grand old trees that provide a foundation for a local ecosystem, they may prove too high a cost for the planet. FSC certified flooring is getting easier to come by, and you'll find it at several of the web shops in our directory.

Reclaimed Wood
Sometimes, old houses must be torn down, and sometimes they leave behind some perfectly functional and beautiful hardwoods, which may be refurbished and reused as flooring. Surprisingly, such options are not that hard to find, and if you think of them as antique floors, you'll come to cherish any irregularities you might discover.

Bamboo
Bamboo's a plant that figures to take on a huge role in our ecological future, and it already makes for a great flooring option. Technically a grass, bamboo plants grow to harvestable size faster than trees, and continue to grow after they've been cut, meaning you can make exponentially more flooring while using the same amount of land.

Cork
There are several reasons cork makes a good, eco-friendly flooring alternative, including price, durability, elasticity and versatility. But the aspects that make it green are particularly good. First of all, it's harvested from the bark of the Cork Oak, which regenerates within a few years. Furthermore, most cork flooring is actually made from remnant materials leftover from making the wood's most popular product: the bottle stopper.

Natural Linoleum
The twentieth century left us thinking of vinyl tiles when we hear the word linoleum, but that's not exactly fair. True linoleum is actually made from the very sustainable flax, and is an eco-friendly, biodegradable product. Because a lot of vinyl flooring is still called linoleum, you will probably have to search fro "natural linoleum" to find the real stuff these days. When in doubt, simply ask.

Recycled Tiles
Whether using recycled glass tiles, stone, plastic or otherwise, the key here is to avoid petrochemical adhesives, and, if possible, to recycle your old flooring in the process. This is usually the option you'll take when you want a specific floor type but don't want to forsake your green values, which means you may have to search long and hard before you find exactly what you want.

Carpets & Rugs

As mentioned earlier, the carpet and rug industry has long been in the practice of using potentially toxic chemicals such as formaldehyde and petrochemical adhesives during production, even when the carpet's comprised of natural fibers. Safer alternatives are available, including untreated wool, hemp and natural grasses like jute and sisal. Whether you're looking for area rugs or wall-to-wall carpeting, green options are easy to find online.

>> Travel & Transportation

The "inconvenient truth" about carbon emissions has us all thinking of how we can reduce our individual output, and it usually starts with one culprit in particular: your car.

The Problem: Any kind of motor vehicular travel damages the atmosphere, and the hospitality industry is notoriously wasteful.

The Culprits: Petroleum-fueled cars, planes and boats, and hotels with environmentally insensitive policies.

The Solution: Take public transportation, ride a bicycle, carpool or find alternate ways to commute. Opt for green destinations and lodging when traveling.

Depending on where you live, using public transportation or carpooling might be the greenest way to get to work or to appointments. In the cases where this is not feasible, there are several environmentally conscious options, some of which may be explored at this site: **CommuterChoice.gov**

EFFICIENT DRIVING TIPS

- Avoid idling: Idling in your car uses more gas than restarting your engine.
- Drive the speed limit: Staying within posted speed limits actually increases fuel efficiency.
- Cruise control: Using cruise control on long drives isn't just easy on your legs; it keeps the engine running smoothly and efficiently.
- Keep it maintained: Improperly inflated tires, dirty air filters and unchanged oil can all inhibit your engine's performance. With gas prices always rising, regular maintenance may pay for itself.

Bicycles

It's no secret that cycling saves gas, and odds are good that your city or town offers bike lanes for both commuting and recreational cyclists. This will only increase as more and more cities recognize the need to reduce car traffic. It may be awhile before pedal vehicles own the road the way they do in Amsterdam, but using bikes has become a reliable, safe and sometimes even quicker way to get around. You may even find folding models to travel and stow more easily, or various racks, baskets and tows to help you transport things like groceries, briefcases and surfboards.

Alternative Fuel Cars

Gas/electric hybrids and Biodeisel engines have received the bulk of the attention as alternatives to the gasoline powered auto, and fuel cell models are reportedly on the way. Unfortunately, these are some of the few products that don't lend well to online sales.

The web does provide a lot of useful information though. The following lists of sites might aid in your research:

General Info on Alternative Cars

Autos.yahoo.com/green_center
EVWorld.com
FuelEconomy.gov
GreenCarCongress.com
GreenCars.com

Hybrids

GreenHybrid.com
HybridCars.com

Biodiesel

BioDiesel.org
E85Fuel.com
NearBio.com

Fuel Cells

Hydrogen-cars.biz

Electric Vehicles

PlugInAmerica.com

Car Pooling, Car Sharing & Taxis

A great option to owning a car is participating in a ride or car-sharing program. The internet's facilitated this to a great extent, and in many cities it is now possible to share a commute or rent a car affordably for an afternoon of errands where public transport or bicycles just aren't feasible.

Taxi Options

BicyTaxi.com
Hitchsters.com

Ride Sharing

CarSharing.net
eRideShare.com
VanPool.com

Car Sharing

FlexCar.com
ZipCar.com

Green Travel

That much-needed vacation from your life doesn't mean you need to forsake your earth-loving values. All over the world, hotels are popping up that value eco-sensibilities by running on renewable energy, using natural cleaners and conserving water. You might even find vacation lodging that is greener than your own home!

GREEN TRAVEL TIPS

When you travel, bring your eco-consciousness with you. It won't take up any extra room in your suitcase, and it will set an example to your friends, family and fellow travelers.

- Carbon offset your travels
- Find an eco-friendly car rental or car service
- Stay at an eco-friendly hotel
- Don't use the amenity soaps, bring your own in small reusable bottles (hotels will toss even partially used ones)
- Turn off lights when you leave your room
- Tell the housekeeping staff they don't need to change your sheets and towels every day
- Encourage management to make more green choices—customers have power!

Eco-Lodging & Eco Tours

Here is a fine collection of web sites that can point you to some green vacation destinations:

AllStays.com	Green travel
BlueFlag.org	Green beaches
ConceptHospitality.com/ecotel	Green lodging
Eco-Resorts.com	Green travel
Ecotour.org	Green travel
EcoTourism.org	Green travel
EnvironmentallyFriendlyHotels.com	Green lodging
GolfAndEnvironment.org	Green golf courses
GreenGlobe21.com	Green travel
GreenHotels.com	Green lodging
Green-Key.org	Green lodging in Europe
Manaca.com	Green travel
NSAA.org	Green ski resorts
Organic-Holidays.com	Organic dining and travel
Planeta.com	Green travel
ResponsibleTravel.com	Green travel
SkiAreaCitizens.com	Green ski resorts
SustainableTravelInternational.org	Green travel
SusTravel.co.uk	Green travel
WildAsia.net	Green travel in Asia

Rental Cars

Slowly but surely, rental car companies are starting to recognize the high demand for fuel efficient, hybrid and electric vehicles. However, high demand means more often than not you will not find them available at the bigger companies. Making a point to ask will put them on notice that they need to beef up their green fleets. In the meantime, check locally to see if a smaller regional company has sprung up to fill this niche.

FURTHER GREEN SAVINGS

These sites will hook you up with some coupons and other savings for eco-freindly products:

OrganicCoupons.org
TheGreenZebra.org

GOOD LUCK GOING GREEN!

HOW GREEN WILL YOU GO?

We've spoken a lot about environmental options that are fairly easy to implement. Of course, there are always some things that are good for the environment, but do involve a pretty serious commitment. Here are a few of the rather great lengths you can take your newly found eco-enthusiasm:

Install Compost Toilets

Not for the idle conservationist, composting toilets (also known as dry or waterless toilets) convert human and household waste into biomass, which may be returned to the environment to nourish trees and plants. As complicated as it sounds—and it's not exactly easy to implement—composting toilets are much different, and better, than septic tanks or other individual waste disposal systems.

Properly assembled, they control odors and do not require constant emptying (though some vigilance, of course, is due). And though they do work along the same principle as compost bins or heaps, they are closed systems, so you will not have to look into any foul holes to check on your progress.

That said, this water conserving technology may not be the best solution for those living in populous areas with decent municipal waste management. However, if you own a rural property, a composting toilet may be your most sanitary and best bet.

CompostingToilet.org

Shape Your Own Green Surfboard

The world's greatest water sport isn't usually as kind to the environment as it might seem, most surfboards are built around toxic foam. Fortunately, you can sidestep these boards and build your own from more earth-friendly materials. All it takes is a little knowhow and a lot of patience, but the odds you'll do it right the first time aren't all that high. Still, who doesn't want to be the ultimate green kahuna?

GreenLightSurfSupply.com

Try UV Water Treatment

When you feel like taking water treatment upon your own shoulders, look into UV Water Purifiers. These relatively high-tech systems expose water to heavy doses of ultra violet light in order to kill or render harmless potentially hazardous microbes such as fungi, bacteria, viruses and other parasites.

As an alternative to using chemicals, it's a relatively eco-friendly way to make local groundwater potable for your household. However, it should used in conjunction with other water filters meant to remove dangerous chemicals and metals. Also, residential systems are not intended for the treatment of sewage, so be careful when it comes to selecting a water source.

WaterCenter.com

Be an Organ Donor

Call it the ultimate in recycling. Any healthy body may participate in an organ donor program so that your healthy body parts can live on helping somebody else live on. Check this site for more details:

DonateLife.net

Go Green Unto Death!

How will you be disposed of when you shuffle off this mortal coil? Returning our bodies to the earth is a timeless practice. However, it's only in recent years that the vessels and preservatives we use to make a better showing at our funerals have started to cause some problems, usually the kind that involve unfriendly chemicals seeping into the earth.

Here are several resources that will help you plan for a green afterlife—well, they will at least clue you in to some environmentally-friendly burial options:

DecentBurial.org
EnvironmentalCaskets.com
EternalReefs.com

NOTES:

_____

_____

_____

_____

_____

_____

_____

_____

_____

_____

_____

_____

_____

_____

_____

_____

_____

_____

Green Shops

Ideally, we would all be able to shop locally for eco-friendly goods, reducing transportation, storage and packaging costs while preserving natural resources. Unfortunately, the world doesn't yet work this way, and to many, finding globally conscious products in local stores simply isn't a reality. Even if you are lucky to have green retailers in your vicinity, the chances they have a wide enough selection to cover all tastes is slim.

So, for now, it makes sense to turn to the web to find the full breadth of available planet-friendly options with any convenience. In doing so, you make a vote with your pocketbook for progress. Ordering online from a responsible provider sends the message loud and clear: a company must be at least as concerned about the environment as I am if it wishes to have me as a customer.

In this section we have gathered the best of such retailers; regional boutiques, homegrown e-businesses, manufacturers and seasoned web stores that understand how making the switch to responsible merchandise is a huge step towards a sustainable future.

Here you will find great selections covering the full range of product categories. Take a shopping spree through the pages of this directory, and you almost can't help making a positive impact.

» thepurplebook green
REQUIREMENTS & STANDARDS

Finding just any online retailer is easy. Finding the good ones—that takes a bit of work. We've scoured search engines, message boards, magazines and web directories in search of great sites, and received recommendations from our readers and friends. Tens of thousands of web sites promised the best prices and the greatest selections, but we took a close look at each one, and held them up to the following list of requirements:

SECURE TRANSACTIONS

Each site must offer a secure credit card transaction that can be completed in a single session. This means we disqualified any sites that only accept fax orders, email inquiries, payments over the phone or PayPal transactions. These methods of payment are both less secure and less reliable than those for sites operating encrypted commerce engines.

CUSTOMER SERVICE NUMBER

Every site in thepurplebook must provide a working customer service number. Finding this number is not always easy, and in some cases we've had to play detective to get it, but we've included one with each site listed in this book, because we've found that a lack of direct contact with a service representative can ruin an otherwise satisfactory shopping experience.

OPEN BROWSING

No site will be listed in thepurplebook that requires consumers to enter credit card numbers or other personal data before viewing its full catalog of products. Such sites usually intend to sell a customer's personal information for profit.

ECO-STANDARDS

In evaluating web shops for this book, we paid strict attention to the types of products they featured to determine whether or not they live up to any environmentally-friendly claims. To warrant inclusion, a site must at least in part offer merchandise that meets or exceeds our standards for one or more of the following green principles: sustainable production, fair trade practices, conservational practices, renewable energy, biodegradability, nontoxicity or use of recycled materials.

If an e-tailer met these requirements, we then subjected it to our own rigorous set of standards, scrutinizing each aspect of the site: Is it easy to use? Does it have a good selection? Are the prices good? Will it download in a reasonable amount of time? We whittled down the selection to include only the finest catalogs, the most beautiful web designs, the best bargains and that occasional ingenious purveyor of a product or service of such unique charm that we couldn't possibly leave it out.

Our final tally includes brick-and-mortar stores that have established a viable online presence, manufacturers who have done the same, internet juggernauts that have managed to survive the dot-com backlash and small businesses, often individuals working out of their bedrooms, who've embraced the virtual marketplace in their pursuit of the American dream. It's a pretty good bunch, capable of fulfilling nearly any online shopping need you may have, and possibly turning you on to something new.

thepurplebook
ONLINE SHOPPING FUNDAMENTALS

Make a habit of using these tips and precautions, and your online shopping experience will be easy, convenient, fruitful and, above all, safe.

USE ONE CREDIT CARD
Dedicate a single credit card for all of your online purchases. This makes it especially easy to spot fraudulent and/or unauthorized charges.

PRINT A COPY
To document your online purchases, print a copy of both your order page (before you click the Submit button) and your order confirmation (receipt) to save for your records.

SAVE ALL CORRESPONDENCE
Online retailers should email a confirmation of your order and/or shipping information. Save these emails until you are fully satisfied with your purchase, as you may need to refer to this information if problems arise.

PROTECT YOURSELF AGAINST IDENTITY THEFT
Never give out credit card numbers or any personal information via email. Emails are not secure, and identity thieves commonly pose as customer service representatives in order to acquire your payment information. Only submit personal data through a secure, encrypted web site.

REPORT FRAUD IMMEDIATELY
If you suspect fraud or other mistakes, notify your credit card company and/or the Federal Trade Commission (877-382-4357) immediately, because identity thieves will not waste any time abusing your information.

USE THE CUSTOMER SERVICE NUMBER

thepurplebook has provided a customer service phone number for every shopping site listed in the book. Do not hesitate to use them. If you have any question not addressed by the web site, speak to a customer service representative before placing an order (you may be required to call during normal business hours).

USE THE COMMENTS BOX

Most online order forms offer a comments box for special requests or any questions you may have. This will be the surest way of contacting the actual humans in charge of fulfilling your order so that they can properly address your needs.

READ THE WEB SITE'S POLICIES

Before you make a purchase, take note of the web site's return and exchange policies, as well as shipping, privacy and security, because once you place your order, you've agreed to their terms and conditions. The FAQ (Frequently Asked Questions) section of a web site often proves a good source of information.

AVOID UNWANTED SOLICITATIONS

When entering your billing and email address, a lot of shopping sites will ask if you're interested in receiving catalogs and/or advertising materials from them and other sites. In most cases, the answer defaults to *Yes*, and you'll need to actively change this answer to *No* if you hope to avoid junk mail and spam.

REPORT BAD BUSINESS PRACTICES

If you do have a bad experience with an online retailer, make a report to the Better Business Bureau, at **BBB.org**.

>> Useful Resources

The following URLs may be useful when you shop online.

BBB.org · *Better Business Bureau site*

Consumer.gov/idtheft · *Identity theft information and warnings*

ConsumerReports.org · *Consumer product reviews*

CountryCallingCodes.com · *International country calling codes*

CPSC.gov · *Product recall lists*

CreditCardGuide.org · *Credit card information*

EquiFax.com · *Obtain your credit report*

Experian.com · *Obtain your credit report*

KidStockMontana.com/sizing.html · *Clothes sizing charts*

LittleShoes.com · *Shoes and clothes sizing charts*

MyUS.com · *Forward packages to overseas addresses*

NetLingo.com · *Glossary of internet terms*

OAndA.com · *Currency converter*

OrganicCoupons.org · *Coupons for organic products*

ShopForDSL.com · *Compare local internet service providers*

SmartQpon.com · *Coupon codes for online retailers*

TransUnion.com · *Obtain your credit report*

WhatsItWorthToYou.com · *Online appraisals*

NOTES:

_____
_____
_____
_____
_____
_____
_____
_____
_____
_____
_____
_____
_____
_____
_____
_____
_____
_____
_____
_____
_____
_____

>> **How to Use thepurplebook**

While we've made every effort to be discriminating, the number of web sites listed in this book does exceed four hundred. Though these comprise a mere fraction of the thousands of sites we viewed, we're well aware that it's a lot to handle. If you're looking for a good place to shop or find a gift, you can browse the alphabetical site listings. If you have something more specific in mind, you can search one of our several indexes for products, companies or key words.

✳ BROWSING

thepurplebook green site listings are arranged alphabetically by URL and presented along with a five-or-six-line review that should give you a general idea of what to expect from the site before ever logging on. Alongside these reviews, you will find icons that evaluate the site's service, selection and usability, as well as a list of key words describing the store's product selection.

Using the icons and key words, you can browse each category to find specific product types, or to locate stores that offer services like gift wrapping or overnight delivery. See the sample site listing below, and the descriptions on the following pages, for further details.

HipAndZen.com Ⓐ   Ⓑ 888-447-6936

Ⓒ As fashionable as environmental-awareness may be, finding accessories and attire that prove stylish as well as eco-conscious has long proven a difficult task—which is exactly why this site belongs on your radar. A small but supremely tasteful selection of chic women's apparel promises to live up to both sets of high standards, and a system of icons let you know specifically which items are natural, organic, fair trade and/or made from recycled materials.

Ⓓ ⚪ Ⓢ ✈ ❋ GC ▦ ℗ ▯▯ ⬡ ⚙ Ⓔ

ACCESSORIES STATIONERY & GIFTS	APPAREL WOMEN	BABIES

Ⓕ

✳ UNDERSTANDING THE SITE LISTINGS

Ⓐ URL

Each site in this book has been listed alphabetically by its URL (internet address). We've left out the standard http://www. that precedes each domain name and extension. In other words, to visit HipAndZen.com, go to the address bar in your browser and type in http://www.hipandzen.com.

Ⓑ CUSTOMER SERVICE NUMBER

We've listed each company's customer service phone number along with its entry (some sites like to hide them). This should help if you can't log on to the site for some reason, or if you cannot find the number listed there. When things go wrong, using the web site's human support staff is often more productive than sending emails.

Ⓒ REVIEW

These reviews are intended to offer some insight into the breadth and scope of the web site at hand, hopefully with a little good-natured fun. After all, we've found that many of the best shopping sites have terrific senses of humor.

Ⓓ CUSTOMER SERVICE ICONS

The set of round, purple customer service icons found throughout the book depict some of the particulars about each store that may come in handy when deciding where to shop: shipping costs, overnight shipping, gift certificates, gift wrapping and user-friendliness.

Ⓔ GREEN EDITION ICONS

The rectangular icons have been included to help you distinguish which sites cover different environmental concepts. The round, green icons will tell you about the shop's dedication to eco-friendly products and policies.

Ⓕ KEY WORDS

At the bottom of each site listing, you will find a list of key words that offer general descriptions of the types of products available from that site. A quick scan of these words should give you a rough idea of whether a site has what you seek.

✳ UNDERSTANDING THE ICONS

CUSTOMER SERVICE ICONS

SHIPPING COSTS

A huge consideration when shopping online is the cost of shipping and handling. High fees can turn what seemed like a great deal into a waste of cash, whereas a cheap shipping policy can mean the difference between competitive prices.

Free, Incentivized or Flat Rate Shipping – Sites marked by this icon either cover shipping costs, reduce the cost of shipping if you spend more or charge a single, preset amount to cover shipment of your entire order, regardless of cost or weight.

Standard Shipping Rates – Sites covered by this icon either charge the same weight-based amount for shipping as determined by the carrier (usually UPS, FedEx, Airborne Express, DHL or the US Postal Service), or compute comparable rates based on the value of the purchase.

Exorbitant or Unknown Shipping & Handling Fees – Sites tagged with this icon either charge excessive handling fees designed to pad their profit margins or do not inform you of an order's shipping charges until after a credit card has been used to make the purchase. A third category of these sites simply ship very large, heavy items that require special companies or even individual trucks, usually at great expense.

OVERNIGHT SHIPPING

When you see this icon, the site in question offers overnight shipping or next-day delivery, in most cases at an extra charge, and often not on weekends. Bear in mind that sites usually have an early-afternoon or morning deadline for one-day delivery, and that time zones may consequently play a big role in your last-minute purchases.

GIFT CERTIFICATES

This icon only appears when gift certificates are available for purchase, in either electronic or paper form. Electronic gift certificates will be sent to the recipient's email address, and therefore make excellent last-second gifts.

GIFT WRAPPING

 Many sites listed within this book offer some pretty great gifts, and most will send your order in a plain brown box. However, some will wrap it up a bit nicer (usually at an extra charge). Such sites are noted by this icon.

USER-FRIENDLINESS

Product selection is the most important aspect to building an online store, but presentation is often what sells, and if using a site to make a purchase is just too much work it may not be worth it. We've ranked each site's performance with the following three icons:

Easy – These sites have gone the distance to make sure that you can find the products you need without hassle and order them with minimal difficulty, either through smart web design or plain common sense. Or the site has only a handful of products to begin with and everything may be viewed or purchased on one page. Either way, we wish all the sites qualified for this rank, but very few did.

Standard – Savvy web shoppers are used to the industry standard—a left-side menu of options, with a few more general choices thrown across the top of the page for good measure. Such sites warrant no complaints, as everything you need is laid out logically so that browsing and buying is easy on the mind, and only hard on the mouse-clicking finger.

Difficult – In some cases, these sites involve failed attempts to create the virtual world's best new shopping technique. On the flipside are the purely bad web designs. Whatever the case, these sites are often impossible to load, browse and/or order from. Ironically, these aberrations wouldn't have made the cut if they didn't offer some of the best the web has to offer.

DEDICATED ECO-SHOPS

 We've awarded this icon to web sites that demonstrate a clear devotion to only offering products that may be considered friendly to the environment. When you see this flower, shop with confidence that you are making a difference.

GREEN PACKAGING

 When a site goes out of the way to ensure its shipping policies are eco-friendly, it earns this icon, which usually indicates recycled and/or biodegradable packaging.

GREEN SHOPS ICONS

CONSERVATION

When you see this icon, it's an indication the shop offers products that will aid in your conservation efforts, either by saving water, lowering power consumption or reducing waste by offering reusable alternatives to disposable products.

FAIR TRADE

When a shop features products that employ fair trade policies, you'll see this icon. It will refer to imported items that have been grown or manufactured at a fair wage, under safe working conditions, by consenting adults.

NONTOXIC/BIODEGRADABLE

When a shop offers chemical-free and biodegradable alternatives to potentially toxic and pollutant products, you will see this icon. Note that this specifically refers to products that are not usually made from natural materials.

RECYCLED MATERIALS

This recycling symbol indicates a product is probably recyclable by virtue of the fact it has already been recycled. Shopping where this icon is found will help you complete the cycle by purchasing reclaimed materials, showing recycled products can be marketable.

RENEWABLE ENERGY

Whereas the Conservation icon above may show you products that will reduce energy consumption, this icon will show you products that produce energy cleanly. They of course may be used in conjunction, but if you can produce your own renewable energy at home, use it up how you see fit.

SUSTAINABLE GOODS

Sustainable materials provide the foundation for most eco-shopping, so when you are on the hunt for responsibly harvested wood products, organic foods, sustainable fabrics or other naturally-raised goods that do no harm to the world around you, shop from one of the many shops marked by this icon.

❉ KEY WORD DEFINITIONS

ACCESSORIES
Accessories may be functional, like wallets and reusable grocery bags, or fashionable, like shoes, jewelry and scarves.

APPAREL
This mostly constitutes clothes made from sustainable fabrics, including casual, athletic, designer and even some formal garb.

APPLIANCES
This key word refers to appliances, electronics and gadgets, most of which are energy efficient, if not energy producing.

BABIES
If you're shopping for anybody under the age of three, you'll want to keep an eye out for this key word, in combination with others.

BUILDING SUPPLY
Whether you're engaging in simple home improvements or some pretty serious rebuilding, these sites will help.

CHILDREN
Sadly, there is not a huge amount of green gear for kids these days, but you will find it all with this, or the *Family* key word.

CRAFTS & HOBBIES
Ranging from sustainable yarns and fabrics to nontoxic art supplies, if you prefer your creativity to have a natural bent, look here.

EPICUREAN
Earth-friendly food and drink is ably covered by this key word, as you will find a lot of tantalizing fare, including wine and coffee.

FAMILY
When a site offers apparel, accessories, furnishings or bath products for someone of every age, we'll note it with this key word.

FURNISHINGS
Looking for furniture, home accents, bedding or bath towels? This would be the key word to watch out for.

HEALTH & BEAUTY
Beauty products make up most of the goods you'll find with this key word, with the occasional alternative health site.

HOUSEHOLD
Keeping house can be a dirty job, so we've noted all the clean, efficient, nontoxic and otherwise eco-friendly household utility products you may find with this key word.

MATERNITY
We didn't find a whole lot of green maternity apparel, so this usually refers to maternity health products and nursing apparel.

MEN
Guys might have the least trouble switching to green accessories and apparel, but some of the beauty products may be a nice surprise.

OFFICE
Your office can get greener all the time, and there are plenty of sites like these that will help you at work or at home.

PETS
They may be the most earth-loving members of your household, so shop where you see this key word to let them join the movement.

SERVICE
Dinnerware, glassware, napkins and other service accessories are important to every household. Shop here to keep it green.

SPORT & OUTDOOR
Most green sports and outdoor options involve fitness apparel, but it's some darn good apparel, often using recycled synthetics.

STATIONERY & GIFTS
Whether it's sending a gift or thanking someone with a card, there's no reason our cultural customs can't be eco-friendly.

TRANSPORTATION
Getting around without burning a lot of gas might be a little easier when you shop from stores marked by this key word.

WEDDINGS
Of course your weeding can be greener! But check out **thepurplebook wedding** for more great shopping suggestions.

WOMEN
Women will not find anything lacking when they shop these clothing, accessories and beauty sites.

✳ USING THE INDEXES

These indexes at the end of the book will help you track down specific products, stores and sites of interest in the most efficient manner.

PRODUCT INDEX (page 242)
A detailed listing of products and the corresponding names of sites that carry them. Note that this is not necessarily a comprehensive list, and that you will be able to find some of these products on sites not mentioned in the index.

KEY WORD INDEX (page 266)
A key word index that can help you locate which stores carry particular types of products within that general category.

COMPANY INDEX (page 278)
This list of brand and company names is simply meant to help you find web sites for companies that may not otherwise be familiar.

FIND ONLY WHAT YOU NEED...
AND LET US KNOW WHAT YOU LIKE
We at thepurplebook are always looking for ways to improve this book, and we welcome all constructive criticism, suggestions and feedback. Visit us at thepurplebook.com for more information.

1Earth1Design.com
888-270-7005

This rather new shop from the state of Washington represents the sort of eco-friendly design focus we're starting to see a lot more of online these days. With a smattering of products selected for sustainable production and materials as well as style, browsing the site's pages is like taking a glance into the future of home service, a future of better health, social consciousness and hope. At this point the limited store still works best as a gift shop, but in time (we hope) it will strongly epitomize a new breed of lifestyle shop enjoyed by idle shoppers as well as consumer activists.

APPLIANCES SERVICE	FURNISHINGS STATIONERY & GIFTS	HOUSEHOLD

2Modern.com
888-240-5333

Since there's no such thing as too modern, we dig this small but appealing furniture and accents site that weighs heavy on embellishments. You'll find plenty of popular ultra-contemporary designers on hand, even in the Eco-Friendly section, which features an assortment of brands with a strong, sustainable focus, whether they make wallpaper, throw pillows, lighting or wood furniture. Supporting this section sends a clear message that modern design and environmentalism may go hand in hand, and ultimately satisfying on both fronts.

FURNISHINGS		

3RLiving.com
718-832-0951

Keeping in line with its own ethos, this Brooklyn retailer has repurposed the classic "Three R's" idea to invoke the slogan "Reduce. Reuse. Recycle." Offering a broad variety of "future friendly products," the most useful options here may be the housekeeping tools and nontoxic cleaners. However, the earnest family business endorses fair trade principles, ecologically sensible packaging and sustainable production as well, so you may be assured that any of its assorted accents and accessories will be ideally suited to your green lifestyle, and will make for particularly satisfying gifts.

ACCESSORIES HOUSEHOLD	CHILDREN PETS	FURNISHINGS STATIONERY & GIFTS

A2BScooters.com
866-333-8686

If the idea of pumping out exhaust fumes while navigating your car through congested roadways has you down, take a moment to check out a web shop like this one, which offers alternative modes of transportation such as electric scooters and bicycles. Depending on the length of your daily commute, you could find yourself saving both time and money running on a precharged engine. And if you can't decide between a powered bike and pedal power, this shop offers an electric version of the classic compromise: a moped.

TRANSPORTATION

AbundantEarth.com
888-513-2784

With the tag line, "saving the galaxy one planet at a time," this site quickly points out that environmental awareness doesn't have to be a humorless endeavor. In fact, there is plenty of fun to be had here, including some pro-environment board games and the wildest assortment of recycled airplane and animal-shaped tire swings you could imagine. Most of this stuff is no joke, though; beautiful organic beds, mattresses and bedding highlight a stellar selection of sustainably produced furniture while hemp bags, nontoxic cleaners and natural/recycled area rugs will make yours a happy universe.

ACCESSORIES GARDENING	FAMILY HEALTH & BEAUTY	FURNISHINGS STATIONERY & GIFTS

AbundantLifeSeeds.com
541-767-9606

Organic gardening begins with certified-organic seeds, which you will find here aplenty, whether your garden furnishes herbs, vegetables, flowers or a combination of all three. However, this seed specialist can also set you up with the proper equipment to keep your soil nutrient rich and all-natural. Organic, biodynamic fertilizers, pest controls and beneficial insects head up the list of necessities, followed by tools, mulch and more. All you'll need is fertile ground, sun, water and the most modest of green thumbs.

GARDENING

Adili.com 55-1258-837-437

The Swahili word for "ethical and just," Adili is a fitting name for this UK shop devoted to global social responsibility. Working hard to "select contemporary styles and validate the ethical position of each brand," the shop picks out clothing, shoes and jewelry that meet some sort of fair trade, sustainable and/ or nonpolluting standard. You might want to take a good look at each product to ensure it meets your own personal standards, but doing so will be no great sacrifice as the vast majority of these hip items for the whole family are beautiful to behold.

ACCESSORIES FAMILY	APPAREL	BABIES

AfterglowCosmetics.com 866-630-4569

Boasting "a truly natural blend of pure mineral make-up with the fabulous, organic infused, highly pigmented color palette you crave," this fully realized makeup brand was established to provide a safer alternative to the petroleum and chemical ingredients found in conventional cosmetics. While the lipstick selections are limited at this time, you'll find eye shadow, blush and foundation in shades to compliment just about any skin tone. The results are beautiful, or at least beautifying, and of course offer a better alternative for the planet as well.

HEALTH & BEAUTY	WOMEN	

AHappyPlanet.com 888-424-2779

With a mission to "improve the quality of life for all creatures...by offering sustainable, quality products which do not compromise labor, animals or the earth," this online shop begins with the basics: underwear. You'll also see some socks and pajamas here, but it's mainly home furnishings to be found, ranging from mattresses and bedding to bed frames and other furniture. Each product is either made from organically-grown fabrics or wood sourced from managed forests, whether you sleep in it or on it.

APPAREL	FAMILY	FURNISHINGS

888-380-5420   AlimaCosmetics.com

Mineral cosmetics lines have been flourishing in recent years as chemical sensitivity and eco-consciousness has been on the rise. This Oregon-based company is only a few years old, but already it's developed a colorful line of nontoxic foundations, blushes, glossy lip balms and eye shadows to rival its synthetic, petrochemical competition. "Free of irritants and 100 percent natural," this makeup is virtually hypoallergenic and thanks to a generous sample program and full ingredients lists posted for each product, you may be sure what you're getting yourself into even before you buy.

HEALTH & BEAUTY

800-361-8292   AllisonsGourmet.com

Making the epicurean's green lifestyle difficult are some familiar temptations: chocolate, cookies and brownies. But if you think a strict eco-consciousness is going to help you resist the lure of these diet-busting sweets, think again. This online vegan bakery specializes in making the socially-responsible delicious, using "only the finest organic ingredients available" to tantalize your sweet tooth in the earth-friendliest of ways. Eat it yourself or turn on loved ones with a gift box, and support sustainability several calories at a time.

EPICUREAN   **STATIONERY & GIFTS**

800-246-7328   AllTerrainCo.com

This small New England-based company want you to enjoy the great outdoors "without having to use harsh chemical products to protect you from the sun, insects and whatever nature throws at you." To this end they offer you a great assortment of hardy, all-natural sunscreens, soaps, repellents and ointments, packaged with recycled, recyclable and biodegradable materials to help you engage the wild world without leaving an indelible mark on it. So feel free to go out and see what you're helping to preserve!

HEALTH & BEAUTY TRANSPORTATION   **PETS**   **SPORTING GOODS**

AlpacAccessories.com 866-662-5722

Although long known to be a rare, luxurious fiber, when alpaca are raised in sustainable ways, these cousins to the llama produce a soft, durable fleece that harms neither animal nor environment. The alpaca sourced by this shawl, scarf and outerwear specialist are traditionally raised in the Peruvian Andes, and the international expansion of alpaca farming has reduced the price considerably, so owning these low-impact products is no longer restricted to royalty.

ACCESSORIES	APPAREL	WOMEN

AltEnergyStore.com 877-878-4060

The "Alt" here stands for "Alternative," as in Alternative Energy Store. Yes, this altruistic retailer may be your best source for energy responsible "solar panels, windmills, inverters, batteries, refrigerators, charge controllers, panel mounts, meters and much, much more." All right, so we don't know exactly what all of this stuff is either. But that's the point: here's a place where we can turn our eco-friendly lip service into actual, environmentally sound progress. Best of all, some states offer up to 50% discounts on some of these items that will, ultimately, render your energy bill obsolete.

APPLIANCES	HOUSEHOLD	

AlternativeApparel.com 888-481-4287

Having mastered the realm of all-cotton casuals, this burgeoning brand is finally starting to make the switch to sustainability, recently launching the Alternative Earth and Eco Heather lines of organic cotton and recycled synthetic blends, respectively. Though everything you see on this site will not be earth-friendly, if you stick close to these growing sections you will find a slim supply of natural basics, including tees, hoodies and good old-fashioned sweatpants. It's great to see a company take an interest in embracing awareness, and with enough encouragement we'll look forward to seeing it continue.

APPAREL	MEN	WOMEN

AlterSystems.com

866-568-5579

Urging you to "go green for life," this Berkeley, California company gives you the opportunity with a number of home renewable energy sources. Chief among them are solar panels by a variety of manufacturers, and even a few models for boats and RV's to prove you can take your environmentalism with you, even if you are powering your journey with gasoline. The site's design is as clean as the air will be once these sustainable power generators are more prevalent, so you should be only slightly deterred by the heavy price tag of these devices: after all, give it a lifetime and your utility savings should even it all out.

APPLIANCES		

Amazon.com

800-201-7575

Little can be said about the internet's oldest and best-known retailer, and we're not going to start by saying the massive bookseller/department store is a green marketplace. However, the fact this store is so massive pretty much means the only way it could avoid eco-friendly products would be to purposefully exclude them—which it hasn't. On the other hand, as of this writing it can be difficult to find the site's Sustainable Living Store. Try searching some of the terms that turn up in this book, such as: organic, hemp, bamboo, solar, biodegradable or recycled, and browse the myriad results wisely.

ACCESSORIES FAMILY	APPAREL HEALTH & BEAUTY	APPLIANCES

AMSOil.com

800-956-5695

When it comes to operating a gas-powered car, there aren't very many earth-friendly choices. However, this synthetic oil specialist offers a few. With a full line of motor oils, lubes, transmission fluids and filters, there are myriad reasons to switch to this petroleum alternative. Aside from the obvious, these products can be expected to improve fuel economy, and due to extended drain intervals, you'll only need to change your oil a minimum of every 15,000 miles (or one year). The substance is not ideal, and should be recycled as you would standard motor oil, but it's regular use can go a long way towards conservation.

HOUSEHOLD		

ANaturalHome.com   866-239-4142

When mass production kicked off the modern era, planned obsolescence and low-cost construction ushered an age of flimsy, throw-away furniture that seems somewhat irresponsible now. Though often gibed for their staunchly traditional ways, the Amish have been living eco-friendly lifestyles all along, and now we can turn to this site to embrace their furniture-building prowess. The solid wood furniture, natural upholstery, organic bedding and hypoallergenic pet products are derived solely from sustainable sources. Better yet, it's built to last, so you'll never see it contributing to the overflow of a landfill.

FAMILY PETS	FURNISHINGS	HOUSEHOLD

AnnaSova.com   214-653-1733

With the mission of reducing "indoor air pollution," this purveyor of "luxury organics" focuses on the bedroom. A dazzling and elegant assortment of linens, pillow shams, duvets, quilts, bedskirts and more may be entirely attributed to organic cotton or silk, utilizing fair trade practices and valuing style as much as sustainability. A growing assortment of towels and even nontoxic paints will secure your own healthy environment, and we can only hope that, in time, this shop will get to the rest of the house.

BUILDING SUPPLY	FURNISHINGS

AntiqNet.com   888-959-1605

As years go by, the definition of what constitutes an antique continually expands to include more and more items from eras past. Of course, it doesn't hurt to consider your thrift store sofa an antique. Antiqnet strives to bring thousands of antique stores together on the web, with more than 5,000 vendors contributing every imaginable kind of searchable item. They will not necessarily be earth-friendly-designed products, but you may consider giving old furniture a new home a charitable act if it makes you feel better.

FURNISHINGS		

214-653-1733   AntiqueDraperyRod.com

Though not technically antique, the drapery and window hardware that stocks this site look good enough to be mistaken as old. The luxurious drapes and bed canopies come in suede, velvet, hemp and silk, while the finials, rods, rings and brackets may be procured in wood, iron, stone or bamboo. As it turns out, the inclusion of earth-friendly materials is no accident: the company is dedicated to sustainability, using organic cotton, eco-safe dyes, recycled aluminum and reforested wood. Don't expect to find better.

BUILDING SUPPLY	FURNISHINGS	

702-219-4174   Apothena.com

What started out as an "obsession…in finding truly natural products" has turned into this comprehensive beauty shop that promises none of the sulfates, parabens, petroleum by-products or other nasty ingredients found in conventional bath, skin care, hair care and cosmetics products. Sometimes it takes a bit of an obsession to avoid such things—as we have discovered assembling this book, a lot of "all-natural" and "organic" claims just don't pan out. These guys are both earnest in their attempts to keep it real, and to find good, fragrant quality items you can trust, leaving you to obsess about better things.

HEALTH & BEAUTY		

212-741-9474   AppellationNYC.com

Dealing a wide range of organic and biodynamic wines, this Manhattan shop believes that "wine making is an expression of the winemaker, their land and passion." They therefore seek out a diverse assortment of naturally rendered wines from every continent not named Antarctica, relishing the distinctive flavors drawn from geographically different regions. Connoisseurs will find no end of quality appellations to sample, while we amateur wine enthusiasts will be thrilled to drink something natural and delicious.

EPICUREAN		

ApplegateFarms.com   866-587-5858

If there's an organic deli in your neighborhood, you probably won't be all that interested in this site. But, seeing as most neighborhoods don't have an organic anything, we're guessing that the hormone, nitrate, gluten and antibiotic-free lineup of meats and cheeses found here will thrill anybody looking to adhere to an all natural diet. Better yet, the site claims its stock only comes from farms that raise their cows and fowl with plenty of space, fresh air and sunshine. In other words, get ready for a lifetime of healthy, guilt-free club sandwiches.

EPICUREAN		

ARENaturals.com   888-245-8342

Because "each whispering act of conservation… rises collectively into a melodic chorus of harmony that echoes across our deep blue seas, rich green pastures and majestic snow-capped mountains," this online boutique offers recycled and sustainably produced gifts to promote eco-consciousness. In truth, you won't find much, but any of the household items or gift baskets will make a great gift for the right occasion, and browsing the entire selection takes about a minute, so you can get in and get out quick, making it almost too easy to do right.

EPICUREAN	FURNISHINGS	STATIONERY & GIFTS

AromaLand.com   800-933-5267

Eco-conscious fans of essential oils—and we figure there are quite a few of you out there—will dig this site, which offers a huge selection, including many certified organic. These oils, along with several all-natural skin care, bath salts and body products, are available in multiple sizes, including bulk orders of up to a gallon, which in the long run will save you money and conserve containers. To that end, you will also find small, reusable containers for these and products purchased elsewhere. This site definitely doesn't stink.

HEALTH & BEAUTY		

AStoreCalledSpring.com
415-673-2065

"For those who wish to manage their home in a greener, safer, and healthier way," this multipurpose home utility shop covers a lot of ground, or floor space as it were. Beginning with a top-notch selection of natural and nontoxic cleaning products, the site aims to remove harmful chemicals from your personal atmosphere, as well as the planet. To this end, the store also offers a good assortment of air filters and is in the process of developing vacuum and body care sections. This is a clean that will be good for all seasons.

APPLIANCES	HEALTH & BEAUTY	HOUSEHOLD

Aubrey-Organics.com
800-282-7394

All-natural hair, skin and body care products are not difficult to find. However, all-organic products are another matter. This beauty line is in the process of certifying all of its herbal ingredients as organic, which means that you'll eventually be able to find all-organic hair color, body wash, shampoo, cosmetics, fragrances, sunscreens and lotions. In the meantime, a great number of the ingredients used have already been certified, and otherwise you'll just have to settle for the fact that everything here is already all-natural.

HEALTH & BEAUTY		

Aveda.com
800-644-4831

As one of the forerunners in sustainable beauty, Aveda is as well-known as it is distributed. However, this site makes it easy to find the entire line of cosmetics, hair care, skin care, bath & body products and fragrances, and to see for yourself just how committed the company is to the environment. Within its assortment of shaving products, men's products and sun protection, the brand is incresingly incorporating organic ingredients and responsible packaging, and encourages economic growth in the communities it sources for materials. In other word, justifying its claim that it "should be emulated as a model of sustainability."

HEALTH & BEAUTY	MEN	WOMEN

AvitaStyle.com

213-670-0000

Fans of cashmere will surely love the limited number of clothes by this flirty and colorful line of apparel, which ranges from "casual day wear to sexy, sultry night apparel." Even more interesting me be the label's exclusive Bamboo Collection. Of course, these anti-bacterial and biodegradable knit tops aren't woody in the least; rather, the spun fiber provides a cool, sensual feel comparable to a silk blend. You may one day find bamboo garments everywhere, but for now you'll definitely want to check out this one of a kind shop.

ACCESSORIES	APPAREL	WOMEN

AzaleaSF.com

866-344-7231

"A keen appreciation for timeless style" is not required to shop from this San Francisco boutique, but it will sure aid in your enjoyment of the several superhip designer collections found on its savvy site. Men and women both will benefit from the denim and other urban fashions (e.g. graphic tees) filling these pages, in partcular the EcoAzalea section, which includes such eco-friendly labels as Loom State, Stewart & Brown, Edun and Del Forte. Meanwhile, the Eco Beauty Bar offers top notch natural skin care items by the likes of Pangea Organics, Kimberly Sayer, Juice Beauty and Nature Girl.

APPAREL WOMEN	HEALTH & BEAUTY	MEN

BaaBaaZuzu.com

231-256-7176

When old sweaters outlive their use they go to Michigan, where this small, homegrown business refashions them into unique, funky outerwear and accessories. The 100% recycled garments are each one-of-a-kind, taking the best surviving portions of secondhand weaves and knits to create intriguing new jackets, gloves, hats and scarves for women and children. Best of all, it may inspire a few ideas of things you can do with some of your own clothes when they start to wear out.

ACCESSORIES WOMEN	APPAREL	CHILDREN

BabyBunz.com

800-676-4559

Whether out of concern for health or the environment, cloth diapers are becoming more popular these days than they've been since disposables crinkled their ways into our lives. This family run business out of the Pacific Northwest makes it easier for all of us to embrace a more natural and less polluting way to control the pre-potty years. Striving to offer only products that are "environmentally sensible, practical, and pleasing to the senses," the specialty shop carries a wide range of cloth diapers and diaper covers, including plenty of all-natural, organic options, and several toilet-training aids that will help make your laundry safe again.

BABIES

BachRemedies.com

800-334-0843

It's tough to explain any health benefits ingesting floral essences might have, and we certainly won't attempt to do so here. Rather, we'll refer you to this niche alternative health site and let it convince you whether its long list of naturally brewed tinctures can alleviate any suffering owed to anxiety, despondence, indecisiveness, irritability or other emotional sensitivities. So far as homeopathic web shops go, this one offers a lot of information that may or may not convince you that plants can unlock the key to your overall health.

HEALTH & BEAUTY

Bamboo4Sale.com

831-685-0152

Not just for tiki styles anymore, bamboo is more frequently being embraced as a durable, sustainable alternative to hard woods. This all-bamboo site focuses for the most part on gardening and landscaping, with lovely gazebos, arbors, bird feeders, deck tiles and plenty of gorgeous fencing; you may even buy live plants, or simple canes to be used in household projects. Never chemically treated or processed, with minimal proper care these products should retain their strength and beauty for years to come.

FURNISHINGS | **GARDENING**

BambooClothes.com   310-538-3051

Used to be any practical use of bamboo was restricted to a stylish rug, a set of wind chimes and maybe a tiki torch. However, it turns out the sturdy, fast-growing grass is much more versatile than most of us ever realized. As this site's name would suggest, it can actually be fashioned into clothing; specifically, a "super soft, moisture wicking, and naturally antimicrobial" weave. Hypoallergenic, and soft like silk, the basic, casual t-shirts, yoga apparel and underwear may not be super hip, but they are comfortable, derived using extraordinarily sustainable methods, and packaged minimally in recyclable, biodegradable materials.

ACCESSORIES WOMEN	APPAREL	MEN

BambooFencer.com   800-775-8641

Homeowners everywhere will be glad to know that one of the most sustainable options when it comes to fencing your property also happens to be one of the best looking: bamboo. This incredible, affordable and durable alternative to wood and aluminum will give your yard a natural but tasteful look, improving any landscape design you may have (even if you don't actually have one). The variety of fences you find here may be purchased by the roll or custom ordered, and we're guessing it will be tough not to follow up a visit to this site with a trip to your local nursery.

GARDENING		

BambooMango.com   866-548-9463

"Manufactured from renewable and eco-friendly resources such as bamboo, mango wood, maple, soy and silk," the products offered by this company, which is either based in New Jersey or Pennsylvania (we're not sure) cover a few different areas of interest. We're particularly enamored of the bamboo serviceware, though, which is colorful, beautifully designed and easily the best reason to visit this site. Or, you might want to suggest a new name for this uncertain company—if they accept it you receive a free Dreamsack, which is essentially a thin, silk sleeping bag, and the other reason to visit the store.

FURNISHINGS	SERVICE	

BareEscentuals.com
800-266-9135

Doing battle with the misconception that beauty and environmentalism must be mutually exclusive, this San Francisco cosmetics line "has been breaking all the rules about makeup" for decades. Promising no additives or irritants, the pure mineral foundations and blush will end your reliance on chemical preservatives, fragrances and dyes. As far as base cosmetics go, this "feather-light" alternative may be about as natural you will find.

HEALTH & BEAUTY	WOMEN	

BarefootYoga.com
877-227-3366

There's no question that yoga is hip, the question here is: are you hip enough for yoga? This is a cool yoga site that'll help you one way or another, with plenty of great rugs and mats, mat bags, lots of clothing (including a line of hemp apparel) and any sundry accessory that might help your stretching exercises. Just take a deep breath, follow the link for Eco-Yoga Products, and step closer to enlightenment.

APPAREL WOMEN	MEN	SPORTING GOODS

BasketsOfAfrica.com
800-504-4656

When a web shop can state its product selection this succinctly in its name, it just makes our job easier. In this case, it gives us the time and space to explain that these fair trade baskets from Kenya, Swaziland, Ghana, Uganda and South Africa are made from natural, sustainable grasses and leaves, and, in some cases, from brightly-colored recycled phone wires. If you're not yet intrigued, let us tell you that these handmade products are finely crafted using traditional techniques and that they are nothing short of outstanding. One look at this site and you'll immediately realize you don't have nearly enough African baskets in your home.

FURNISHINGS		

BeeswaxCandles.com
888-350-4929

You might not immediately think of candles as a big ecological problem and, in truth, they don't rate super high on the list of priorities. However, when reminded that their primary function is to burn, we do start to wonder: just what sort of substances are they releasing into the air? With the vegetable, palm, soy and beeswax candles of this Colorado company you won't have to worry—they never include lead wicks or paraffin (a petroleum byproduct), and even the scented varieties use essential oils. These are candles you can burn all day, if you like, but they are probably best used at night.

STATIONERY & GIFTS

Beklina.com
408-688-6281

Proving once again that women are in no danger of running out of eco-friendly apparel to browse, this small online boutique covers a decent amount of ground with an ever-changing selection of stylish threads. Popular sustainable labels like Park Vogel and Stewart+Brown reign supreme, but skirt the edges of the assortment and you'll discover a few lesser-known designers who're contributing new looks to the planet-loving world.

| APPAREL | WOMEN | |

BetterForBabies.com
877-303-4050

Touting "natural, organic and uncompromising baby products," this truly inspired shop holds true to its word, beginning with an unparalleled assortment of diapers and diaper covers, made from hemp, organic cotton and organic wool and in some cases surprisingly stylish. The same standards apply to a variety of baby slings, clothes and blankets, and even a few accessories to help out mom and dad. The stellar selection is capped by a smattering of nontoxic personal care and household cleaning products, proving this shop is actually better for everyone.

| ACCESSORIES HEALTH & BEAUTY | APPAREL HOUSEHOLD | BABIES |

BetterWorldClub.com

503-546-1137

Supporting "a cleaner environment and alternative modes of transportation," this new generation auto club does things a bit differently than you might be used to. For example, though its twenty-four hour roadside assistance coverage may not offer drivers any more perks than they'd receive elsewhere, the fact that it includes bicycles in its coverage could prove priceless to the avid and adventurous cyclist. Even if you do drive, knowing that a portion of this company's revenue is donated to environmental charities should at least in some small way counter your car's exhaust.

TRANSPORTATION

BeyondSkin.co.uk

44-845-373-3648

Fully aware that "attempts to combine fashion and ethics have generally resulted in one side of the equation being sacrificed," the designer behind this women's footwear has endeavored, successfully, to create hip boots and pumps that are both cruelty-free and handmade with earth-friendly materials. Even the packaging has not overly taxed the environment and, although you will come across some faux leathers and even the occasional polyester, the label strives to use the lowest impact alternatives available to create shoes that will last through several seasons.

ACCESSORIES **WOMEN**

BiCoNet.com

800-441-2847

There are billions of tiny reasons why mankind turned away from the all-natural agricultural methods that have been successfully employed for millennia: pests. Insects, rodents, birds and other tiny creatures can thwart the greenest of thumbs on a bad day, and toxic though they may be, chemicals have proven a wholly effective weapon. This ancient-looking site offers more eco-conscious arsenal, including traps and nonchemical insecticides and repellents. If you'd rather fight fire with fire, the shop's lengthy list of beneficial insects provides an even greener means of defending your garden against the hordes.

GARDENING

BigBrandWater.com
818-340-7258

With water usage on the rise and water resources on the decline, it doesn't take a mathematician to see problems ahead. This water filtration specialist offers myriad solutions to improve the efficiency of your water usage, primarily by making it possible for you to collect and recycle water from local sources (ground or sky) and treat it for safe home use. Even if you merely implement some of the available filters in your faucets, the improved taste of your tap water should save you from resorting to the plastic bottle variety.

BUILDING SUPPLY	HOUSEHOLD	

BiodegradableStore.com
303-449-1876

The idea of disposable plates, cups, bowls and eating utensils doesn't usually sit well with environmentalists, but this biodegradable service specialist might change all that. Made from corn-based PLA, sugar-based Bagasse, potato-starch foam and recycled-content paper, these party and picnic supplies will compost and biodegrade within months. You will even find straws, soup containers, coffee sleeves, trays and biodegradable garbage bags to help you dispose of these products responsibly. Few solutions are ideal, but this one comes pretty close.

HOUSEHOLD	SERVICE	

BlueCanoe.com
888-923-1373

Creating a line of organic comfortwear well-disposed towards physical activities such as yoga or Pilates, this small line of mostly-women's attire offers surprising breadth of athletic styles. The occasional percentage of lycra gives some of these clothes a little extra stretch, and the vibrant variety of colors may be attributed to low impact dyes, but most remarkable aspect here is that good taste may be applied to such organic threads, right down to the functional undergarments.

APPAREL	MEN	WOMEN

BotanicalDog.com

843-864-9368

Promising "a dog free from harsh chemicals and unsafe ingredients," this small line of dog health and grooming products from South Carolina forsakes the use of toxins for natural and organic ingredients, many of which were used in pet care long before the advent of synthetics. Lustrous coats, healthy skin, pest and itch control can be had without paying that extra chemical cost, and with the great variety of supplements and shampoos available here you might just find away to eliminate that smelly dog odor from your life once and for all.

PETS

BountifulGardens.org

707-459-6410

With a truly impressive variety of "untreated open-pollinated seed of heirloom quality for vegetables, herbs, flowers, grains, green manures, compost and carbon crops," this nonprofit organization serves all of your gardening needs. Including trees, shrubs, unusual, medicinal and super-nutritional vegetation among its many-splendored wares, the Northern California cooperative will also hook you up with the knowledge it takes to raise such rare finds properly, along with the requisite tools and eco-friendly plant foods to raise a rich, colorful and delicious crop time and again.

GARDENING

BranchHome.com

415-341-1824

Rightfully pointing out that worrying over whether the items you purchase are globally responsible "can really sap the joy from a fun day of shopping," the folks behind this brilliant San Francisco furnishings and housewares shop have "done the challenging thinking for us." They've managed to find a superb assortment of furniture, serving pieces, decorative accents and gift ideas, all of which combine principles of sustainable production and modern design. There's no joy lost shopping here.

ACCESSORIES SERVICE | **FURNISHINGS STATIONERY & GIFTS** | **HOUSEHOLD**

BreezerBikes.com

415-339-8917

Getting around gets breezier when you pick up one of this company's folding bikes. Ride to catch the bus or train, then fold it down small enough to fit in a duffel bag and take it with you. Ideally suited for commuters and city-dwellers with limited storage space, they may not be the most stylish bikes you've ever seen but with carriage space, they might be the most functional. Make sure to check the limited models available for online sale to make sure they are suitable to your height, and whether they have enough gears to handle your local terrain.

TRANSPORTATION

BrewOrganic.com

800-768-4409

There are a few brands of organic beer out there, but finding them can be difficult, and variety is rarely an option. Here's the chance for you to brew your own. Whether you're an experienced brewer or need everything from equipment to know-how, this Oregon shop can hook you up with books, brewpots, fermenting equipment and a ready supply of organic malts, hops and yeasts. It might take you awhile to discover your own palatable recipe, but while you wait you can always delve into roasting your own organic coffee beans. Your morning cup will never taste fresher.

CRAFTS & HOBBIES **EPICUREAN**

BrilliantEarth.com

800-691-0952

The past few years, shoppers have developed conflicted attitudes toward diamonds. On the one hand, the unbreakable stone's traditional place atop engagement rings stands as one of love's most lasting symbols. On the other, growing awareness of the horrible impact diamond mining has had on the land and people of Africa casts the luminous gem in a foul light. Fortunately, this site offers jewelry that is both literally and figuratively conflict-free. Sourced from Canadian mines, with minimal environmental impact, these diamonds sport a luster even the most socially-conscious bride-to-be can show off.

ACCESSORIES **STATIONERY & GIFTS**

888-395-2135   **BTCElements.com**

The words stylish, high-quality and sustainable have rarely ever been seen together anywhere near women's fashion. Fortunately, shops like this one are out to prove that global awareness isn't limited to the age-old hippie panache, and that you can find smart, sexy, even work-appropriate attire that suits all of your expectations. Comprised of hemp, organic cotton, bamboo denim, recycled cashmere and/or factory surplus fabrics, this en vogue apparel even meets fair trade standards, leaving you to wonder why you ever shopped differently.

ACCESSORIES WOMEN	APPAREL	STATIONERY & GIFTS

800-292-4838   **BuildingForHealth.com**

"Leading the way in environmental living," this massive Colorado-based retailer offers an impossibly large array of green building materials, energy efficient appliances, energy generators, household cleaning supplies, furniture and accents. It winds up being a little too much for the site's simple navigation, and eventually finding a product doesn't mean it's available for purchase without a phone call. However, should you locate the hard-to-come-by reclaimed wood, sustainably forested lumber, heating system or filtration device you need, it might be worth placing an order to be sent from warehouses around the country.

APPLIANCES GARDENING	BUILDING SUPPLY HOUSEHOLD	FURNISHINGS

888-455-2800   **Bulbs.com**

While this site's obvious specialty is light bulbs, there are two reasons in particular that we like it. The first is a larger-than-average selection of compact fluorescent bulbs. These burn brighter and longer than conventional incandescent or halogen bulbs, and use much less energy in the process (look for the site's compact fluorescent categories). The second reason might be better than the first: light bulb recycling. The problem of what to do with your spent bulbs may be solved by the company's mail-in recycling program; simply order the prepaid return packaging for the bulbs in question, send your bulbs and they will do the rest.

HOUSEHOLD		

ByNature.co.uk

44-208-488-3556

With a well-established cluster of earth-friendly brands at their disposal, it sometimes seems that looking at UK eco shops is like seeing the future of environmentalism. With graceful casual fashions, lovely assortments of gifts and a thorough dedication to sustainable practices, looking at this site you might almost forget unsafe practices ever existed. The downside for us, of course, is having to ship across the Atlantic; however, within just about every category there's a lovely, practical and/or perfectly stylish product that you just can't easily find at home.

APPAREL FURNISHINGS	BABIES MATERNITY	FAMILY SERVICE

CaliforniaOrganicFlowers.com

530-891-6265

Lovingly grown and selected flowers make a reliably romantic gift for nearly any occasion. Make sure those flowers are organically grown, and even the hardest of hearts will melt. This California grower offers gorgeous dahlias, sunflowers, lilies and more, with a selection that varies seasonally and is sure never to disappoint. With limited options available at any time, it makes sense to View All Products and simply choose the picture that most inspires feelings for your intended recipient.

STATIONERY & GIFTS		

CambriaBike.com

888-937-4331

Cars are very expensive in addition to polluting, and though more eco-friendly, the bicycles you'll find here are pretty expensive too. However, if you're interested in cutting down on your day-to-day emissions by getting around on peddle-power, a durable, quality bicycle that will get you around efficiently might be worth the investment. This shop offers a comprehensive variety of bike builds and styles, with all the accoutrements, ensuring you will find a vehicle best suited to your level of fitness and local geography, safely and cleanly.

TRANSPORTATION		

Canvasco.de
49-421-2219-880

The concept of recycling discarded materials into new, usable products is pretty well-known these days. This German company does just that, reclaiming discarded sailing canvas to turn into stylish handbags. Oh, and there's an added twist: the women making on these bags are in prison. We suppose you could look at it as reclaiming labor lost to the German penal system and enjoy the contribution the business is making towards their rehabilitation. We're guessing you'll just enjoy the varied patterns and styles, and your freedom to buy the bags here.

ACCESSORIES	WOMEN	

CardboardDesign.com
212-255-4489

A unique take on what can be done when we successfully recycle paper, this small furnishings company specializes in cardboard furniture. Clever design is the key to these items' durability; the 100% recycled cardboard is woven into a tight network of honeycomb cells and glued with a vegetable-based adhesive. The results are funky, less fragile than they look tables, desks and shelves, and a particularly interesting divider screen. We've never seen anything like it, but keep recycling and we might see it again, and again.

FURNISHINGS		

CavendishFruitcake.com
800-536-7899

It might sound unlikely, but this Vermont-based bakery has done it: created an all-natural, certified organic fruitcake. The perennial holiday gift cake has never looked so good. "Dark, fruity, laden with nuts and cold-aged long enough to let the brandy and orange liqueur permeate and moisten each slice," you may very well wish to pick up an extra one for yourself. Otherwise, it's great to know you can keep up the tradition without betraying your impulse to go green.

EPICUREAN	STATIONERY & GIFTS	

Chabah.com   240-491-7022

Great sandals make excellent shopping quarry even when they aren't made from sustainable materials, and when they look as good as the ones you'll find here, you might not care what goes into them. But, for the record, it's mostly "hemp, woven grass, and sack cloth," along with some recycled plastics and foam, handmade in Thailand "under responsible working conditions by fairly-compensated adult laborers." A dozen or so models give you plenty of reasons to buy a single pair, but if you're a fan of summery footwear, the looks and prices suggest you'll get at least two.

ACCESSORIES	WOMEN	

CheckGallery.com   800-354-3540

Welcome to "America's leading environmentally-friendly bank check printer." No kidding. It turns out, you don't have to order your checks through your bank. And why would you, knowing that you can custom order them here? A wide variety of patterns may be selected, ranging from antique designs to animal themes. Simply enter your bank account information (scary, but it's encrypted), and within a couple of weeks you'll receive personalized checks, printed on recycled paper, using soy-based ink. You may also order address labels and business cards, but what better way to promote a green lifestyle than with your pocketbook?

STATIONERY & GIFTS		

ChildOrganics.com   865-933-0819

This family business out of Tennessee offers a fun, hand-picked variety of baby stuff, from unique baby carriers and slings to cozy baby blankets and bedding. Plenty of great gifts may be found, along with more necessary items such as cloth diapers and covers. Of course, it's all natural, often organic and fair trade in accordance to the high standards of the shop's resident parents. You'll find bigger selections elsewhere, but rarely one compiled with so much care.

ACCESSORIES HEALTH & BEAUTY	APPAREL	BABIES

ChocolateBar.com

800-293-0160

As if it weren't enough that this Indiana company offers delicious, ethically traded and organic chocolates, it also donates a portion of profits to wildlife and environmental charities, all while working out of a LEEDS-certified green building. In other words, with every bite of these candy bars you will not be merely satisfying your sweet tooth, but also supporting as socially responsible a business as you're likely to find in the world of candy, which is definitely a world worth preserving.

EPICUREAN

ChoiceOrganicTeas.com

206-525-0051

Subject of ceremonies and religious rituals dating almost to the beginning of mankind, tea has often possessed spiritual associations, so it makes sense that you'd like to take your tea without any ethical qualms. This organic, fair trade tea line proves perfectly suited to the globally aware, with a deep selection of green, white, black, oolong, chai and herbal teas. Buy the tea loose leaf or bagged, in small packets or the more efficiently-packaged bulk buys, and you'll have only to find a place of repose to sip your earth-friendly brew.

EPICUREAN

CleanAirGardening.com

214-370-0530

If gasoline prices have got you down, why pay at the pump to keep your lawn manicured? This site offers plenty of earth-friendly ways to tend your yard and garden. While a push-reel mower might seem like a lot of effort, an electric mower is simple to charge when you need it, giving one cause to wonder why gas mowers were invented in the first place. It doesn't stop at mowers, with plenty of tillers, trimmers and blowers contributing to your curb appeal without polluting the air. Eco-purists will also benefit from compost bins and rain barrels, and all will appreciate the hand tools and ornaments populating the rest of the site.

APPLIANCES | **GARDENING**

CocoaVino.com
646-418-7634

Created by a pair of French Culinary Institute graduates, this New York City chocolatier is all about trying new things with chocolate, creating a constantly changing selection of artisan confections for gifts or your own enjoyment. Another new thing they do is focus on organic, regional and fair trade sources for their high quality ingredients while running their kitchen on wind power and using ecologically sensitive packaging. It all adds up to brilliant, unexpected flavors like fig caramels and plum/lavender bonbons. With a new taste to try every month, this is probably one you'll want to revisit.

EPICUREAN

CocosShoppe.com
303-775-2461

Leave it to Colorado to provide us with this "concept boutique mingling the most coveted fashion and beauty care with sustainability and eco-consciousness." Heading up a new generation of boutiques that combine green sensibility with up-to-the-minute trends, this store excels by offering a long list of clothing labels like Bahar Shahpar, Deborah Linquist and Burning Torch; handbags by Ananas and Ë bella; and several natural beauty lines. Whether it's made from repurposed silk scarves, bamboo, organic cotton, cashmere, hemp or viscose, the vast majority of these stylish items highlight a bold new direction for women's fashion.

ACCESSORIES WOMEN | **APPAREL** | **HEALTH & BEAUTY**

CoffeeTraders.com
800-345-5282

It's a phenomenon of recent years that purchasing coffee has become an ethical act for Americans, even a form of activism. This coffee specialist should satisfy the more globally and ecologically aware caffeine addicts, offering a rich assortment of coffee beans produced using sustainable agriculture and purchased from free trade farms. In the site's Organics section, the conscientious coffee consumer will find beans that have been grown "in harmony with the rain forest," and justly supports the hard-working folk who help kick-start your morning.

EPICUREAN

CometSkateboards.com

510-625-9045

For a vehicle that can get the adept rider across town quickly on kick power and gravity alone, the skateboard is small enough that it doesn't really consume much in terms of resources. But even skaters can get greener with this line of eco-friendly boards. The brand's many models incorporate sustainably harvested woods and low-VOC finishes to create durable decks with minimal global impact. As if the world needed more evidence that skaters are cooler than drivers.

TRANSPORTATION

Composters.com

877-204-7336

Composting may seem like some dirty business, but this clean conservationalist site makes it easy for you to make a foray into recycling organic waste. With the largest assortment of composting bins and materials we've come across, you can engage in this household environmentalism with your sense of landscaping taste intact. To that end, you'll also find a terrific assortment of electric and push lawn mowers, as well as several gardening tools, water conservation items, recycling bins and even a few green waste management systems for your pets. Everything neat and tidy, planet included.

GARDENING | **HOUSEHOLD** | **PETS**

ConservaStore.com

800-805-9207

The name of the game here is conservation, and the shop offers a variety of practical items to help your household do just that. It begins with flow control shower heads, efficient toilets, hands-free faucets and a variety of plumbing retrofits to help you reduce water usage. When it comes to energy we find simpler buys: rechargeable batteries, long lasting light bulbs (including LED), dimmers and even the occasional solar powered product. When it all adds up you'll discover a lot of happy subtraction: you'll have saved water, used less electricity and lowered your utility bills.

APPLIANCES | **BUILDING SUPPLY**

ContainerStore.com

888-266-8246

Although the vast majority of the products found here are made of plastic, or prove otherwise less-than-eco-friendly, wise shopping here can actually set you up to minimize waste. Begin by checking out the reusable food storage options and water bottles, which will help eliminate plastic baggies and disposable water bottles from your lifestyle. You will also find a healthy assortment of reusable containers for your beauty and grooming products, whether you want to take them on the road or refill them with local or bulk purchases. Either way, it adds up to clean.

| EPICUREAN TRANSPORTATION | HEALTH & BEAUTY | HOUSEHOLD |

CottonClouds.com

800-322-7888

A good yarn can captivate and delight a receptive audience, or it can make a great sweater. This site specializes in the latter, with a fine selection of yarns, each in a variety of colors. The shop has recently added some green fibers into the mix (also in a variety of colors) including a comprehensive assortment of 100% bamboo. The quickly replenishable grass is a story we're fond of telling, which means the durable, sustainable material makes for a good yarn, both literally and figuratively.

| CRAFTS & HOBBIES | | |

CottonFieldUSA.com

888-954-1551

These purveyors of "earth-honoring clothing" specialize in organic cotton, throwing in the occasional hemp and bamboo for spice. That might be the only spice you encounter, as the casual men's and women's apparel tends to veer towards basic fashions: t-shirts, simple skirts, no-frills blouses and undergarments, often so natural as to even forsake dyes. However, you may be assured that everything here is fair trade, sustainably sourced and in no way harmful to the planet.

| APPAREL | MEN | WOMEN |

CowgirlCreamery.com
866-433-7834

Stock up on your organic artisanal cheese with this Bay Area California creamery. Though small in selection, these cheeses are big on taste—and size as it turns out. You may only order online in three pound increments, which means you spend a bit of money up front. However, properly stored these cheeses could last you awhile, and, hey, you might just enjoy the high brow flavors more upon further consumption. You still may want to start with just one, though, and then wait to see what next season's flavors are.

EPICUREAN		

CozyBabies.com
845-321-2187

Among a much greater variety of all-around baby stuff, look for the Shop Organic Baby Bedding link of this site. Here you'll find the entirety of the family-owned business's eco-friendly selection, which primarily consists of blankets and crib sets. However, we were particularly drawn to the small but rarely seen assortment of organic Moses baskets and bassinettes. Hand-woven maize fiber and organic wool mattresses contribute to these beautiful and sustainably produced nursery must-haves. Here's hoping this green selection grows.

BABIES	FURNISHINGS	

CranberryLane.com
800-833-4533

To get a first-hand understanding the sort of things that go into natural bath and body products, spend some time using the crafts kits and recipes available from this make-it-yourself beauty site. In no time, the ingredients going into your daily regimen will be under your sole discretion. Even if you're not feeling so handy, you might get good use out of the reusable Containers and Bottles section, along with some simple and natural bath salts, massage oils, essential oils and soaps to keep them refilled for months.

CRAFTS & HOBBIES	HEALTH & BEAUTY	

Crispina.com
800-824-1143

"It is Crispina's mission to teach thoughtful consumption by offering domestically produced, high quality home accessories made from recycled raw materials." But don't let this deter you, the site's offerings are actually much more fun than that—at least, as fun as blankets and throw pillows can be. As they're made from recycled clothing (completely cleaned, processed and recut), each of these items offer slight variations in look and feel, resulting in a very homey style that's as comforting as it is comfortable.

FURNISHINGS	SERVICE	STATIONERY & GIFTS

CustomPaper.com
888-294-1526

Though convoluted layout and an occasionally confusing ordering process plague the site of this family-owned stationer out of Seattle, the handmade paper, invitations and cardstock make a visit worth your while. Somewhere in here you get to choose between tree-free (cotton) and recycled paper, usually infused with flowers, herbs and vegetables and featuring several custom options. In particular, the invitations stand out as beautiful way to put your eco-sensibilities into practice, as the company's designs aim to minimize the amount of paper used in the first place.

STATIONERY & GIFTS	WEDDINGS	

CyberCanine.com
410-766-5151

Just like people, some dogs have allergies and/or a heightened sensitivity to chemical household and cleaning products. This homegrown business was developed to provide organic solutions to this problem in the form of hypoallergenic and non-toxic grooming products, and things like gluten-free dog biscuits. Homegrown or not, though, this site looks about as slick as any other on the web and, having viewed their adorable Customers picture section, we're quite glad to know they are around.

PETS		

800-393-6075   # DagobaChocolate.com

If you were going to judge chocolate by its impact and the lengths its makers took to give back to the earth, this would probably be the best on the planet. With a variety of fair trade, organic chocolate bars, baker's chocolate and hot cocoas, there's a good chance it is close to the top in flavor as well. Sourcing cacao from places such as Costa Rica, Peru and Madagascar, the Oregon-based company is dedicated to replanting deforested areas and even offers reusable silk packaging with its gift boxes. All this for chocolate. How could you not love it?

EPICUREAN

626-305-5624   # Dahon.com

Specializing in ultra-light, compact bicycles for the urban rider, this manufacturer is probably best known for it's many models of folding frames, which allow you to easily store or travel with your ride. However, the company also makes a variety of full-sized, performance bikes, both for off-road and on, all of which are available here for easy online purchase. And, since these are lighter than your average bicycles, the shipping costs shouldn't be quite high as you might expect.

TRANSPORTATION

888-701-2333   # DakotaOrganic.com

When this site claims to offer "beef in its purest form," it's not kidding. Farming cattle on certified organic pastures, they are raised humanely with constant access to grass and the outdoors. The cows are then "finished" on certified organic grains to increase nutrient content as well as flavor. Most organic beef is raised entirely on grains, while most grass-fed beef can not be certified organic. This terrific option offers the best of both, and though it offers only a few cuts and grounds, any carnivore may eat them confidently, and without ethical qualms.

EPICUREAN

DeansBeans.com   800-325-3008

This wonderful site for a small New England coffee roaster makes it almost too easy to find fresh, fair trade, shade-grown organic coffee; and it doesn't stop there. Among the various roasts, water-processed decafs and flavored coffees you'll find an intriguing Design Your Own Custom Blend option that even lets you personalize the product label for gifts. To further entice the java enthusiast, the shop offers about a dozen varieties of green beans, which may be roasted at home, perhaps using one of the available coffee roasters. Organic sugar, hot cocoa and baker's chocolate round out a selection sure to satisfy your morning craving.

EPICUREAN

DermaE.net   800-521-3342

As well-equipped as any natural beauty line to cover the steps of your daily regimen for radiant, healthy skin, this brand goes a step further to offer a thorough assortment of anti-aging and healing treatments. Including itch-relief, vanishing creams and scar reducers, such products complement beauty maintenance with dermologic health, and might just compete with toxic alternatives now, and almost certainly for the long term.

HEALTH & BEAUTY

DiamondOrganics.com   888-674-2642

Taking the natural-grocery concept to a new level, this fantastic shop offers nothing less than organic fruits and vegetables, available seasonally and delivered fresh. Still, you may want to eat this stuff quick, as your produce will not be tainted by synthetic preservatives, fertilizers or pesticides. Additional sections such as Soy Dairy, Mushrooms, Macrobiotics and Herbs should entice health-food lovers and gourmet connoisseurs alike, though we're not exactly sure what segment of the population will be drawn to the Edible Flowers category.

EPICUREAN   **HEALTH & BEAUTY**   **STATIONERY & GIFTS**

DirtCandles.com

866-436-3865

At least a little bit better than they sound, the lovely gift candles found here come in a variety of scents comprised of essential oil, floral and herb blends. They are also made from organic soy wax and encased in recycled glass, so whether you're buying it for yourself or a friend you'll know your gift has had minimal environmental impact. This might explain the candles' popularity in the press, or it could just be that delicious aromas such as Gingerbread man or the apple-infused Curb a Peel treat the nose as well as these products treat the planet.

STATIONERY & GIFTS

DoggieWalkBags.com

877-364-2247

Sometimes it's your civic duty, sometimes it's mandated by law; either way, cleaning up after your dog is just being a good neighbor. Problem is, more often than not, poop gets tossed out in the trash inside a plastic baggie. While this might seem a good use for the ubiquitous plastic grocery bag, the plastic will be around for a long time, making a bigger mess than your dog ever could. Lines of biodegradable dog waste bags like this enable you to keep your parks and streets clean, and your landfills… well, hopefully it will help keep your landfill out of your backyard.

PETS

DolphinBlue.com

800-932-7715

All these guys really ask is that we "please be cognizant of the volume of paper being consumed on our globe." If you are ecologically aware, you will definitely appreciate this site, which exclusively sells recycled office supplies. Pretty much comprised of recycled and tree-free bulk printer paper, envelopes, post-its, organizers, folders and recycled toner cartridges, this stuff all gets the job done, just without additional deforestation or land-fill dumping. Here's hoping they expand the operation.

OFFICE | **STATIONERY & GIFTS**

DoodleGreetings.com
240-426-4206

Greeting cards allow you to make a gesture of congratulations, condolence, thanks, well-being, love and much more. With a little help from this earth-friendly stationer, you can add a tacit gesture of hope with each greeting. Printed on 100% post-consumer recycled paper, the company is extremely proud to say that "no virgin wood fiber is used in the production of any of the paper we use," including packaging. We can't think of a better way to let someone know you are thinking of them... and the planet.

STATIONERY & GIFTS

DownBound.com
416-890-4355

Promising sweatshop free, cruelty free and organic wares, this site works hard to deliver on all counts, and if we thought the proprietors believed in guns, you can bet they'd be sticking to them. Though various categories cover a wide range of products, your best bets are in the Cosmetics, Bags & Wallets, Dog & Cat Food and Footwear sections. Come looking for any of these items and we're sure you'll leave satisfied. Take a look at what the rest of the site has to offer while you're at it, and you'll probably leave happy.

| **ACCESSORIES** | **EPICUREAN** | **HEALTH & BEAUTY** |
| **MEN** | **PETS** | **WOMEN** |

DrHauschka.com
800-247-9907

Promising that the "vast majority of ingredients...are Biodynamically and organically grown and harvested," this eco-conscious skin care line aims to put the welfare of people and the planet over profit. That said, these are relatively high-end products, so as long as you don't go in expecting a great bargain you should leave happy. However, if you wish to apply only quality, natural ingredients to your delicate body, this is the place to look. Knowing that no workers have been exploited in the process should give your skin an additional glow no chemicals can reproduce.

HEALTH & BEAUTY

800-378-4786   **Drugstore.com**

No, this massive online pharmacy hasn't switched its entire selection to eco-conscious products... yet. It has, however, provided a neatly organized Natural store within a store. Here you will find nontoxic cosmetics, pet products, household cleaners, toiletries and bath & body items. Of course, there are a lot of other things to buy on this site that aren't enviro-friendly in the slightest, but if you take advantage of the free shipping incentive to order a healthy mix of green and not-green products into one order, it sort of balances out.

HEALTH & BEAUTY	PETS

877-538-2382   **DucDucNYC.com**

This New York City line of modern, sustainable wood furniture for babies and kids is about as good as you're going to find. Culled from managed forests and painted with non-VOC lacquer, the assorted desks, cribs, dressers, chairs and beds are more earth-friendly than they are numerous, but the slim selection's hallmark is a clean, modern design that should be durable to endure at least a couple of childhoods, and stylistically almost until adolescence. While we're not crazy about the crib bedding, this young furniture site is definitely no goose.

BABIES	CHILDREN	FURNISHINGS

877-447-1521   **EarthFriendlyGoods.com**

Determined to get it right, this eco-department store deals mostly in hemp products, but also endorses "organic cotton, soy, flax, wool, and other earth friendly resources." These will primarily be found in the various apparel and accessories sections, where every member of the family will find basic, sustainable attire, occasionally even with a bit of flair. Pets can get in on the act with some green toys, collars and leashes, and if you're handy with a needle and thread you will delight in the selection of hemp fabrics available. This is precisely the sort of shop you would think of when you hear the word "sustainable."

EarthMamaAngelBaby.com   503-607-0607

Skin care's always a complicated issue, particularly during pregnancy and especially when you're trying to stick to all-natural products. Well, this small line of maternity, nursing and baby personal care products takes on the challenge, and what's more it does it with certified organic ingredients. The "diverse blend of nurses, herbalists, labor and postpartum doulas, childbirth hypnotherapists, childbirth educators, women, mothers and grandmothers" behind the brand combine an incredible amount of expertise to contribute healing, softening and soothing creams, oils and salves to what was originally a very natural process.

BABIES	HEALTH & BEAUTY	MATERNITY

EarthPak.com   888-532-7847

Synthetic fabrics didn't get to be so popular by being useless, and one particularly practical application of petroleum-based materials is the common backpack. Light, sturdy and often water-resistant, a synthetic backpack has its benefits and, thanks to this site, you can still own one with a clear conscience. Breaking down the plastic from recycled soda bottles and weaving it into a proprietary fabric colored with low-impact dyes, the company promises waterproof bags with durable seams that should easily carry your stuff into the next decade.

ACCESSORIES	FAMILY	

EarthSake.com   877-268-1026

Each year many of us struggle to find an appropriate way to celebrate Earth Day, and most of us probably don't wind up starting an eco-friendly business. However, some people do, and this natural furniture and bedding shop was founded to celebrate the occasion's twentieth anniversary. Aside from a variety of sustainable towels and linens, the California Bay Area store offers a very nice assortment of furniture made of wood taken only from managed forests. Come to think of it, shopping here might be a good way to observe your next Earth Day, even if it's still several months away.

FAMILY	FURNISHINGS	

800-434-4246   # EarthsBest.com

Finding the purest and most sustainably made baby food doesn't get any easier than with this site, even if the site can be a little frustrating to use at times. The all-organic food producer delivers with three levels of jarred foods for infants, as well as soy and regular formula, juices and even a few healthy snacks for toddlers. You will be satisfied that you're providing all-natural, nontoxic and nutritious meals for your little ones, and, presuming you can get the airplane to fly into the hangar, your children will also be well-fed.

BABIES	EPICUREAN	

718-797-6898   # EarthSpeaks.com

Here's a site for all the professional women out there who never thought they'd see the day they could wear organic cotton attire to work. This "sweatshop-free manufacturer" offers a small but terrific range of classic, tasteful designs that have been made using renewable resources and all-natural materials, all for an affordable price. And it's not all business here, by any means. You'll also find some decidedly hip pants, skirts and blouses, and a even a few surprisingly elegant evening gowns. A few visits here and you can forsake synthetics altogether.

APPAREL	WOMEN	

877-548-3387   # EarthTechProducts.com

Many green sites look back to traditional, natural methods to lessen the impact of humans on the earth—this is not such a site. Here, new technology is embraced to (often quite literally) light our way out of ecological problems (tough to say where the recycled dinnerware fits in, but it's nice). Combining fun (solar backpacks and gadgets) with functional (LED light bulbs, energy conservation products and wind-up radios), the bulk of the products are not made using sustainable methods or materials, but generally offer the best-bet alternatives to similar conventional products. Definitely worth keeping an electronic eye on.

APPLIANCES SERVICE	BUILDING SUPPLY	HOUSEHOLD

Eco-Artware.com 877-326-2781

Drawing the fine line between art and accessories, this vastly compelling shop does so with a palette of discarded materials. Thus, scrabble tiles become a pair of earrings, old sweaters turn into stuffed animals and street signs somehow get fashioned into switchplates. Sometimes functional, often kitschy, occasionally sublime, this stuff really does promote recycling by demonstrating an element of artistry, and there's no question you can find a terrific gift here for just about anyone. It's true what they say: one man's trash is another man's cufflink.

ACCESSORIES STATIONERY & GIFTS	FAMILY	OFFICE

EcoBags.com 800-720-2247

You wouldn't think that a store offering grocery bags, produce bags, lunch bags and totes would have much impact on the planet. However, these reusable bags, typically made from sustainably produced or recycled fabrics, promote a routine awareness that disposable paper and plastic bags aren't necessarily conducive to an earth-friendly lifestyle. You'll find a variety of bags designed for all manner of daily uses, and when you consider the amount of paper or plastic you might save in just one year, it's easy to see how small change adds up.

ACCESSORIES		

EcoChoices.com 626-969-3707

The clear and important emphasis of this site is that living an ecologically sustainable lifestyle is a choice we can make as consumers; at least, now that we know about this lifestyle shop we can make the choice to purchase environmentally sound products. Most of the products here, such as the clothing and furniture, have been made from organic materials. Others are comprised of recycled materials, some made of hemp or, as in the case of the bath & body products, all natural herbs and vegetables. Whether you're shopping for towels, coasters, toys or a new mattress, this shop can keep your shopping and your home green.

APPAREL HEALTH & BEAUTY	FAMILY PETS	FURNISHINGS STATIONERY & GIFTS

800-733-3495   EcoExpress.com

Boasting "Uncommon Gifts for the Common Good," this site succeeds by devoting itself entirely to green gift set baskets. Beautifully arranged and delivered with recycled and biodegradable packaging, the dozens of options here can't go wrong. Whether you opt to give gourmet sweets, eco-sensitive baby stuff, tea sets or organic beer collections, here you may be assured of finding delightful gifts for colleagues, friends or loved ones, whether or not they know they're environmentalists yet.

EPICUREAN	STATIONERY & GIFTS	

877-204-7336   Eco-Furniture.com

Offering what has to be the largest collection of eco-sensible furniture anywhere, this member of the Green Culture ring of shops makes a great effort to make sure their manufacturers adhere to sustainable sourcing of wood, low-impact finishes and nontoxic upholstery. Although they cannot claim to succeed across the board, for the most part these items are at least greener alternatives to most conventional furnishings, and with thorough descriptions that pinpoint exactly why they are. The trouble here will be less about figuring out what is earth-friendly and more about which option goes best with your interior design motif.

FURNISHINGS		

305-674-0433   Ecoist.com

How far can we go to recycle? Check this handbag specialist to find out. Its "one-of-a-kind, handmade items made from repurposed materials like discarded food packages, candy wrappers, movie billboards, and soda can tabs." It sounds crazier than it really is, and really does have to be seen to be believed. Some of these items are not merely tolerably hip, but beautiful as well, as since the erstwhile fair trade retailer promises to plant a tree for every purchase, you'll probably want at least a couple.

ACCESSORIES	WOMEN	

Eco-Lights.com
877-204-7336

If not for this site's name, we might not even have noticed that its wares were environmentally-friendly. After all, the extensive variety of chandeliers, wall sconces, outdoor fixtures, lamps and other lighting are so beautifully rendered that one would never suspect they were made using sustainable practices. It's true, though. Incorporating "recycled materials, ecologically harvested timber, and other earth friendly ingredients," these "enlightening" products are all at least partially constructed with the planet's welfare in mind.

FURNISHINGS

EcoPaper.com
805-644-4462

If you think of paper as something strictly made from trees, this site begs to differ. All of its organic, tree-free paper products are made from—are you ready for this? Cigars, bananas, coffee, lemons and mangos. Based in Califonia, the company combines agricultural waste from Costa Rica with post-consumer, recycled paper to create handmade journals and notebooks printed with vegetable dyes, usually with an animal or environmental theme. You'll also find envelopes and printer paper that will most likely offer more texture and durability than your office is used to. You'll never view your morning cup of joe the same way.

STATIONERY & GIFTS

EcoParti.com
877-473-8257

Weddings are beautiful, inspiring, celebratory events... but they can get a bit messy. Here's one small way to make a wedding a little less of a strain on the environment, specifically when it comes to the part of the ritual that, in a way, promotes littering: the wedding toss. The "Ecofetti" featured here provides a vibrant, biodegradable alternative to boring old rice or soapy bubbles. Your guests will simply fill the air with bright colors, and within a couple of days the starch-based confetti will have dissolved. It may not be the great eco-solution the world is clamoring for, but we like it.

WEDDINGS

EcoSmartInc.com
888-329-2705

As frustrating as it can be to find some amazing eco-friendly building materials or appliance on this site, only to find the words "Quote Request," there are a number of terrific flooring, passive heating, solar heating, insulating and water conserving materials and systems available for online purchase. It's often very pricey, and much of this stuff will require a competent builder, more than likely a contractor, to install. When you do stumble into an item unavailable for online purchase, a series of phone calls should do the trick. After all, no one said green building was easy, only that it's worth it.

APPLIANCES	BUILDING SUPPLY	

Eco-Terric.com
866-582-7547

Always striving to "create beautiful, colorful and environmentally friendly living spaces using healthy materials that are also socially responsible," this furniture specialist with stores in San Francisco and Montana features a great variety of earth-conscious wares. The wood and organic, nontoxic furniture incorporates sustainable and recycled materials, offering an elegance to eco-home décor that probably hasn't existed for a hundred years, and which conventional furniture manufacturers would like to have you believe can't be found today. But it can be found, and this is one place you'll definitely want to look.

FURNISHINGS		

EcoVineWine.com
805-688-4455

If you or a loved one appreciate good wine and sustainable practices, but don't have the time to sift through all the wines of the world to find the finest organic bottles, check out this organic wine club. "Every selection that is offered to [their] members has been taken through a rigorous tasting and evaluation process," so you may just sit back and wait for the next month's bottle to arrive, gradually becoming well-versed with the quality end of the burgeoning organic wine industry. A great gift for enthusiasts and would-be connoisseurs alike.

EPICUREAN		

EcoWise.com   512-326-4474

When it's time to upgrade your home to match your ecological lifestyle, you won't want to miss this outstanding "earth-friendly-everything store." You don't even need to wait, as the site's fairly well-equipped to handle routine needs such as organic toiletries, hemp apparel, chemical-free cleaning agents, natural pest control and recycled disposable service ware. However, it's definitely your bigger household projects that benefit most, whether you wish to find energy efficient appliances, eco-friendly flooring, air filters, composting equipment, nontoxic paint and plenty of green building supplies. Wise is an understatement.

BUILDING SUPPLY STATIONERY & GIFTS	GARDENING	HOUSEHOLD

EdibleNature.com   703-637-9377

Ineffectual browsing design sometimes makes it difficult to find what you need in this discount naturals and organics market, but it only highlights the wide selection available here. Categories like Healthy Foods and Bulk Goods cover a lot of edible ground, while plenty of Wellness, Beauty and Household Items prove that keeping your home and body clean, pure and natural doesn't have to be a luxury.

EPICUREAN STATIONERY & GIFTS	HEALTH & BEAUTY	HOUSEHOLD

ElectricTransport.net   866-895-2289

Weaning yourself off of petroleum can be as easy as visiting this specialty shop, which features electric bicycles, scooters and golf carts that will help you get around town sans carbon emissions. However, if you really want to blow some minds, follow the Electric Cars link. Here you'll find a small selection of highway friendly electric vehicles. Worried about style? Well, it just so happens you can choose between a Rolls Royce and a converted Porsche! If all else fails, you may at least get the gear to convert the car you already own.

TRANSPORTATION		

Elixir.net

310-657-9300

This site may be the modern-day version of traveling shysters selling tonic and elixir "miracle cures" out of the backs of horse drawn wagons. Then again, this could be the dawn of a new era in American health care, one in which people are becoming increasingly disenchanted with insurance and pharmaceutical companies, and are ready to turn to some long-standing and natural remedies for minor ailments. The answer probably lies in your willingness to pursue this course of therapy, combined with your body's ability to sustain a healthy and natural balance. Either way, these guys are here, and you might feel better knowing so.

HEALTH & BEAUTY		

ElseWares.com

866-578-0730

This "catalog of unique products from independent designers and entrepreneurs" is more than capable of providing a most unusual gift for that funky friend or curious loved one. But we're mostly interested in the potential of its Recycled/Eco section of its Gift Ideas menu. look for the link on the bottom-right of the page and you'll quickly find a smattering of unique gifts that make use of discarded items like socks, bicycle chains and soda cans, the result usually being a kitschy accent or accessory that will tell the world: "I recycle."

ACCESSORIES	STATIONERY & GIFTS	

EnergyFederation.org

800-379-4121

Devoted to conservation of energy for more than a quarter century, this company's product selection is predicated on the idea that embracing efficiency does "not necessarily require sacrifices in people's quality of life." Quite the opposite, in fact, as energy and water-efficient products "often perform better than conventional" ones, and in the long term will preserve your bank balance as well. Here you'll find the necessary tools to accomplish such feats, including water-saving shower heads, longer-lasting light bulbs, energy-saving insulation products, rechargeable batteries, solar panels and more.

APPLIANCES	BUILDING SUPPLY	HOUSEHOLD

EnvironGentle.com 760-753-7420

Anytime you come across product categories like Biodegradable, Recycled & Reusables and Hemp Products, you just know a shop is earnestly dedicated to the health of the planet, and this one definitely is. The San Diego-area small business has been operating for more than fifteen years as a source of eco-goods and a local showcase for green ideals, and in that time has developed a tidy assortment of products covering a wide range of needs; anything from organic socks and linens to biodegradable doggy bags and surf wax. Leave it to beach-lovers to get it right.

ACCESSORIES	APPAREL	FAMILY
HEALTH & BEAUTY	HOUSEHOLD	STATIONERY & GIFTS

EquaClothing.com 011-44-7968-144275

Wanting its clothes "to be desirable for desire's sake, as well as having an ethical story," this "first" of its kind Central London boutique prides itself on finding designers just as committed to fair trade principles and sustainable fabrics. They chiefly succeed with regard to women's clothing, and to a lesser extent accessories, offering an interesting collection of garb for the girl of mixed casual and fashionable tastes. Here's hoping other boutiques will quickly follow suit.

ACCESSORIES	APPAREL	WOMEN

ErbaViva.com 877-372-2848

If you're into naturals, and want your child to be as well, start by checking out this site whose name means "living herbs." Basically, it offers soothing and sweet-smelling ointments and salves that are "100% pure, certified organic," and designated baby-friendly. Treat the whole family to this line of products, and you may one day have to answer some tough questions from your kid—like, "What's a chemical?"

BABIES	FAMILY	HEALTH & BEAUTY

781-878-5397   **ExtremelyGreen.com**

As green as green gets, this organic gardening specialist helps you put together a beautiful lawn and garden while fostering "thoughtful, cautious stewardship of the biosphere." Though products often lack detailed descriptions or even photographs, you will find tips and information about their use elsewhere on the site. Likewise complicating things, the shipping terms may be unclear, as some products (beneficial insects, for example) will include free express shipping, while others will incur a two-dollar handling fee. Nevertheless, we give the shop a couple of green thumbs up.

GARDENING		

866-492-4841   **FaeriesDance.com**

Sticking to clothing that only uses "environmentally sensitive fabrics and dyes" is only one way this small, Southern California store actively promotes green living. Its practice of reusing packing materials and commitment to charity contributes just as much, as does the fact its affordable wares are accessible to a wide range of women. What do you get from such a positively inclined retailer? Eco-friendly jewelry and fashionable dresses, tops and bottoms for women, made from such sustainable fabrics as hemp, tencel, soy, bamboo and organic cotton. A role model for other shops, it couldn't do more to deserve your business.

ACCESSORIES	APPAREL	WOMEN

866-327-4344   **FashionDig.com**

This clothing site devoted to "exploring 20th century style" aims to satisfy those with vintage cravings. You can browse through the Mod Shop, the Fabulous Fifties or the always intriguing Couture, and you'll easily be met with some truly fashionable attire that is just outdated enough to appear fresh and new. Better yet, you will be extending the life cycle of some chic manufactured materials, thus reducing the need for overproduction. It might not work out exactly like that, but you will look good, so no one's complaining.

APPAREL	MEN	WOMEN

FlorCatalog.com

866-281-3567

Mosaic meets rug on this curious site, which sells modular carpet, 380 square inches at a time. The roughly 20"x20" self-adhesive squares of carpet come in a range of colors, and may be arranged and rearranged as you see fit. Cover a small area or go wall to wall; follow a checkerboard pattern or keep it simple. Although only a few of the available tiles are actually made using sustainable materials, look and you will find them. Otherwise, take comfort in the fact the company is commited to zero-waste production practices, even going so far as to recycle its own product when you stain one square and need to replace it with another.

FURNISHINGS

ForOtherLivingThings.com

408-739-6785

It's rare to find a good, earth-friendly pet store, especially one that takes more into account than dogs and cats. Although everything in this store doesn't qualify as eco-conscious, the owners have made an effort to include natural and/or organic products where possible. So while shopping for your chinchilla or rabbit may not save the planet's resources entirely, it's a start, and whether it's a dog, cat, hamster or bird, stick with this store and, in time, there might be a little something more for every living thing.

PETS

FoxFireFarms.com

970-563-4675

You have to admire an operation that stands behind its product, and this Colorado farm puts it on the line, saying, "we feel confident that the lamb we raise and sell will be the best organic grass fed lamb you have ever had in the world." Well, odds are still low that most of us have yet tried other organic grass fed lamb, let alone raised free range, which makes this site all the more special. If you're going to eat lamb this year, try it here first.

EPICUREAN

011-41-43-210-3252   Freitag.ch

Presenting endless variations of a good thing, this Swiss manufacturer offers hundreds, if not the alleged thousands of bags made entirely from recycled materials. With "used truck tarpaulins, bicycle innertubes, car seat belts and used airbags" contributing to the waterproof durability of these handbags and totes, the limited models feature colors and patterns that vary as wildly as their industrial sources. Though fashionable, these materials did perform burly tasks in their first incarnations, so these might not be the most dainty of your accessories, but you can bet these rugged items will get the job done.

ACCESSORIES		

866-326-2111   FreshUnlimited.com

To those who would say that finding gifts for environmentalists is too difficult, we offer this thoughtful and well-stocked gift basket specialist. Adherent to the principles of sustainability as well as the concept of indulgence, the shop features a surprisingly diverse assortment of gift ideas for different budgets and occasions. Particularly inspired are the Spa, Executive and Gourmet options, made all the better for their devotion to organics. It's almost too easy.

STATIONERY & GIFTS		

212-239-8230   FriendlyRobotics.com

What if we told you that you could mow your lawn without lifting a finger and still minimize your negative impact on the planet? Well, log on to this site and get ready to believe. Here you will find the innovative product teenage boys have been waiting for since the beginning of time: the robot lawnmower. The rechargeable electric mower proves that future technology can seamlessly blend convenience with social conscience, almost without trying.

GARDENING		

FrontierCoOp.com
800-669-3275

These guys have been around selling all-natural and organic products for a quarter century, meaning they were doing it long before it became a fad. In that time, they've developed a rather thorough bit of information, some of which they're willing to share here, though most of your time is best spent in the Aromatherapy and Herbs & Supplements sections. Join the co-op, of course, and you'll receive discounts and dividends, making this a good candidate for repeat business.

EPICUREAN	HEALTH & BEAUTY	

FuzBaby.com
801-282-6895

This family business out of Utah makes some products so popular it has trouble keeping them in stock, and when you find out what they are you might be shocked: cloth diapers. Not your ordinary diapers and covers, though. You might be equally surprised to know the notoriously unfunky state is home to the funkiest diaper covers you'll find anywhere. Featuring charming and colorful patterns in organic cotton and wool, just seeing the variety is worth a visit, which may be all you can do as the growing company strives to keep up with high demand. Who knew there could be all this fuss over something designed to catch poop?

ACCESSORIES	BABIES	

Gaiam.com
877-989-6321

This increasingly popular online department store was created "to provide choices that allow people to live a more natural and healthy life with respect to the environment," and thanks to its growing selection of information, health products, fitness equipment and housewares, adhering to an eco-friendly lifestyle has never been easier. Proving that sustainable living is not just a fad, the excellently designed shop offers items as aesthetically pleasing as they are functional, which almost takes the fun out of curbing your reliance on chemicals and plastics for the sake of the planet.

APPLIANCES HOUSEHOLD	BUILDING SUPPLY SPORTING GOODS	GARDENING STATIONERY & GIFTS

Gardeners.com

888-883-1412

Few of the gardening sites we've covered in this book have as diverse a selection as this one, and none as complicated. The massive gardening site maintains an earth-friendly stance, while occasionally falling back on more conventional wares to round out the selection. The complicated part is you'll occasionally find items that are positive one way, negative another, such as hearty outdoor furniture made from sustainably harvested wood, topped by polyester cushions. Such is the give and take of the green lifestyle sometimes; if you think you can spot the dangerous items, do so. If you're uncertain, your best bet is to move on.

FURNISHINGS	GARDENING	

GardenHarvestSupply.com

260-589-3384

As environmentalists, we aim to be at peace with animals, preserving their habitats and promoting biodiversity. However, it's hard to maintain any kind of lofty stance when some of the peskier species invade your space. When this happens, turn to this garden supply shop for a pretty savvy assortment of environmentally-friendly pest controls. Electronic and chemical-free solutions should keep common and even more surprising animals at bay, including snakes, rodents, birds, bugs, raccoons, skunks, deer and rabbits. This way you may humanely strike an agreement: I'll stay off your turf if you stay off mine.

GARDENING		

GardenKids.com

541-465-4544

Using organic and colorgrown cotton, with the occasional low-impact, phosphate-free dyes, this small Oregon business doesn't make extravagant, trendy nor overly expensive baby and children's clothes. However, they do happen to make eco-friendly products that are remarkably adorable, and often unlike those churned out by the competition. In particular, the assorted longjohns and pajamas will keep your youngsters cute as well as cozy, and promise to maintain their charm through repeated washings, and indeed through several kids.

APPAREL	BABIES	CHILDREN

GardensAlive.com   513-354-1482

What does it take to make your garden grow? Obviously, there's water, sunlight and fertile soil, but what nature gives nature can take away in the form of insects, fungi and other botanical threats. The tendency is to add chemicals to the mix. But come on, this plant life flourished for millennia without the help of pollutant artificial supplements, so why should they stop now? Instead, check this site's "environmentally responsible products that work" for beneficial insects, non-chemical fungicides and other nature-friendly products to aid and protect your lawn and garden.

GARDENING		

GDiapers.com   866-553-5874

This could be your best source of disposable diapers online. "What's that?" you ask, "Don't disposable diapers exemplify the overfilling of our nation's landfills?" Well, yes. But these aren't your typical disposables. In fact, technically speaking, the diapers themselves aren't disposable, just the liners. And the liners aren't designed to be thrown away, rather flushed. The nonplastic, predominantly biodegradable liners are by no means a perfect solution to the problems of diapering, but this unique site offers plenty of information to sway you, and at least serves as another option for young parents to know about.

ACCESSORIES	BABIES	HEALTH & BEAUTY

GetKnu.com   616-741-9663

You can get to work on greening up your home office by visiting this new (or knu, as it were) furniture manufacturer. Desks, bookcases, filing cabinets, chairs and tables are comprised of certified sustainable wood, recycled steel and low-VOC adhesives and finishes. The company even takes great efforts to offset carbon emissions and use alternative energy sources to power operations, making this the sort of eco-conscious business we love to see. And did we mention this furniture looks good? We like to see that, too.

FURNISHINGS	OFFICE	

GildenTree.com
888-445-3368

Giving the full treatment to your hands and feet, this altruistic spa products specialist offers your extremities a chance for natural relief, and features an extremely comfortable-looking selection of robes to cover the rest of your body. Although its cotton products are not technically certified organic, they do describe an earnest, sustainable process used from growing on through manufacture, and detail their commitment to educate the women of Pakistan who put these products together, as well as their children. Taken at its word, this company offers relaxation for mind, body and soul.

APPAREL	FAMILY	HEALTH & BEAUTY

GiveMode.com
877-365-8800

Proponents of the green lifestyle are prone to preach to friends, family, even fellow bus passengers about the merits of sustainability, but the surest and most-welcome form of activism might involve eco-friendly gifting. It's at the very least the most generous way to share your globally conscious attitudes, and few gift sites will spread the good word so deliciously as this organic and naturals gift box specialist. Featuring mouth-watering selections of heirloom and organic produce, organic cheeses, honey and delectable desserts, these gifts definitely get the point across: you don't have to sacrifice quality or taste to save the planet.

EPICUREAN	STATIONERY & GIFTS	

GladRags.com
800-799-4523

All things being equal, every month, women place a little additional strain on waste disposal systems, and it really can't be helped—unless you make the switch to alternative, nondisposable feminine hygiene solutions. This site has a lot of them. The homegrown business out of Oregon offers a variety of reusable cotton and organic cotton pads, as well as menstrual cups and sea sponge tampons. Finding the right solution might take a little time and consideration, but there's no saying a fact of life has to impinge upon the Earth.

HEALTH & BEAUTY	WOMEN	

GlobalGirlfriend.com
303-730-3680

Devoted to improving women's rights and financial independence worldwide, this fair trade apparel and accessories shop also promotes the use of organic cotton and recycled materials in the majority of its products. You'll find come pretty cool belts, scarves and handbags, and some funky, fashionable jewelry that makes reclaimed products beautiful again or, in some cases, for the first time. Although limited, the Apparel section offers some lovely, simple and affordable dresses, which will make you feel both feminine and strong as you realize you've done something positive for the woman who made it.

ACCESSORIES	APPAREL	WOMEN

GoodBaker.com
800-615-7059

The good baker in this scenario is you, whether or not you have a knack for it. This small brand's specialty is organic baking mixes; all-natural, whole-grain, low-sugar mixes you can prepare alone or with the kids to make tasty snacks that are wholesome, unprocessed and designed to be delicious. A variety of muffins, cookies and brownies are sure to delight, while assorted cake mixes, pancakes and waffles will be something special.

CRAFTS & HOBBIES	EPICUREAN	

GoodCommonSense.net
347-623-8131

Good and sensible, yes, but we'd hardly call this sincerely altruistic home site common. Offering a variety of appliances, devices, conversion items and household upgrades, the shop covers a great list of big and small changes you can make around the old abode to tweak yourself in a healthier, ultimately less expensive and greener direction. Energy efficient washer/dryers, longer-lasting lightbulbs and area rugs made from recycled materials just give you a glimpse of what to expect, but in every smart category there is plenty to behold, a lot to learn, and probably something you'll want to order.

APPLIANCES OFFICE	BUILDING SUPPLY SERVICE	HOUSEHOLD STATIONERY & GIFTS

GrassRootsStore.com
888-633-5833

"Green washing," as this growing Toronto environmental retail chain tells us, refers to the sad fact that "anyone can claim to make an environmental product." Unwilling to fall for false claims, this store "carefully sources and investigates products" to make sure they live up to its own stringent green standards. This mostly benefits shoppers in bath and body, but you will also find a great assortment of household cleaners, a few solar energy products and an always improving assortment of housewares. US orders will may accrue an additional customs fee in transit, but shop wisely and this should be a good green bet.

APPLIANCES STATIONERY & GIFTS	HEALTH & BEAUTY	HOUSEHOLD

GreenBabies.com
800-603-7508

To avoid any misunderstandings, let it be known that we at **thepurplebook** believe babies to be wonderful and extra-special no matter what color they happen come in. We just happen to be fond of Green Babies because they use 100% organically grown cotton. Yes, newborns up to 24 months of age may be securely nuzzled in these rompers and cushy hats that use toxin-free dyes on top of being ecologically sound. Sure, the kids won't be able to say, "ecological," let alone understand it, but they'll sure understand what cozy means.

ACCESSORIES	APPAREL	BABIES

GreenBatteries.com
800-790-7866

Where do batteries go when they die? It's a question the earth-loving, landfill-hating soul probably doesn't want to answer. However, as this site shows, powering your portable electric devices doesn't have to be a source of internal conflict. With an extensive selection of rechargeable batteries (and chargers), you'll be able to find Lithium Ion or Nickel Metal Hydride varieties in standard sizes (C, D, AA, etc) as well as for the occasional digital camera model.

APPLIANCES		

GreenBuildingSupply.com   800-405-0222

Construction of environmentally sound *green* buildings has just started to catch on, but thanks to this site it's not too late to improve your existing home's eco-compatibility. It can be as simple as using the nontoxic cleaning solvents, paints, sealers and stains, or as involved as installing low-water toilets, energy-conserving appliances and natural flooring. You'll find it all here, as well as some helpful air and water filtration systems, earth-friendly insulation and lovely wood furniture. The site tends to offer too much information to make for easy shopping, but there shouldn't be any lasting damage for cluttering up the web.

BUILDING SUPPLY	HOUSEHOLD	

GreenCulture.com   877-204-7336

Actually a conglomeration of sites, including Eco-Furniture.com and Composters.com, this rather large umbrella retailer endeavors to cover an increasingly vast range of sustainable and nonpolluting products for your home and garden. The home page menu appears to list categories such as Pest Control and Water Conservation, but will actually take you to these separate stores, and you must visit each shop separately to view the truth wealth of items covered. This works if you have a lot of time on your hands; otherwise you'll want to stick to whichever eco topic currently interests you the most.

FURNISHINGS	GARDENING	HOUSEHOLD

GreenDepot.com   800-238-5008

Drawing obvious comparisons to a popular national home store, this greener alternative in no way features as massive and varied a selection as other "depot" stores might. However, it has assembled a bunch of earth-friendly products for home improvement projects and household utilities. The shop has sustainable flooring and carpeting well-covered, as well as nontoxic floor cleaners, but its most significant contribution is found in the assortment of low-VOC paints, finishes, adhesives and sealants. The value of such products cannot be overestimated, and their use will go a long way towards giving you a greener home.

BUILDING SUPPLY	HOUSEHOLD	

GreenEarthMarket.com

800-781-8837

Taking interactivity to the next level, this green supersite urges you to be in touch if you cannot find the products you seek. This could prove challenging, as the altruistic, carbon-neutral family business offers a comprehensive assortment of eco-friendly products. Push lawn mowers, hemp accessories and all-natural dog food only hint at the vareity you may expect, all of which, to some degree, has been chosen with sustainability in mind.

ACCESSORIES FURNISHINGS	APPAREL GARDENING	FAMILY PETS

GreenEarthOfficeSupply.com

800-327-8449

The office always presents a challenge when you're trying to adjust to a green lifestyle, so when it's time to restock and replenish your workplace it's best to visit a retailer devoted to eco-considerations. This site certainly fits the bill. With a no-frills approach the shop fills in the big picture with little details, whether it's recycled paper clips, hemp briefcases, remanufactured printer cartridges or forest-friendly paper. After all, if you're going to work, it might as well be for the environment.

ACCESSORIES OFFICE	APPLIANCES STATIONERY & GIFTS	CRAFTS & HOBBIES TRANSPORTATION

GreenFeet.com

888-562-8873

Green is our other favorite color here at **thepurplebook**, in part due to this shop, which delivers a diverse selection of "high-quality, truly natural products that you can trust." We've gotten used to seeing the eco-lifestyle represented online, but every time we visit this site we're still surprised at just how varied its products are. With entire sections devoted to Housekeeping, Personal Care and Hemp, it's hard enough to go wrong, but with assorted other items to improve your day-to-day life, we're guessing you'll be back for large purchases often.

ACCESSORIES HEALTH & BEAUTY	FAMILY HOUSEHOLD	FURNISHINGS PETS

GreenFibres.com 44-1803-868-001

It usually doesn't make much sense to buy products shipped from the UK, but for well-made, comfy looking socks, underwear and sleep attire like this, we might be willing to go for the transatlantic shipping. The organic cotton, organic wool, silk, and fabric blends of this British manufacturer are beguiling in their own simple way, and with options for every member of the family you can maximize your order with a single purchase to cover everybody's essentials.

APPAREL	FAMILY	

GreenFieldPaper.com 888-402-9979

For more than fifteen years this San Diego company has been exploring ways to make paper more sustainable. What have they come up with? Hemp paper, paper recycled from the company's own junkmail, plantable seed-embedded paper and more. Not bad, huh? These come in the form of stationery sets, journals and greeting cards, but really any way you go it's tough to go wrong. We're particularly fond of the invitations and announcements, which tend to be handmade, contain the aforementioned seeds, and will spread your joy far and wide along with a clear message that the earth matters.

STATIONERY & GIFTS	WEDDINGS	

GreenFloors.com 703-352-8300

Oftentimes, the only thing getting between you and a clean Earth is the carpet or floor on which you stand. Not so when you shop from this Virginia carpet and flooring source. The site may not look like much, but within you will find an unparalleled variety of tiles, woods, carpet squares and rolls, as well as padding and adhesives. All the products are either made from recycled materials, sustainably harvested, produced using low-impact methods, free of volatile organic compounds or all of the above, and many are LEED certified, making this one an invaluable stop on the road to a green home.

BUILDING SUPPLY		

GreenGlass.com
715-355-1897

We're betting you've recycled a lot of glass bottles in your life, only to see them made into more glass bottles, recycled again, and so on. If you'd like to give some glass a slightly longer incarnation, check out this North American representative of an interesting South African company whose sole purpose seems to be turning recycled glass into attractive service ware. Colorful, stylish and made to last, the glassware here will occupy a special place in your kitchen cabinets for some time to come... or at least until you recycle it again.

SERVICE

GreenHome.com
877-282-6400

As "your source for environmentally superior goods, services, and information," this excellent, multifaceted lifestyle shop shows us just how easy it can be to go green. It of course covers organic clothing, long-lasting lightbulbs, all-natural bath products, nontoxic cleaners and renewable energy sources, but as you browse you soon realize that technology has brought the concept of sustainable living to a wider range of products than previously imaginable. We'd recommend this as your go-to home store, because chances are you'll find just about any functional product you need here, and it will be green.

ACCESSORIES BUILDING SUPPLY | **APPAREL FAMILY** | **APPLIANCES FURNISHINGS**

GreenHomeOutfitters.com
830-833-5948

Because few things are as exciting as environmentally sound home improvement, we direct you to this "source for nontoxic green products." Actually, when you get past the low-VOC paints, stains and sealers, finish browsing the many cleaning supplies and marvel at the solar attic fan, there are some pretty cool things to be seen here. In a word: flooring. Although there are several carpeting options, the real gems will be found in the selections of kirei, cork, marmoleum, bamboo and certified reclaimed hard woods. Allowing you to eat your cake and have hardwood floors too, it seems there is some fun to be had being green.

BUILDING SUPPLY | **HOUSEHOLD** |

GreenKarat.com   800-330-4605

When we think of recycled metals, we usually envision aluminum or steel. However, gold, platinum and other precious metals are also obvious candidates for recycling, and this site will show you how doing so can lend an extra special beauty to engagement rings, wedding bands and a smattering of other fine jewelry. Procuring your baubles from this altruistic shop won't necessarily put an end to intrusive mining practices around the world, but it might help get the ball rolling.

ACCESSORIES WOMEN	MEN	WEDDINGS

GreenLightConcepts.com   415-702-5655

Aptly named, this green lighting shop is mostly about the concept. Apparently, US cities across the map are upgrading their traffic lights to embrace more efficient technology (which is good). However, "giant truckloads of red, yellow, and green lenses are tossed into land-fills" as a result. That's where these guys come in. They take these pieces of glass and fashion them into striking modern lamps and lighting fixtures. The results are a bit limited, but good-looking and undeniably clever.

FURNISHINGS		

GreenLinePaper.com   800-641-1117

Though this shop's main thrust is eco-friendly office supplies, there are a few interesting items to be found other than recycled paper, correction fluids and file folders. Specifically, there's a great assortment of biodegradable disposable dinnerware. As conservationists we wouldn't typically want to embrace disposable anything, but we also know that with large group gatherings such as barbecues or beach parties, lugging and washing utensils, plates and cups isn't generally a viable alternative. These PLA wares may not be ideal, but neither will they still be around in a landfill somewhere when it's our children's turn to throw a party.

OFFICE	SERVICE	

888-473-6466 **GreenNest.com**

"Creating healthy homes," this site's mission is to help you eradicate toxicity where you live. This begins with clearing your indoor atmosphere of volatile organic compounds, which means air filters, water filters, HEPA vacuums and VOC-free paints. The shop further offers organic bedding, mattresses, baby stuff and pet food (so your dog or cat may be protected as well). Finally, you'll find general household cleaning products, because once your homes surfaces are free of chemicals you'll want to keep them that way. The results will be improved health for you, and a reduced harmful impact on the world outside your door.

APPLIANCES FURNISHINGS	BABIES HOUSEHOLD	BUILDING SUPPLY PETS

520-394-2571 **GreenPlanetPaints.com**

There was a time when paints were typically divided between oil and synthetic bases, but that time has past, and now it's possible to paint your home in a variety of rich colors that won't contribute to global carbon output or pollute the air you breathe every day. The certified zero-VOC paints of this small Arizona company are made using clays, minerals and other mostly natural ingredients "that have been carefully selected to minimize environmental impact." Need we say more?

BUILDING SUPPLY		

44-1364-644036 **GreenShoes.co.uk**

Click on this site's "ecotan range" link to discover why some of the leather shoes, boots and sandals featured by this UK footwear specialist live up to green standards. Basically, any shoe you see that is tagged by the shop's "E" icon is made of leather tanned "using pure plant agents and oils," available in "gently dyed and toxin free colours, or natural tones." With a variety of models on hand for men, women and children, the only recently available ecotan offers a new means of leather production that may be friendlier to the earth than it is to cows, but signifies a good first step in protecting the environment with your feet.

ACCESSORIES		

GreenSpeed.us   949-715-2345

Here's a unique source of travel alternatives that might seem peculiar. Basically, this Southern California bike shop offers bicycles, scooters and skateboards that run on electricity, as well as conversion kits to help you make the switch. Now, as to why you would forsake pedal power, the greenest of all mechanized travel, we should note that the object of these vehicles isn't to replace the bicycle—you always have the option of pedaling instead of running the electric motor. Rather, these are meant to be alternatives to cars, enabling you to get up hills and quickly travel long distances that might be a strain on conventional biking.

APPLIANCES	TRANSPORTATION	

GreenStreetGreetings.com   646-290-5331

Next time 'tis the season to send out holiday cards, and you're once again reminded that the traditional gesture is probably pretty devastating to a few forests, remember this site. Its specialty happens to be bulk orders of holiday greeting cards that employ 100% postconsumer recycled paper, chlorine-free processing and vegetable-based inks. The carbon neutral company even powers its web server with wind energy, which you'll be prone to forget as you browse the quirky collection of vintage and seasonally-themed photographs. Better yet, if you can't find one you're thrilled with, you can actually upload one of your own.

STATIONERY & GIFTS		

GreenWithGlamour.com   888-831-3176

A full service home and fashion boutique based in Chicago, this small retailer gives you plenty of great products to look at without having to throw a massive selection at you. High style is the objective, but every item seen here in some way takes the environment into consideration, whether it's a dress shirt made from organic cotton, a hip top assembled from recycled silk, dinnerware finished with earth-friendly glazes or sunglasses with wooden frames. You'll also find a sweet and sustainable assortment of baby gifts that prove the environment never stands in the way of a beautiful gesture.

ACCESSORIES MEN	APPAREL SERVICE	BABIES WOMEN	

GroundsForChange.com

800-796-6820

Serving coffee that is triple certified (fair trade, shade grown and organic), this family-owned, carbon neutral Washington state coffee roaster proves itself highly committed to a long list of environmental protocols. But how's the coffee? In a word: fresh. The coffee beans aren't roasted until your order has been placed, meaning your beans or grinds will be as few as two days old, depending on the shipping options you select. These guys put in more effort than is typically expected from American businesses, and yet still manage to offer great prices. Those are ethics that're easy to get behind.

EPICUREAN		

Handmade-Paper.us

800-727-3740

The .us extension of this site may mislead, as what you'll actually find is a variety of handmade papers from all over the globe. It's quite the stunning array, and though not all the selections are strictly eco-friendly, paper categories including Lokta, Mulberry, Silk, Recycled Organic and Tree Free make the sustainable stuff easy to find. The latter includes Cotton and the not-as-disturbing-as-it-sounds Elephant Dung Paper, which would take the cake if it weren't for the ancient cultural resonance of Papyrus. It's also a great source of invitations and note cards, and boasts some of the most beautiful green journals you'll ever see.

STATIONERY & GIFTS	WEDDINGS	

HannaAndersson.com

800-222-0544

If for some reason the apparel on this site looks familiar, that's because these soft fabrics and colorful designs draw inspiration from the clothes worn by Swedish schoolchildren. It's not surprising, then, that this clothing line excels in winter clothes, stuff like longjohns, sweaters, mittens and especially a wild selection of knit caps. What might surprise you is that for several years now the company has been making the move to organic cotton, and currently boasts more than half of its products are made certified free of harmful toxins, right down to the buttons. Come to think of it, you might want to check out the Women's section.

ACCESSORIES CHILDREN	APPAREL WOMEN	BABIES

HannasDream.com — 208-683-2051

It turns out, Hanna's dream is "to see organic, sustainable clothing become common place in America." The small family-owned shop out of Idaho may one day succeed in this, offering a wonderfully rich selection of primarily colorgrown cotton attire for babies and children. These earth-savvy, organic garments represent a handpicked assortment, combining popular American eco-brands with harder-to-find domestic and European clothing labels. Even those who aren't looking for organic fabrics will find everything they need, as ultimately, the only thing that's hard to come by with this web shop is disappointment.

APPAREL	BABIES	CHILDREN

HazelnutKids.com — 888-869-1901

This Michigan toy shop offers any number of reasons to avoid plastics in favor of nontoxic, natural toys made from wood, bamboo and organic fibers, but you can ignore those pages of this web site and just focus on the toys. The great dolls, ride-ons, games, puzzles, art supplies, trucks and more make a better argument to stick to natural toys than any amount of science could, as these quality speak a language even younger kids will understand: fun.

CHILDREN	STATIONERY & GIFTS	

HealthGoods.com — 888-878-2497

This better home environment shop offers a wealth of information on such topics as why organic beauty products are healthier, or why you're better off with nontoxic household cleaners. The interesting articles may cause you to forget there are also products here to browse. Although the site's aim is to protect sensitive souls from common indoor pollutants, its selection goes to show that the green lifestyle is a healthy one, with plenty of natural alternatives to hazardous items, with water and energy conservation products such as rechargeable batteries to flow control shower heads thrown in to remind you this more than just good reading.

APPLIANCES HOUSEHOLD	FURNISHINGS	HEALTH & BEAUTY

HealthyHome.com
800-583-9523

With fifteen years of experience selling green building supplies, this Florida retailer has plenty to offer your ecological home, including water filters, air filters and low VOC paints. But the most exciting selections here will be found behind the Flooring link, where you'll find sustainable hardwoods like palm, cork and bamboo, as well as natural linoleum, recycled ceramic tiles and several natural, nontoxic carpets. It's a great place to start when you're ready to build your earth-friendly house from the ground up.

BUILDING SUPPLY

HealthyPetNet.com
877-387-4564

The quest to feed our pets with all-natural and on occasion organic ingredients leads us to this small online pet shop devoted to giving animals the best possible diet for their health. Some of these foods are actually designed to emulate what the dog, cat or horse might actually eat in the wild (at least nutrient-wise—it's tough to imagine a wild cat fishing shrimp out of the ocean). Ultimately, these endeavors result in real food, untainted by artificial colors, flavors or preservatives, and with a few nontoxic/biodegradable grooming products as well.

PETS

HeathCeramics.com
425-332-3732

Delighting in "simple and authentic" beauty, this tableware specialist offers a very small but breathtaking assortment of classic yet contemporary ceramic place settings, the likes of which you won't find anywhere else. Most pottery pieces consume vast quantities of water and energy in production, and often pollutant glazes, but this Northern California manufacturer takes care to use low-impact materials and production processes. If you take care of these plates and bowls, years of gorgeous service should balance things out nicely.

SERVICE

HempBasics.com   888-831-3747

More evidence of the growing popularity of hemp in this country, this site offers a few garments and accessories that are more likely to blend in with the rest than turn your head. However, this shop does offer probably the best variety of hemp fabrics for your own apparel and household good projects. Sourcing fairly traded, sustainably grown hemp from Romania and China (since the US still frowns on hemp agriculture domestically), the assortment of yarns and weaves available include silk and cotton blends, and taking the New Jersey shop's offer to order a swatch to test the softness might be a good idea.

CRAFTS & HOBBIES		

Hempest.com   617-421-9944

True to its name, this site really is the hempest; or at least it may be the most complete of all the online hemp stores. The selection of well-made casual and subtly stylish clothes for men and women is so thorough that it exceeds the bounds of mere hemp, incorporating bamboo, soy, silk and organic blends to create weaves that are durable, soft and as friendly to the planet as they are complementary to your wardrobe.

ACCESSORIES WOMEN	APPAREL	MEN

Hemp-Sisters.com   866-465-4489

This hemp specialist lends a little substance to your style, mostly in the form of casual accessories for men and women. While we would like to see many, many more products populate these pages, the Binghamton, New York, retailer's devotion to sustainable fabrics, use of recycled materials and fair trade makes it an extremely attractive destination for the eco-aware shopper. That, and it's also got a terrific assortment of hats.

ACCESSORIES MEN	APPAREL WOMEN	EPICUREAN

619-445-4888

Hempys.com

Although branded with the sort of nickname only a cowboy politician could truly appreciate, this "eco-technology clothing brand" actually uses organic cotton and recycled materials in addition to hemp. The accessories manufacturer particularly excels at beanies and wallets, although you'll also see other hats, some bags, belts and backpacks. The company's designs stay true to its San Diego roots, providing stylish basics that invoke laid back lifestyle and a potential new moniker for fans of a certain fabric.

ACCESSORIES	MEN	WOMEN

888-631-5055

Her-Design.com

Finding a good handbag has never been difficult—at least, not since the advent of internet shopping. But finding one that's kind to animals and the environment may sometimes be a tall order. This designer handbag label makes every effort to correct that, "opting for eco-sensitive inks, glues, and solvents when possible," and although some of the purses here are made from synthetic fabrics, you will usually find comparable designs in hemp, linen and organic cotton. Best of all, the bags look good enough to suit nearly every wardrobe, so whichever material you choose, you won't have a hard time finding a terrific accessory.

ACCESSORIES	WOMEN	

800-687-6707

HighFallsMercantile.com

With an eclectic wealth of vintage products like teapots and table linens, this small shop set in the New York countryside makes use of some quaint and quirky old products. Shop carefully, as there are a few new products and antique reproductions that don't necessarily live up to green standards, but a great deal of these rustic furnishings and service wares are more than capable of overcoming their slightly-worn status to provide many more years of functional and beautiful use.

FURNISHINGS	SERVICE	STATIONERY & GIFTS

HighVibe.com 212-777-6645

We know processed foods, heavy oils, fructose, pesticides and preservatives wreak havoc on our bodies, but can we really flush them out of our system and start from scratch with a new, completely healthy approach? Maybe not, but with the help of this site you can come pretty damn close. The raw-foods, organic and natural-products specialist covers a wide range of health and dietary concerns, with a breadth of products ranging from produce to skin care items, self-help books and exercise guides. Rare is the web site that can make you feel so good after visiting.

EPICUREAN	HEALTH & BEAUTY	

HipAndZen.com 888-447-6936

As fashionable as environmental-awareness may be, finding accessories and attire that prove stylish as well as eco-conscious has long proven a difficult task—which is exactly why this site belongs on your radar. A small but supremely tasteful selection of chic women's apparel promises to live up to both sets of high standards, and a system of icons let you know specifically which items are natural, organic, fair trade and/or made from recycled materials.

ACCESSORIES STATIONERY & GIFTS	APPAREL WOMEN	BABIES

HistoricTrees.org 800-320-8733

It's hard to gauge whether you'll learn more about trees or American History on this site. By associating different species of trees with historical figures, places and events, this conservation organization hopes to provoke the imagination. As it turns out, the group offers you a chance to propagate the offspring of trees that, while they themselves may not necessarily be famous, might once have been owned or seen by someone who was. No, the cherry tree George Washington chopped down isn't here (we checked), but when it comes down to it, it's the beauty of a new tree you've planted that you'll ultimately remember.

GARDENING		

877-232-5359   HolisticBeauty.net

"Offering Natural Beauty Solutions and health products that meet the demands of eco-wise people," the founder of this Ohio shop has a surefire way of determining whether a beauty product has unnatural ingredients: she has a strong physical reaction. She also has a background in skin care and cosmetics. What this all means for you is that while you shop this vast selection of makeup, skin care treatments, bath products, toiletries, massage oils and hair care products, you can be sure it's all natural and occasionally organic, meaning healthy for you as well as the earth.

HEALTH & BEAUTY	MEN	WOMEN

610-866-7370   HomeAndPlanet.com

The "largest retail store in the nation dedicated to high style, earth friendly home furnishings and gifts," this Pennsylvania brick-and-mortar shop offers no real product focus, but does feature a smattering of unique household items derived from recycled materials, organic fibers and sustainably harvested wood, whether it's a bamboo stool or glass tableware. We might take exception to the claim this fairly small site is the "largest" such retailer out there, but it's certainly one of the more interesting ones.

FURNISHINGS	SERVICE	STATIONERY & GIFTS

866-436-7869   HTNaturals.com

At first glance just a limited line of wardrobe basics like t-shirts and hoodies, one might easily look past this site without realizing how diverse it really is. Part of it has to do with the color variety, but primarily it's the savvy use of sustainable fabrics we like. Along with mainstays like hemp and organic cotton, here you will find soy, bamboo and recycled polyester. It's not incredibly stylish stuff, but so far as staples go, these stand up well to a second look.

APPAREL	MEN	WOMEN

Importica.com   541-420-6871

It's rare enough that wrapping paper is eco-friendly; when it's also vibrant and beautiful, it's almost an occasion worth celebrating in-and-of itself. The wrapping paper offered by this family-owned Oregon business is sustainably sourced, created without harmful chemicals and, above all, gorgeous. Handmade in Thailand from the shed bark of mulberry trees, this variety of papers includes patterns derived from Hindu, Buddhist and Native American traditions, all of them brightly colored with nontoxic dyes. The selection may be limited, but it is definitely special.

STATIONERY & GIFTS		

IndikaOrganics.com   800-458-3106

"Made of the finest Peruvian organic cotton, plant and vegetable dyed, with prints inspired by ancient wooden block patterns," the high-quality linens made by this small company out of Montana are fine enough to compete with any other sustainable bedding line, but more interesting to look at than most others you'll see. You'll also find hemp/silk blends, so you might like to request a sample to see how it feels before settling on one design or another. Actually, you may want to request a few samples as all their fabrics are also available by the yard.

CRAFTS & HOBBIES	FURNISHINGS	

InfiniteHealthResources.com   888-667-0563

Follow the Green Store link of this massive and informational site to find a wide-ranging assortment of earth-friendly products, many of which you might have seen on the *Real Savvy Moms* TV program. It seems obvious to say there are a lot of healthy products here, but aside from health foods, beauty products, essential oils, natural hair colors, organic cosmetics and maternity skin care treatments, you'll find great assortments of organic teas, pet supplies and nifty gizmos like a solar oven. Browsing can seem infinite, as some categories are just too deep to explore in a single sitting, but if you have the time, this is a good place for it.

EPICUREAN	FAMILY	HEALTH & BEAUTY
MATERNITY	PETS	

877-224-6663

InMod.com

Modern makes for a better planet when you check out the Eco-Friendly Furniture section of this designer home store. Would that the entire fanciful site were green, so we could enjoy the likes of bubble chairs and marshmallow sofas with a clear conscience. However, as it is, the green furniture selections are about as whimsical as it gets, so avoid the temptation of a humongous selection of modern furniture and accents, head straight to the Eco-Friendly Furniture link on the home page, and revel in what bamboo can do for you.

FURNISHINGS

800-643-4221

InterNatural.com

This alternative health superstore has been in business for more than two decades, and thus is "NOT new to the industry trying to make some fast bucks as part of the Internet boom,'" and it shows. Rather, these guys are quite serious about the aromatherapy, biomagnetics, massage therapy, herbal supplements and other natural healing products they carry, to the point that the massive selection is underscored by a wealth of information. Unfortunately, there's neither a pill you can take nor an incense to burn that will make browsing easy, so you may want to meditate on the virtue of patience before you log on.

HEALTH & BEAUTY | **SPORTING GOODS**

314-781-0743

IrieStar.com

There are a number of reasons hemp isn't a more popular fabric in the United States, chief among them being a ban on its domestic cultivation. But another tends to be the feeling that hemp manufacturers fail to put a lot of imagination into their clothes, resulting in well-made, sturdy basics, but not necessarily fashion. This fascinating family-business out of St. Louis completely repudiates this notion by offering hip, funky attire for women. The sustainably produced clothing covers new and perpetual trends exceedingly well despite an all-too-small selection. It will forever change the way you think about hemp.

APPAREL | **WOMEN**

IslandHemp.com

808-337-1487

The spirit of aloha is alive and well in hemp, as evidenced by this Hawaiian island wear dealer. Board shorts, plumeria dresses, smoking pants and boxer shorts feature classic leafy patterns while blending hemp and organic cotton. Of course, chief among products here are the aloha shirts. Available in a variety of sizes and colors (although popular sizes do tend to sell out from time to time), these might just offer your best bet at living a green island lifestyle. Obviously, we'd recommend going to Hawaii to pick up your order in person.

APPAREL	MEN	WOMEN

iXiBike.com

800-474-6615

Just when you thought bicycle technology had plateaued, along comes this innovative, quickly dismantled bike that uses a rubber belt instead of a chain. The unique frame is also designed to stow emergency materials, and a series of add-on accessories allows you to build a bike suited to your daily needs. You can tell with a single glance that this is not your typical ride, and though the site repeatedly asserts high levels of comfort and ease, it will really take a test drive to know for sure if this kinky take on a classic works for you. To that end, take a look at the money-back guarantee—they're clearly confident you will like it.

TRANSPORTATION		

JohnnySeeds.com

800-879-2258

When you're ready to scour long lists of flowers and vegetables, go to this site, which offers just about all the seeds you could want to add beauty and/or nourishment to your garden. Along with plenty of heirloom seeds and a full section of organically produced choices, the site also offers a comprehensive assortment of tools and supplies; everything you'll need to keep your thumb as green as can be.

GARDENING		

JoliBebeBoutique.com
480-988-5622

While the market for sustainable baby clothing is booming, for some reason finding eco-friendly garments for the young mother has fallen behind. This small line of organic cotton and soy fabric attire covers both, and though there are adorable layette options here, clearly more remarkable is the limited but great-looking Nursing Line. With luck the incredibly tiny smattering of designs and colors will increase over time, but due to how lovely these tops are, and given what's out there, we're guessing you'll find this selection more than satisfying.

APPAREL	BABIES	MATERNITY

JoMamaCo.com
866-663-5334

If there's one thing we can say for sure about green shopping online it's this: there are a lot of eco-friendly baby shops out there. But there are none like this one. The small Venice Beach, California retailer carries unique and delightfully funky toddler t-shirts and vintage outfits, using organic cotton and recycled fabrics. Limited editions mean three things: 1) No two items are exactly alike, 2) You won't want to sit around mulling over your order for a week or the precious baby item could be gone and 3) You'll want to come back and check out the next new selections available from this terrific site!

ACCESSORIES	APPAREL	BABIES

Jonano.com
877-327-9753

Amid this fair trade, luxurious eco-fabrics brands casual and flirty fashions you will find a unique assortment of Eco-Scrubs, which one would assume could only be worn by the hippest, most stylish earth-friendly doctors and nurses. In actuality, these designs would make terrific loungewear even for nonmedical professionals, and make a delightful supplement to the yoga wear, t-shirts and dresses found elsewhere on the site. Don't let the "designer organic clothing" tag line fool you—these clothes are as affordable as they are lovely.

APPAREL	MEN	WOMEN

Jurlique.com

800-845-1110

"No chemicals and no compromise" is the motivating motto behind this company's holistic approach to skin care. All-natural products are infused with minerals, herbs and any such manner of ingredient that promotes a healthy skin and body; everything from cleansers, moisturizers, cosmetics and aromatherapy oils. Yes, beauty has come a long way on this somewhat difficult but functional site that boasts "the purest skin care on earth." If you're looking to boost your body's natural aversion to aging, Jurlique might be a winner.

| FAMILY | HEALTH & BEAUTY | |

KaeliBodyCare.com

888-329-9993

Bringing aromatherapy down to earth, this homegrown company incorporates essential oils into a small line of all-natural bath and body products. In addition to bath salts and soaps, you'll find safe facial cleansers, masks, moisturizers, massage oils and even the occasional aftershave balm. In one corner of the site you'll even find a section devoted to baby-friendly formulas. This smart application of aromatherapeutic principles makes it much easier for those of us who barely understand the practice to enjoy its fragrant benefits—or, to just find beauty products that smell good.

| BABIES | FAMILY | HEALTH & BEAUTY |

KaightNYC.com

212-680-5630

Of the sort of fashionable boutique women travel to New York to visit, this one offers an important distinction: a preference for environmentally conscious designers. Hopefully, one day, they'll all be this way. For now, the bulk of this merchandise is comprised of organic cotton, bamboo, repurposed cashemere and silk. If you were actually in the Manhattan shop you might feel pressured to buy it before someone else snatched it up. Online, you may just casually move on. After all, even if everything here isn't green, it is all pretty hot.

| ACCESSORIES | APPAREL | WOMEN |

KasperOrganics.net
818-988-3924

A chance to stock up on the basics is what this "affordable and socially responsible" organic cotton and hemp specialist offers. The San Fernando Valley retailer features staple items like socks, underwear and t-shirts, meaning any man, woman or child can build a wardrobe that is sustainable to the core. You'll also find assorted towels, bed linens and napkins, and, if you're lucky, a smattering of decent casual clothes to get started on the rest of your eco-friendly wardrobe.

| APPAREL | FAMILY | |

KateQuinnOrganics.com
877-760-2997

As one of the top names in sustainable baby clothing, you don't need to look far across the internet landscape to find Kate Quinn's extremely popular kimono-style onesie. However, there is a lot more to found in the growing organic cotton line, and here you'll find the full selection, ranging from stylishly simple shirts to breathtakingly cute dresses. If you can't find it elsewhere, you'll find it here, and given how widely dispersed some of these products are we fully expect to see a lot more variety pop up here in the years to come.

| APPAREL | BABIES | |

KenanaUSA.com
800-708-8583

Stuffed animals aren't hard to come by—if you have any skills with a joystick you can pluck one right out of an arcade game. But to find one that's not stuffed with dubious materials, made with synthetic fabrics or colored with toxic dyes you might have to look as far as Kenya. The beauty of this site is that it offers a wide variety of adorable plush dolls, all constructed of wool, each handmade by rural Kenyan women and made using vegetable dyes. You'll feel good knowing these fair trade crafts support families in agricultural areas, but your children will simply be delighted by how cute they are.

| CHILDREN | | |

KidBean.com   828-299-3608

This altruistic homegrown baby business might be the most ardently eco-friendly shop of its kind—so stringent are its founder's standards that it's a wonder she found anything to sell at all. However, dedication and hard work have paid off, and the result is a terrific selection of baby necessities, maternity products, household cleaners, recycled paper goods and more. It would take hours, if not days for you to find all these terrific items in other shops, but here you may simply add it all to a single shopping basket and be assured that even the packaging will be as,sustainable, labor-friendly and cruelty-free as everything you've purchased.

ACCESSORIES CHILDREN	APPAREL FURNISHINGS	BABIES HEALTH & BEAUTY

KimberlySayer.com   212-414-7701

As the daughter of organic farmers, Kimberly Sayer grew up using natural ingredients of skin and body care, then bolstered that experience by earning something called a Beauty Therapy degree. The result is this globally renowned, high end line of spa, skin and anti-aging products that will be "absorbed by the skin, identified as food, therefore achieving maximum results." Natural as can be, and known to be effective, once your skin has felt these cleansers, masks and lotions, it will undoubtedly be hungry for more.

HEALTH & BEAUTY		

KokoGM.com   800-210-0202

These guys offer environment-friendly products to "detoxify your body" and "detoxify your world." Both seem to be good ideas, and what with the all-natural soaps, household cleaners, water filters and baby-care products, they seem to be fairly well executed. Further exploration uncovers other fantastic items such as biodegradable trash bags, sun-simulating Chromalux light bulbs and powerful air filters that will still keep your home's atmosphere chemical free if you happen to use a product you didn't buy here.

EPICUREAN	HEALTH & BEAUTY	HOUSEHOLD

KushTush.com

888-336-3017

Reminding us that organic bedding was "once called just blankets," this family-owned retailer from Illinois is devoted to making such earth and health-friendly options easily available again. Luxury bedding, crib bedding, towels, robes and bathroom accents are available in certified-organic cotton as well as silk, either domestically produced or imported adhering to fair trade practices. Shopping may get frustrating, as specific items seem to go in and out of stock unexpectedly, but the passion of the proprietors is evidence in the wealth of information available, while the quality products speak for themselves.

BABIES	FAMILY	FURNISHINGS

KusiKuy.com

866-587-4589

Specializing in Bolivian and Peruvian knits, this Vermont-based company touts the organic and fair trade practices used to create its line of accessories and outerwear, which is great. But better still are the products themselves. Featuring warms scarves, wraps, beanies, sweaters and jackets, the small company sources herds of naturally-raised Andean llamas and alpaca, the latter producing yarns that are "stronger than mohair, finer than cashmere, smoother than silk, warmer than goose down," and yet somehow breathe well. Beautiful, cozy and surprisingly affordable, this one's just about perfect for everyone.

ACCESSORIES FAMILY	APPAREL	CRAFTS & HOBBIES

LagniappeGiftWrap.com

617-281-8236

Any kid will tell you that a well-wrapped gift makes you even more curious to own whatever's inside. However, if you've ever seen a post-birthday-party stack of colored paper and ribbons, you know, deep down, that forests wind up paying the price for this artful suspense. Not so when you shop from this site, which specializes in an earth-friendly alternative: reusable gift bags. The natural fabric bags add every bit of teasing mystery, but when the party's over they're still around to wrap again. For added satisfaction, you might stick to the Organic Collection, which is limited, but an even greater gift to the earth.

STATIONERY & GIFTS		

LaptopLunches.com   831-457-0301

Spawned by the simple idea to send kids to school with nondisposable lunch containers, this small business partnership takes the classic Japanese Bento box and turns it into an everyday conservational effort. A variety of bento options lets you pack something nutritious at home without resorting to plastic or paper bags or throw away drink containers. You'll even find nontoxic, biodegradable, resuable ice packs to keep things cool. Not that these lunchboxes aren't cool already.

ACCESSORIES	CHILDREN	

LarrysBeans.com   919-828-1234

With the express purpose "to sell awesome-tasting coffee in ways to make the world better," this small North Carolina specialist aims high and hits the mark. The founder (Larry, of course), considers himself a "hipster coffee zealot," his team spreading the message of fair trade and sustainability far and wide with humor, sincerity and great tasting coffee. You'll find a fresh, global selection that invigorates the planet as well as your taste buds.

EPICUREAN		

LaurenCeleste.com   800-890-7857

Here's another line of baby clothes that's exquisitely small, so tiny in fact that the merchandise would really have to be something special to warrant a visit to the site. Clearly, we think its a worthwhile stop, as the adorable designs just happen to be hand-knit with soft organic fabrics. The handful of infant outfits are reason enough to shop here, but if you're looking for more, maybe the idea of a personalized recycled fleece blanket will win you over.

ACCESSORIES	APPAREL	BABIES

877-528-3727   **Lavera-USA.com**

The idea of 100% natural beauty products always sounds... well, beautiful. This cosmetics, skin and hair care line originating out of Germany takes this concept to new levels by offering a wealth of certified organic and vegan ingredients along the way. From anti-aging treatments to men's shaving products and covering a lot of ground in between, the always growing brand promises protection from toxics as well as excessive sun, attempting to enhance and protect beauty rather than manufacture it, which isn't just earth-friendly but people-friendly too.

HEALTH & BEAUTY	MEN	WOMEN

877-253-4273   **LegareFurniture.com**

The concept of modular, assemble-it-yourself furniture is not new; it's become one of the biggest industries in the world. However, in most cases it's made of laminated particle board, typically involving toxic adhesives and environmentally reckless manufacturing processes. This modular furniture company, on the other hand, sources FSC-certified lumber to create plywood furnishings "with very minimal formaldehyde content resin adhesives," usually with nontoxic paints and finishes. The result is durable, affordable furniture that uses less wood than solid pieces and demonstrates a more responsible approach to a big business.

FURNISHINGS		

888-438-5346   **Lehmans.com**

We love finding a store with character, and this Ohio general store (est. 1955) definitely has it. It also has a charming Eco Friendly Goods section. Founded to help the local Amish community retain their values and self-sufficiency, most of these products adhere to their standards, and quite a few also manage to fit the green lifestyle as well. Particularly intriguing are the Hand-Cranked items and Appliances and Energy Savers sections, which include some rare finds sure to infuse some extra personality into your green home.

APPLIANCES	GARDENING	HOUSEHOLD

LilGreenHouse.com

866-473-3607

However big or small your home is, this online retailer encourages incremental changes that will, over time, not only make it healthier and more efficient, but also friendlier to the world outside its walls. A hefty assortment of water conservation options will get you started, as will some biodegradable garbage bags and other household supplies. When you're ready to make some bigger changes, check out the excellent selection of sustainable flooring and low-VOC paints, whatever color you want your green home to be.

BUILDING SUPPLY	FURNISHINGS	HOUSEHOLD

LittleTwig.com

866-545-8944

When it comes to bath time, getting squeaky clean is always the objective, but it's just not that much fun if harmful products irritate your child's delicate skin. This line of soaps, shampoos and bubble baths should prevent that from happening, using all natural ingredients to create "extremely gentle, non-irritating and hypo-allergenic" formulas. It's a simple idea, carried out in simple fashion, but proves incredibly effective when it comes to peace of mind.

BABIES	CHILDREN	HEALTH & BEAUTY

LivingNature.com

415-373-6011

New Zealanders are well-aware just how blessed they are to have such beautiful, raw expanses of uncorrupted nature, and you get the feeling that environmentalism on their side of the planet is viewed more as a privilege than as a struggle. This small line of beauty products from down under adds an element of good health to its earth-friendly mission, refusing to incorporate any toxic or even questionable ingredients to its all-natural skin care, bath and cosmetics offerings. Although you won't find a huge selection, odds are good you'll come away with a big order to justify the trans-pacific shipping (which will also make it free).

HEALTH & BEAUTY		

800-260-5534   LivingTreeCommunity.com

Begging the question, "Just how alive are your nuts?" this Berkeley raw, organic foods specialist delivers a small but naturally nutritious range of products. With close ties to California farmers, the small shop features fresh, raw nuts, including almonds, cashews, pistachios, macadamia, walnuts and pecans, as well as associated nut butters. You'll also find some "living oils," edible seeds, agave nectar and organic honey. The site might be of particular interest to vegans and vegetarians, but really people of all diets may benefit from this wholly nutritious, earth-friendly distributor.

EPICUREAN		

831-475-8150   LocalHarvest.org

If you don't know where to find your local farmer's market, this site will tell you. If your local market isn't so local, or you have to miss it one week, the site also offers all you've come to expect from it, and probably a bit more. It begins, of course, with fresh produce, and if you shop wisely you'll be able to pick out heirloom and organic selections. You'll also find grass-fed beef, nuts, seeds, herbs, cheese, syrup and baked goods. There are even free range goose and duck eggs, which they will actually send to you through the mail, if you're brave enough to order them, and plenty of wools, which should easily survive the trip.

CRAFTS & HOBBIES	EPICUREAN	GARDENING

423-837-7181   LodgeMfg.com

Once you're eating sustainably, you may start to consider the tools you're cooking with. Making cookware out of hemp and bamboo clearly don't offer a practical solution, but this company makes pots and pans that are. The cast iron skillets, cookers and bakeware you'll find here present a good alternative to the popular but chemically treated "nonstick" varieties. Naturally seasoned to create a "nonstick, rustproof finish," these pans promise durability and heat retention to help you conserve energy while cooking, without the potential for toxins to be released into your food during preparation. Unless, of course, you're cooking with toxins.

SERVICE		

LollDesigns.com 877-740-3387

You don't typically think of plastic outdoor furniture as being eco-friendly, but the way this company does it, you might want to reconsider ever buying wood tables and chairs for your patio or deck. Made from recycled plastics, the Adirondack and contemporary style pieces promise to be durable and weatherproof, living up to the brand's ethos that "using green products should not entail that you have to sacrifice anything; it should be better in every way than its uneco-friendly counterpart."

FURNISHINGS

LuckyCrow.com 206-910-3997

Nondisposable gift wrapping options may someday be the norm, and one way to get this trend up and running is to start the circle of reusable gift bags now. This is one of several sites that offer unique, regiftable bags—all you need to do is drop in your gift, pull the ribbon to close it up, and encourage the recipient to pass it on. We'd like to see the bags made from organic materials and low impact dyes, but for now we have to settle for the idea that every step is progress, and these hip bags might just keep some landfills wrapping paper free for a cleaner future.

STATIONERY & GIFTS

LumberLiquidators.com 800-366-4204

Sourcing green building materials is an ongoing issue across the country, and though cross-country delivery of lumber for your hardwood floors can be incredibly expensive, if you simply cannot find wood culled from managed forests locally, this site provides a viable option. Shipping aside, the prices here are very competitive, and the selection is top-notch, covering maple, mahogany, walnut, hickory, teak, oak, bamboo and cork, as well as a couple dozen or so other varieties. Keep an eye out for the Antique/Reclaimed section for some particular deals that will ensure no new trees have been cut on your behalf.

BUILDING SUPPLY

866-440-1290   LumiaOrganic.com

An open flame is not the only potential for danger found in a common candle; most are made using petroleum-based paraffin and prone to give off toxins while burning. This candle specialist avoids this problem by creating wax from soy oils and infusing it with essential oils to make safer, healthier scented varieties. They even do us one better by only using certified organic soy, and by casing some of the candles in recycled glass. This wax even cleans up easier than the conventional variety, begging the question: why have candles ever been made differently?

STATIONERY & GIFTS		

718-802-9757   MadImports.org

As angry as it might sound, this importer's product line prove bright and cheery. We're talking about woven handbags, constructed from the native grasses and by the native women of Madagascar and Kenya. The beautiful fair trade accessories cover a variety of patterns and styles, each one abundant with color and flair. Materials like raffia, sisal and jute lend the bags durability tempered by a daintiness that is perfect for spring and summer outings.

ACCESSORIES	STATIONERY & GIFTS	

888-750-6004   MaryJanesFarm.com

Fresh from Idaho comes this farm-loving site aimed to promote a simpler life. For our purposes, this means checking out the Food Pantry section. In addition to organic pantry items, it features some easy-to-make hot meals and snacks, from the appropriately rustic mac'n'cheese and potato soup to more exotic fare like couscous, curry and jambalaya. Proving that it doesn't need to be unhealthy to be quick and convenient, these foods will help your on-the-go green lifestyle like few others.

EPICUREAN		

MEC.ca   888-847-0770

This Canadian outdoor equipment outfitter is not, technically speaking, an eco-shop. However, it puts a lot of effort and resources into sustainable business practices, and with each year is increasingly better able to serve its customers with a green mindset. It begins with the organic cotton of its proprietary clothing, continues to making its brick-and-mortar stores environmentally sound and at the very least includes biodegradable packaging. You will still find lots of outdoor products here that don't meet ecological standards, but if you shop carefully you will manage to visit nature without feeling complicit in its degradation.

ACCESSORIES SPORTING GOODS	APPAREL	FAMILY

MessageProducts.com   800-243-2565

Printing custom checks allows you to express your identity during financial transactions; buying your checks from this specialized printer lets you endorse an environmental charity, which might just have a little more impact. Printed on recycled paper with soy-based inks, these checks promote such organizations as Greenpeace, the Sierra Club and the World Wildlife Fund. Basically, every time you send off a bill or pay for your groceries, everybody who sees that check between you and the bank is reminded about the good work being done to preserve our planet's resources.

STATIONERY & GIFTS		

MethodHome.com   866-963-8463

The fight to clean up the planet starts in your home, as this company wouloud have it. Run by "people against dirty," this nontoxic household cleaning specialist is rapidly changing the way people wash their sinks, countertops, dishes, laundry and hands. With a growing variety of products mingling natural scents with safe-for-any-surface ingredients, these guys will keep you feeling clean and fresh, and mostly just happy you gave up your old chemical cleaners for good.

HOUSEHOLD		

858-755-0055 # MissionPlayground.com

"Preserving the present" is this hip clothing manufacturer that prefers to work in organic cotton. The men's, women's and children's casual apparel includes jeans and hoodies, as well as a growing assortment of other nifty finds and a slew of graphic t-shirts, most of which advocate a natural, earth-friendly lifestyle and aim "to make environmental awareness exciting, appealing." Obviously, they do this in a youthful way, so this isn't the stern environmentalism of ardent activists; don't forget your sense of humor when shopping here.

APPAREL WOMEN	CHILDREN	MEN

206-782-5518 # MommyAndKaiNaturals.com

Do you like looking at baby pictures? If so you will delight in this homegrown shop that features babies photographed in 100% organic clothes. All the products here—accessories, diapers, clothes and bedding—are made from organic cotton or wool, all of it fair trade or domestically produced using low-impact dyes and without toxic chemicals. The results are well-dressed, adorable, healthy and happy tots. Log on and see for yourself.

ACCESSORIES FURNISHINGS	APPAREL	BABIES

503-236-7542 # MonsterVintage.com

Don't go thinking that classic tastes can't be accommodated by online shopping. If this site's any indication, you can still piece together a slick, nifty and/or keen wardrobe without leaving your home. Covering vintage styles across the board, including Motorcycle and Westernwear, we're particularly impressed with the Oregon shop's Suits, Hawaiian Shirts, Outerwear, Denim and Big & Tall sections. Browsing may take some time, but as each item is pictured with exquisite detail and described with exact measurements, we're pretty sure you'll like what you'll find.

ACCESSORIES WOMEN	APPAREL	MEN

MoonriseJewelry.com   866-338-9109

Jewelry may not be the first thing that comes to mind when you think about environmental awareness, but even the brightest baubles seem to dim when cast in the light of detrimental mining practices. Which is why the talented designers behind this site espouse an "ethical sourcing program," incorporating fair trade protocols and "natural, recycled, and renewable materials" in the development of their "Premier Eco-Jewelry Collection." Look for the link, and adorn yourself with mindful indulgence.

ACCESSORIES

MotherNature.com   800-439-5506

If you're as interested in personal health as you are the environment (and why wouldn't you be?), you might want to check out this store, which has been offering all-natural and organic supplements, food and beauty products for more than a decade. Shopping the Organic section is probably the surest way to find what you need, but as the site offers a wealth of informative articles and other resources, a bit of browsing could turn you on to plenty of the other items carried in these pages.

EPICUREAN   **HEALTH & BEAUTY**

MountainRoseHerbs.com   800-879-3337

A deep assortment of certified-organic and wild-harvested herbs, spices and essential oils may be found is this all-natural Oregon shop, anything from Acacia to Yucca. In fact, there are so many bulk products here, you probably would have had to devote your life to the study of aromatherapy to know them all. No problem. The site offers in-depth descriptions of each ingredient and its potential uses, both in contemporary culture and folklore. Available in as little as 4 oz quantities or, with discounted prices up to multiple pounds, feel free to try new herbs in small amounts, then really stock up on those you love.

EPICUREAN   **HEALTH & BEAUTY**

877-875-0689   MountainsOfTheMoon.com

To those who thought no Deadhead would never amount to much, we'd like to point you to this terrific hemp apparel specialist based in the Midwest. Once set up in the parking lots outside of Grateful Dead concerts, the founder stepped up business in the late 90s and has turned it into a fashionable source of sustainable women's clothing. Skirts, pants and dresses rule here, and a special selection of hand-crocheted goods is not to be missed. All this without having to smell any Nag Champa, unless you want to order that too.

APPAREL	WOMEN	

877-226-5073   MrSolar.com

Chances are, you don't know enough about particular photovoltaic cell brands to make a discerning choice between them. Nevertheless, when you decide to convert to solar power, this online specialist offers various models by over a dozen different manufacturers. A few helpful worksheets and other resources are designed to help you choose, but when it comes down to it, you are left with plenty to decide, between wattage, size and your home's capability. If the sheer volume of choice addles your brain, look to the wind power section; it's much smaller.

APPLIANCES		

203-321-1218   MySigg.com

Keeping hydrated doesn't have to mean you carry around a disposable plastic water bottle all the time. This company with a peculiarly narrow focus offers more than one hundred reusable water bottles. The specially designed aluminum bottles are "manufactured in an ecologically-friendly environment and are 100% recyclable after their very long lives." As durable as it gets and promising to be both nontoxic and antibacterial, the real kicker is that they won't retain the lingering flavor of the last fluids you drank, meaning you could be drinking from these bottles for twenty years without any bitter aftertaste.

ACCESSORIES		

NaturalAreaRugs.com 800-661-7847

Knowing it can be tough to pronounce some of the materials used in carpet fibers, we think you'll appreciate this natural alternative. Featuring easy-to-pronounce materials like wool, mountain grass, paper, sisal, jute and bamboo, you can be confident that these area rugs will feel as cool as they look, even if you don't exactly know what sisal and jute are. Available in many sizes, alongside a lovely assortment of shag rugs, these natural-fiber floor coverings may be some of the nicest things you ever step on.

FURNISHINGS

NaturalBuiltHome.com 612-605-7999

Greening your home requires a lot of studious planning and research, but you might catch a shortcut if you take a look at this site. A variety of water saving fixtures, floor tiles, lighting fixtures, sinks and counter tops may be easily perused, and most of them turn out to be crafted from recycled materials. You'll also find nontoxic paints, sealants, insulation and finishes. Last but certainly not least is an intriguing product called kirei board, a wood alternative constructed of compressed sorghum with a look all its own (you might have to look up what sorghum is).

BUILDING SUPPLY **FURNISHINGS**

NaturalGardening.com 707-766-9303

This "oldest certified organic nursery in the United States" belies its age by putting up a very well-designed site. One look at the pictures offered for each fruit or vegetable will have you clamoring to grow it yourself from seed or, if your impatience runs high, from a seedling that you may nourish to adulthood. Although the herbs and spices may not look as delicious, they are sure to be, and while the flowers won't inspire any pangs of hunger, you will certainly want these beautiful varieties in your bed. A case unto itself why organic gardening is the way to go, this California Bay Area nursery is not one you'll likely forget.

GARDENING

Natural-Lifestyle.com

800-752-2775

From a small city in North Carolina comes this mail order natural grocer with a quirky online presence. Making organic products a priority (when possible), the shop supplements its sustainable selection with otherwise natural and best-alternative products, such as enamel cookware and macrobiotic foods and sea vegetables. Your best bet, however, lies in the Natural Pantry category, where you'll find a host of organic staple foods like beans, noodles and grains, as well as essential baking ingredients. Get around the loosely designed site a little bit and you may find a few decent personal care items, and some cute teapots as well.

EPICUREAN	HEALTH & BEAUTY	SERVICE

NaturalPetMarket.com

800-460-1549

If you've embraced an ecologically friendly, all natural lifestyle, there's no reason you can't include the care of your dog or cat, at least while this site is operational. Offering a deep selection of food, healthy treats and a long list of natural treatments for specific animal health issues, including allergies, eye care, flea and tick control, immune support and a healthy skin and coat, the site's even equipped to serve vegetarian animals. There aren't many sites for all natural human health care that are this thoroughly stocked.

PETS		

NaturalSpaces.com

877-877-4929

The ethos of this Oregon family-owned home store is plainly stated: "If it's glass, metal or plastic, it's recycled. If it's wood, it's either reused, salvaged or certified sustainably grown. Textiles are natural or organic fiber with no chemical dyes or bleaches." The products that meet such lofty criteria are often the results of other small businesses, meaning you're not likely to find a lot of it where you live. Primarily, we're thrilled by the glass- and dinnerware selections, but you'll also see some natural table linens, organic cotton towels and door knockers made from recycled bullet casings. Talk about turning a negative positive!

FURNISHINGS	SERVICE	

NaturalZing.com   888-729-9464

Promising "only the healthiest products for you and the Earth," this healthy grocer offers a deep selection of raw, organic, vegan and otherwise nutritious foods and supplements. The fact that it's a fully committed green company makes us like it all the more. Along with such stuff as sea vegetables, flax seed cookies, nut & seed butters and organic food bars, you will find plenty of great condiments, oils, cereals and all kinds of healthy snacks. If you're waiting for us to say something negative about the Maryland shop, we won't. After all, it turned us on to the nutritional benefits of Goji berries.

| EPICUREAN | HEALTH & BEAUTY | |

NatureNeutral.com   800-656-1961

Green building supplies are hard to come by—in the real or virtual world. Which is why this user-friendly home improvement shop is worth a look despite it's one major shortfall: it doesn't offer most of its items for online sale. You can buy earth-friendly paints, stains, caulks, adhesives, carpet cleaners and other such alternatives to typically toxic products, as well as natural fiber insulation. But the terrific flooring, carpeting, plumbing and lumber options require phone orders at the time of this writing, which is still a step in the right direction.

| BUILDING SUPPLY | HOUSEHOLD | |

NaturesHardware.com   866-354-5337

When it comes to decorative hardware, it can be difficult to find green alternatives to the conventional plastic and polished metal varieties. This Oregon-based site offers quite a few options to meet your ecological standards. Incorporating "either natural, renewable or recycled material," these products vary in how sustainable they are, but with bamboo, recycled glass, bone, antler and stone mixed in to the assortment of knobs, pulls and tiles, a little bit of browsing should find you a good bet. As of this writing, the proprietors are working on a classification system to highlight green options, which will definitely open the door to easier shopping.

| BUILDING SUPPLY | | |

NaturesPet.com

201-796-0627

"Modern physics, various eastern philosophies and ecology all have shown that we live in a unified field." This says it all, does it not? At least, it explains why this retailer sells "natural and holistic products designed to enhance and extend the lives of your pets." These include some natural foods and grooming supplies, along with a few stranger things worth exploring. This one does deviate from the beaten path a bit, but you can't shake a stick at natural products and treatments for a variety of animals. Unless, of course, shaking a stick is one of the recommended treatments.

| PETS | | |

Nau.com

877-454-5628

As it's thoroughly fond of telling you, this company offers a sustainable alternative to the vast outdoors wear market, blending organic cotton and recycled synthetic fabrics to create stylish, performance-based apparel for men and women. It's not entirely for camping trips, though, as most of these clothes will slide right into your day-to-day wardrobe and make you look all the better for it. The jackets, shirts, pants, dresses and skirts are casually hip, almost to the point of dressing up, while the base layers will keep you warm when the weather turns.

| APPAREL WOMEN | MEN | SPORTING GOODS |

NearSeaNaturals.com

877-573-2913

Whether you'd like to knit or stitch your way into organic apparel, this solar-powered, family-owned business offers a lovely assortment of yarns, knits and weaves made from organic cottons, wools, hemps and blends. Any non-natural colors and patterns are either the result of colorgrown plants or low-impact dyes, and you can always find out for sure by reading the product description, while ordering a swatch first will let you know how soft or durable each fabric is. As for how the clothes will fit—that part's up to you.

| CRAFTS & HOBBIES | | |

NepalesePaper.com   707-665-9055

Now entering its second decade, this eco-conscious stationer "has been practicing Fair Trade since before it was called Fair Trade, when it was just called 'the right thing to do.'" The beauty of its wares hinge on traditional Nepalese designs and handmade Lokta paper, which is made from the trimmings of a bush of the same name. Hence, the journals, note cards, stationery sets, photo albums and wrapping paper are gorgeous as well as green. Add affordability to the mix and these guys have accomplished an earth-friendly hat trick.

STATIONERY & GIFTS	WEDDINGS		

NestNaturalHome.com   443-535-0212

This "little shop with a big mission" is intent on "offering products that support independent artists, fair-trade importing, organic farming, and recycling," and the only thing we don't like about it is that part about being small. We'll go ahead and hope that the earnest Maryland boutique finds a way to build upon its tiny but stellar selection. In the meantime, we'll just have to content ourselves with the lovely recycled glass and bamboo tableware currently populating these pages.

SERVICE			

NestPlease.com   413-467-2086

Defying the misconception that products made using sustainable materials, recycled goods and fair labor practices will be lacking in style, this family-run children's furnishings manufacturer offers very appealing modern design elements for your brethren's healthy, green bedroom. Though the selection is small, it definitely consists of kid-sized furniture and storage items that everyone in the house will love, and should be durable enough to pass on. .

CHILDREN	FURNISHINGS		

NigelsEcoStore.com

44-800-288-8970

Nigel's just a British guy who wants the best sustainable options available to serve the needs of his lifestyle. That's what makes this UK store special; its unerring devotion to finding interesting, unique and functional products that will take some of the environmental sting out of your daily routine. Considering the transatlantic shipping costs and unfavorable exchange rates with the pound sterling, you'll probably want to be cautious about ordering products you could find at home, but there are a few here even we haven't seen before, and considering the effort Nigel's put into his catalog, you can at the very least get some nice ideas.

ACCESSORIES HOUSEHOLD	APPLIANCES OFFICE	FURNISHINGS STATIONERY & GIFTS

NimanRanch.com

510-808-0340

To the carnivores among us, merely to mention a great selection of ribs, roasts, steaks, chops and braising cuts is mouth-watering enough. So imagine the results of invoking "the finest tasting meat in the world" cut from "livestock [that] are never given growth hormones or sub-therapeutic anti-biotics" might be. From the sound of it, this is meat as pure as it gets, and to be sure this beef, pork and lamb, culled from a sustainable ranch in Northern California, will arrive about as fresh and tasty as the postal system allows. If you live next to a slaughterhouse, you're set. Otherwise, this one's worth considering.

EPICUREAN		

NordicWoollens.com

877-858-9665

The long underwear, baby layette and cloth diapers found here aren't from Norway, they're from Canada. Not only that, but they're not necessarily made of wool. However, all of these ultra-comfy undergarments consist of fabrics culled in "an ecologically sensitive manner... devoid of any chemical processing." So whether they're merino, organic cotton, a bamboo/silk blend or some combination of the three, these base layers will keep the entire family warm in any country.

APPAREL	BABIES	FAMILY

NunoOrganic.com   914-762-6159

No need to look to European retailers to find continental baby accessories, apparel and toys, because this Danish brand distributes its adorable wares through an office in NYC. The organic layette, toddler's clothes, baby blankets, pajamas, booties and bonnets don't rely on bright colors or cartoon characters to call attention to themselves; they are just cute, sustainably-made basics to wear around the house or to social occasions. In the toys category, standouts include organic plush dolls, along with nontoxic crayons and paints, assuring your children can live and play without exposure to industrial chemicals.

ACCESSORIES STATIONERY & GIFTS	APPAREL	BABIES

OfficeDepot.com   888-284-3638

As you may be well aware, this chain carries a lot of products that can hardly be considered earth-friendly. In fact, looking at this home page you might never guess the company has endeavored to support the environment. However, enter any product category and you should be able to find a Featured Stores menu that includes a handy Buy Green link. This section lets you focus on a healthy variety of office supply products, whether energy efficient, nontoxic or made in part from recycled materials. It's not ideal, but buy online and you may pick up your order locally, cutting down on packaging waste, which is good business sense.

OFFICE		

OliviaLuca.com   503-753-2787

Having your clothes custom-made is one way to ensure you can dress in sustainable fabrics, and this rather intriguing site makes it easy to do just that. While it recommends you are measured professionally before ordering, and only shows illustrations of the various formal dress and skirt designs, it makes up for all of it by offering a wide assortment of fabrics and colors, as well as wedding appropriate garments and maternity dresses. Selecting a silk, hemp, organic cotton or tencel blend is up to you, but the result will be a great-fitting, eco-friendly gown just for you—brides take note!

ACCESSORIES WEDDINGS	APPAREL WOMEN	MATERNITY

OnlyNaturalPet.com

888-937-6677

Doing right by your dog or cat doesn't have to mean forsaking your earthly values, which is made abundantly clear in this online pet shop that promotes such things as organic diet and holistic remedies. Covering a wide range of grooming and nutritional needs, the entire catalog is promoted as all-natural, whether you're searching for flea shampoos, cat litter or vitamins. The dog and cat food selections are so great that organic options get special categories, meaning there's plenty more to choose from if Fido or Fluffy don't like your initial selection.

PETS		

Oompa.com

888-825-4109

Determined to find toys free of synthetic materials and unnatural finishes for her young children, the founder of this site turned to Europe, where she found a great bounty of playthings for kids six and under. Here she offers them in terrific fashion, without plastics, covering a wide range of fun including organic plush dolls, wooden toys, pretend play, ride-ons, art supplies and educational puzzles and games. Even exposed to television and movies, kids will find satisfaction and joy in these great gifts that are sure to inspire, and always safe to have around.

BABIES	CHILDREN	STATIONERY & GIFTS

OrganicBouquet.com

877-899-2468

There are dozens of great places online to shop for floral arrangements and boxes of chocolates, so how can you choose? Well, if you like to encourage organic and other ecologically sustainable growing practices, this shop wins hands down. With fine bouquets of roses, lilies, tulips and more, this proves a satisfying and easy way to promote your environmental agenda without sacrifice. The flowers look absolutely gorgeous, of course, and while we can't vouch for the flavor of the chocolates, they are also beautifully presented and will surely taste delicious to the green sweet tooth.

EPICUREAN	STATIONERY & GIFTS	

OrganicFruitsAndNuts.com   760-749-1133

Raw, whole and organic foods are available on this not very slick looking site, and it's much easier than it seems at first to find them. It's not all dried fruits and nuts, either, although these definitely make up some of the better-stocked categories. But you'll also get bulk grains, beans, spices, pastas, trail mix, oils, vinegars, candies and baking ingredients. As healthy as it is earth-friendly, the selection might take a little getting used to if you're accustomed to ready-made, flavored snacks and food out of a can, but if want nutrition, look no further.

EPICUREAN		

OrganicSelections.com   888-216-9917

You've probably shopped for organic clothes, eaten organic foods and even brushed your teeth with organic toothpaste. But if you'd like to see the full breadth of products that may be manufactured using organic materials, take a look at this site. The family-owned, Iowa-based department store offers an incredibly varied assortment of goods ranging from housewares and linens to accessories and apparel for every member of the family. Aside from certified organic items, you'll notice various all-natural, nontoxic, recycled and sustainably sourced products, any of which you'd feel good about buying, all at once, to minimize packaging.

ACCESSORIES FURNISHINGS	APPAREL HEALTH & BEAUTY	FAMILY STATIONERY & GIFTS

OrganicVintners.com   800-216-3898

Offering "the best-tasting international wines from the best organic wineries in the world," this site is an eco-friendly epicurean's dream come true. The shop's proprietors believe in healthy as well as fine living, and though you won't find those bottles coveted by serious collectors, you will find good taste. The flat-rate shipping policy and further discounts on bulk orders will encourage you to try a wide variety to start, after which you may even make organics your top choice for everyday sipping wines.

EPICUREAN		

310-666-8675

OrganicWearUSA.com

Though it may sound like an organic basics retailer, this small Los Angeles store is actually more of a baby gift shop. With a narrow but lovely range of 100% organic, naturally processed cotton and wool products, it will take you no time at all to browse the selection of healthy, ecological baby gift sets, clothes, blankets, bedding and toys. Highlights include a simple, double-breasted suit for infants and a soft sheep music box that plays "Sleep Baby Sleep."

APPAREL	BABIES	STATIONERY & GIFTS

541-347-3326

OrganicWinePress.com

Leave it to this small coastal Oregon retailer to track down domestic and international organic wines for your enjoyment. Freely pointing out that in the past two decades, wine aficionados have been slow to come around to the concept of sustainable production, and that an "organic wine label has gone from working against the wine, to becoming a big plus." Featuring a small but pleasurable variety, we can only hope this shop, and others like it, might provide a place for a new breed of environmentalist connoisseur.

EPICUREAN		

203-364-1484

OurGreenHouse.com

Grown organically out of an environmental testing company, the wide but limited selection of this house and family site features products used by these professionals to help people "keep their homes safe." Basically, while you may forfeit a modicum of choice here, you can rest easy with the knowledge that by shopping here, you're turning your home into a natural, nontoxic place. The exceptions to this are a lovely assortment of baby clothes and a great variety of cleaning products. Guess which of these we think are adorable.

BABIES HEALTH & BEAUTY	FAMILY HOUSEHOLD	GARDENING PETS

Pangaya.com   800-872-6618

Here's an "online eco-chic retailer that cares about two things: sustainability and fashion." It may sound a bit blunt, but in selecting fashions by some of the better eco-friendly clothing labels out there, their simply stated efforts clearly pay off. In fact, you'll even notice a little bit of overflow into the area of dinnerware. However, clothes reign here, whether you're looking for something appropriate for exercise or that first date with a fellow environmentalist—see if he can tell you're dressed all green.

ACCESSORIES	APPAREL	FURNISHINGS
SERVICE	SPORTING GOODS	WOMEN

PangeaOrganics.com   877-679-5854

Offering a product line "as honest as it is organic," this "ecocentric bodycare" producer thoroughly details its ingredients list to assuage any concerns you may have about what touches your skin, and it's little wonder the small company is quickly garnering a global following. However, as positive as its internal practices are, the brand's strong reputation probably has as much to do with the quality of its cleansers, soaps, toners and creams. You may even find the occasional 'conventional' aesthetician recommending Pangea—not because it's all-natural, but because it puts most synthetic beauty products to shame.

HEALTH & BEAUTY		

PaperBagPrincess.com   310-358-1985

If you get excited by names like Prada, Chanel, Galliano, Gaultier, Pucci, Versace and Dior, this site will excite you. Vintage dresses and gowns get the most notice, as do some suits that might just be too good for any office. Shopping on this busy site turns out to be slow loading, but otherwise easy, even if you want to shop secondhand designer fashions that have been consigned by some popular celebrities. We'll let the celebrities in question remain a mystery. Suffice it to say that poor taste has nothing to do with their contributions to this fascinating shop.

APPAREL	WOMEN	

800-340-4631 **Paporganics.com**

"Inspired by the idea that environmentally sound paper can be beautiful too," this greeting card and wrapping paper company succeeds on both counts. The former is accomplished printing organic cotton, hemp and recycled papers with soy and vegetable-based inks. The latter with simple, tasteful patterns and colorful fruit themes. We're particularly impressed by the eco-friendly ribbons and tissue paper, recognizing that proper disposal is a crucial step of all green gift-wrap efforts.

STATIONERY & GIFTS

800-638-6464 **Patagonia.com**

One of the bigger names in earth-friendly business, this popular outdoors outfitter continually makes great efforts to cease any practices that are detrimental to the environment. It has upgraded its shipping facilities to meet green building standards, manufactures using only organically-grown cotton and restricts its use of synthetic fibers to reclaimed and recycled fabrics. A prime example of how companies can change their ways, this one also happens to make top-quality gear for the whole family.

APPAREL | **FAMILY** | **SPORTING GOODS**
TRANSPORTATION | |

626-795-8400 **PathToFreedom.com**

Viewing themselves as "urban pioneers," the Los Angeles-area family behind this small but growing shop/organization is out to keep the frontier spirit alive by advancing the green lifestyle. Composting and water conservation products top the list of reasons to visit this site, though admittedly that list isn't very long. However, the occasional handpicked items you'll come across browsing these pages will catch your eye with its ingenuity, usefulness and/or charm, and you wouldn't be likely to find these things anywhere else, especially in your local outpost.

APPLIANCES | **GARDENING** |

PeacefulValleyGreetings.com   866-626-3321

Driven by a love of nature, the proprietor of this Oregon e-tailer seeks out "unique gifts and specialty items made with a conscience" to populate her site. The result is an eco-friendly gift shop offering recycled and sustainably produced wares for each member of the family. Although any particular category will only offer a few products, quick perusal should guide you to something suitable to the occasion; if not, simply browse on to the next section and find it there (your best bets are the jewelry, stationery, journals and gift wrap).

ACCESSORIES STATIONERY & GIFTS	FAMILY	FURNISHINGS

PeopleTree.co.uk   44-20-7739-0660

Quietly operating out of the UK, this small apparel shop delivers some great and (despite the currency exchange rate) affordable men's and women's fashions. Devoted to fair trade practices and organic cotton, the site makes room for incoming seasonal collections by rotating older designs out with some excellent clearance discounts. The results are spectacular, whether you're trying to keep abreast of current trends with a green mind, or simply looking for something good that you can't find domestically.

APPAREL	MEN	WOMEN

PerformanceBike.com   800-727-2433

A great selection of bikes makes this a good place to get your cycling career started, or at least to help you kick it up a level or two. Otherwise, you can always shop by part, building your dream ride piece by piece, or peruse the Outlet section for good deals. They also feature special store for female riders, and a family store with cool rides for youngsters, including some sturdy strollers and bike-trailers that will help you cart things around town and more completely make the transition away from your car.

TRANSPORTATION		

PixelModernPieces.com

213-746-0024

When it comes to people, cool and friendly too rarely go together. But whether your interior decorating tastes prioritize cool looks or environmental friendliness, this small green furniture manufacturer has you covered. With hip modern pieces to go with some pretty slick bedding, there's not a lot to view yet plenty to like. And that's not even considering the baby half of the site, which is cool enough for the next generation.

BABIES	FAMILY	FURNISHINGS

PlanetNatural.com

800-289-6656

If all the necessary supplies for earth-friendly, organic gardening and lawn care are what you want, visit this massive Montana retailer. Or, if you're one of the roughly 299 million Americans that don't live in Montana, visit this, its well-assembled web site. Featuring push mowers, organic fertilizer, composting bins, greenhouse equipment, nontoxic pest control and more, your first visit may not be enough, as it will surely entrench you deeper in the world of gardening. No need to worry, though, as your needs advance, the site will still be here to serve them.

GARDENING	HOUSEHOLD	

PlanetReworks.com

804-502-1539

Here's a site offering a fine selection of "old tires, typewriter parts, broken windows, wine bottles, and junk mail." No kidding. Fortunately, these detritus of the consumer wasteland have been reclaimed and refashioned into stylish personal and home accessories. You'll find such things as handbags crafted from billboard vinyl, garden accents constructed from recycled aluminum, glassware made from wine bottles and myriad objects created with old LP's. Surprisingly stylish, these are fashion statements that actually make a statement.

ACCESSORIES MEN	FURNISHINGS WOMEN	GARDENING

PlantablePaper.com

760-271-1727

This small Malibu, California stationer offers only three general products, but the concept behind them is so ingenious you'll probably be interested in at least two of them. The note cards and wrapping paper will feel special on any occasion, whereas the party favors may require an occasion to make special. All are made from recycled cotton, infused with "flower petals and other natural inclusions," and embedded with wildflower seeds. This means they can be planted, paper and all, and rather than pollute the earth, will make it more beautiful.

STATIONERY & GIFTS

PMOrganics.com

703-627-1512

Crafty souls on the lookout for sustainable fabrics will want to know about this textiles specialist, which began as a cooperative of work-at-home moms "who got together to purchase a large quantity of organic fabrics at wholesale prices." They found a small variety of knits and weaves of organic cotton, hemp and tencel blends, including a small variety of natural patterns and bright colors. Today, it's these same women offering close to wholesale prices online, ensuring industrious people everywhere can go green.

CRAFTS & HOBBIES

PoshVintage.com

305-609-6398

If you have a taste for vintage styles and nurture a healthy appreciation for high fashion, this may quickly become your favorite site. Browsing here is done on a one product per page basis and, though each garment is beautifully presented from multiple angles, if you try to click through the entire selection, you may wear yourself out. However, all is not as difficult as it seems. Select the Start Show link within each category, and you can sit back and watch the vintage designer dresses, jackets, lingerie or tops and bottoms flash by like a slide show, which actually works beautifully, and turns out to be quite an enjoyable experience.

APPAREL | **WOMEN**

800-488-4340

Positive-Energy.com

Behind the uplifting name of this conservation site is the urge to actually reduce the amount of energy we're consuming, primarily when it comes to heating and cooling our home environment. With products such as tankless water heaters, energy saving ventilation systems and programmable thermostats. Some of these products involve a heftier price tag than comparable, less-efficient models, but reduction in gas and electricity consumption will be priceless.

APPLIANCES	BUILDING SUPPLY	

800-557-7262

Prana.com

Athletic apparel is generally not known for its reliance upon natural materials; advancements in the way synthetic materials wick, insulate, breathe and fit have long since seen to that. However, this innovative manufacturer has taken a renewed interest in reversing the trend. Among the yoga, outdoor and sporty casual apparel here, you'll find sections devoted to 100% organic materials. Look elsewhere on the easy-to-browse site and you'll come across other garments and accessories that although not necessarily all-natural, make up for it by trying to incorporate only recycled plastics.

APPAREL WOMEN	MEN	SPORTING GOODS

866-776-4543

ProgressiveKid.com

You're rarely going to come across a shop this fun that also promotes conservation and diversity to children. Somehow, through its assortment of games, graphic t-shirts, picture books, party packs and lead-free lunch sacks, it manages to make the world a better place for kids while teaching them to make the world a better place, and without ever being pedantic (well, rarely). Though every single product on this site may not be organic or even all-natural, the shop's policies and product selection is all about positive impact, both on the planet and its children, and in that sense it's hard to go wrong with this outstanding green e-tailer.

ACCESSORIES CHILDREN	APPAREL STATIONERY & GIFTS	BABIES

PupLife.com
773-620-0050

Though myriad products carried by this Michigan-based online retailer will delight pets and owners alike, we're particularly drawn to the site's Earth Friendly section. Amid scattered natural and organic soaps, treats and foods you will find one of the web's better variety of eco-friendly dog and cat beds. Choose among those made from sustainable materials or that include recycled filling, and add some gourmet doggy treats if you're feeling generous. If your eye should wander to the other parts of the store, well that's up to you.

PETS		

PurBebe.com
877-850-3313

Pampering your baby is the natural thing to do, so pampering your baby naturally must be the thing to do. This beautifully-designed site offers myriad ways to keep your tot adorable and clean without exposing him or her to anything detrimental to the planet. With a simple system in place to help you identify which bath and clothing products are made from organic materials, nontoxic ingredients and/or with fair labor practices, you may easily browse the likes of soy clothing, all-natural lotions and organic cotton accessories.

ACCESSORIES HEALTH & BEAUTY	APPAREL	BABIES

PureBeginnings.com
866-787-2229

Rarely deviating from its objective to provide 100% organic cotton bedding, apparel and accessories to globally minded families, this small baby brand keeps it all refreshingly simple on this user-friendly site. Even when it does branch out, say into wool diaper covers, plush dolls or gentle, non-toxic skin care products, you can be sure the same aesthetic and socially-conscious sensibilities apply, with classic designs, soft colors and every cozy comfort considered.

ACCESSORIES FURNISHINGS	APPAREL HEALTH & BEAUTY	BABIES

219-926-7604   PurrfectPlay.com

Striving "to use only organic, chemical free, fair-trade materials" in construction of its pet toys, collars, treats and bedding, the genuine love this small business from Indiana has for animals is obvious. Any eco-conscious dog or cat owner will be glad to have shopped here, whether you're after organic catnip toys, fair trade silver collar charms, biodegradable waste bags or hemp products ranging from chew toys and leashes to Frisbees. There are even a few adorable puppy greeting cards made of recycled fine art paper to elicit an "awww" from folks even outside America's heartland.

PETS

877-729-4367   Rawganique.com

Easily one of the most comprehensive hemp specialists anywhere, this shop takes its commitment to the Earth to levels high enough to warrant a bookmark in your web browser. The apparel alone makes your visit worthwhile, and although by far most of the certified-organic hemp products are meant for casual occasions, you might just be surprised by a bridal gown or two. The bedding, table linens and other household necessities will also impress, but if we were to pick one section that we'll be sure to visit again it's gotta be the shoes!

ACCESSORIES FURNISHINGS   **APPAREL**   **FAMILY**

800-339-9748   RealMilkPaint.com

You have only to be exposed to regular paint fumes to know that oils or acrylics contain ingredients that are unhealthy to people as well as the environment. As an alternative, take a look at this line of all-natural, organic, nontoxic paints and tung tree wood finishes. Arriving in powder form, to be mixed with water, the shipping is nevertheless a bit pricey, so it behooves you to order the brand's color stick samples first, so you may select the right hues for your home improvement project.

BUILDING SUPPLY

RecyclingBin.com   800-910-4757

One simple way to encourage recycling is to designate receptacles for your papers, plastics, metals and more. Whether it's for your kitchen, office or party venue, this single-minded company offers specially-designed bins that will streamline the recycling process for you and your guests. Special perks like self-closing lids that will "eliminate odors" and the fact the bins themselves are made of recyclable plastic give these some appeal, but they will primarily serve as a visual reminder to separate materials and minimize your contribution to the dump.

HOUSEHOLD

RedFlowerWorld.com   212-966-1994

"Entirely botanically based," and blended with "environmental consciousness," this perennially growing bath, body and fragrance line captures floral essences and utilizes the nourishing properties of the plant kingdom to create some of the most refreshing, aromatic gifts a woman could want. Particularly popular is the selection of beautiful scented candles, which reads like the inventory of an English garden.

HEALTH & BEAUTY | **STATIONERY & GIFTS**

RedSnail.com   541-482-2060

You're going to wish you'd known about this small travel specialist before your last camping trip or global excursion! The Ashland, Oregon-based retailer is wholly devoted to eco-friendly travel accessories, with a tiny but fantastic assortment of bags, travel towels, travel pillows, waterproof pouches and toiletries. The only thing we could possibly fault them for is not having more products to buy, but we'll certainly be singing their praises while shopping and planning for our next adventure.

ACCESSORIES | **TRANSPORTATION**

336-510-0585   RefreshinglyFree.com

Although founded to serve those suffering multiple chemical sensitivity, the eco-friendly implications of a shop devoid of harmful chemicals is impossible to ignore. Nontoxic health, beauty and household cleaners are found here in abundance, including cosmetics, toiletries and sensitive baby care products. The family-owned business out of North Carolina has been developed with environmental awareness in mind, because when you think about it, the Earth is sort of sensitive to some man-made chemicals as well.

HEALTH & BEAUTY	HOUSEHOLD	

800-426-4840   REI.com

Select the link marked Eco Sensitive and this popular outdoor activity retailer's web page will turn you on to their burgeoning selection of earth-friendly outdoor gear and fitness attire. Whether it's made from sustainable fabrics or recycled materials, this stuff is intended to keep you warm when you tackle extreme cold, or cool when you need to sweat. Hopefully they will eventually stock a full complement of sporting goods as well, but in the meantime they're getting off to a good start.

ACCESSORIES SPORTING GOODS	APPAREL	FAMILY

888-707-3873   ReusableBags.com

In only a quarter of a century, the common plastic bag has essentially overrun the planet, disperse by the billions every year, either winding up in a landfill or, worse, at large in the general environment. This site's aim is to hook you on reuseable alternatives—in other words, to simply use a bag you own instead of amassing your own collection of plastic trash. To that end, you'll find plenty of great recycled, hemp and organic cotton bags among this selection, often designed for explicit purposes such as carrying your groceries, lunch or produce. You have only to select your style and continue to shop wisely.

ACCESSORIES		

RobbinsPetCare.com — 916-342-4370

Taking a holistic approach to pet care, this California retailer strives "to offer product choices [that] have a positive impact on the environment." On occasion, you will find a chemical additive or something mixed in among these natural remedies; on the other hand, you may also find food dishes made from recycled products, organic chew toys, hemp collars and organic bird seed. For the most part, this well-stocked shop has the right intentions, and it should be easy to take care of minor health matters and pet basics without exposing your animal to problems that man made.

PETS

Roots.com — 800-208-0521

Although most of its products can not expressly be viewed as green, this Canadian company shows a strong commitment to the environment in its business practices and charitable commitments. And it's eco-selection is growing. Take, for example, their burgeoning collection of vegetable tanned leather accessories. Follow the Leather Bags link and click Roots Zerum Collection from the menu. The small but colorful assortment of handbags features leather manufactured with a low-impact process, and we're sure in time this company has a little more planet-friendly tricks up its sleeve.

ACCESSORIES | **MEN** | **WOMEN**

RubyLane.com — 415-864-4563

Ruby Lane serves as a virtual street where you can find a wide dispersement of unique fine art, crafts and antiques dealers, easily accessible through one site and commerce engine. Of course, things can get a little complicated and confusing, and to be frank, we're still not entirely sure how it's all organized, just that it generally works and you can definitely buy stuff here. Not only that, but some of these things are great finds, proving that there can be plenty of life left in vintage products, reducing the need for our society to manufacture something new.

FURNISHINGS | **STATIONERY & GIFTS**

RustyZipper.com

503-233-2259

There aren't many stores where you can find leisure suits, disco shirts, Hawaiian shirts, bell bottoms, swing-era skirts and hippie dresses all in one place. This is just such a store. Featuring one of the best vintage apparel selections of all times, the site takes it a step further, offering a quick-and-easy search function that allows you to pick through thousands of items by decade, clothing article, size and price range without even a second thought. Individual items are displayed well, both in text and pictures, with special note given to the garment's condition: in most cases, very cool.

| ACCESSORIES WOMEN | APPAREL | MEN |

SaffronRouge.com

866-322-3227

While you might typically associate the word "organic" with your grocer's produce section, this site proves that you can opt for sustainable beauty and health care, as well as fruits and vegetables. Products here delve into dental care, hair care, cosmetics, acne treatments and lip balms, all chemical-free and never tested on animals. It's an incredibly slick site that arranges its products by category as well as brand name, but we mostly like it because it helps to make you feel good even as you look good.

| BABIES WOMEN | HEALTH & BEAUTY | MEN |

SageBabyNYC.com

646-241-3848

Aware that parents want "only the purest materials next to their baby's skin," this New York baby brand assembles clothes, toys, bath products and even non-gassing nursery furniture to minimize a child's toxic exposure. Obviously, such actions are also great for the planet, particularly the heavy use of organics. The clothing selection starts off very basic and gets a bit more diverse as the sizes reach toddler age, when the babies apparently begin to add fashion sense to their inherent wisdom.

| APPAREL HEALTH & BEAUTY | BABIES MATERNITY | FURNISHINGS STATIONERY & GIFTS |

SameUnderneath.com

503-223-3592

As the creator of this line of sustainable men's and women's apparel points out on his MySpace page: "bamboo naturally acts like a technical fiber in that it wicks sweat, does not pill, shrink or lose color like cotton." He makes it sound like a miracle fiber, and he's maybe not far off the mark. Check out this site to see how bamboo works on you, whether you're on the lookout for some basic tees, simply stylish dresses or light jackets. With luck the seasonal offerings will grow with time, then like the quite renewable grass, grow again.

APPAREL	MEN	WOMEN

Sckoon.com

877-671-2145

Finding dozens of ways to make 100% Egyptian organic cotton adorable, this New York City baby brand delivers such things as reuseable diapers, monkey pants and kimonos for your tot. Incorporating sustainability with fair trade practices and use of low-impact dyes (or no dyes at all), the company takes an ecological turn with most of its practices, which is great for the earth, but also pretty fantastic for babies, who have enough new words and concepts to learn to add "pollution" to the list.

ACCESSORIES	APPAREL	BABIES

SeaBags.com

888-210-4244

With a very particular focus, this site's full selection will probably take you less time to view than this review will to read. Nevertheless, we feel it worthwhile to mention that all of the bags found here were created from recycled sails. As in, they once were used to catch wind and power boats through the water, or possibly as a means of escape for a pirate with a clever dagger. The latter may be unlikely, but it would serve to explain why the canvas is now better used in these stylish totes, which still often feature classy, seaworthy graphic designs.

ACCESSORIES	MEN	WOMEN

SeaVeg.com

207-565-2907

Because not all produce is grown above sea level, this terrific New England small business began sustainably harvesting sea vegetables more than a quarter century ago and has never looked back. The certified organic dulse, laver, alaria, bladderwrack, sea lettuce, nori and kelp packed an incredible nutritional punch, and the Recipes link will give you some ideas on how to incorporate small amounts of the stuff into your healthy meals with out overwhelming the flavors of your other ingredients. Done right, it can be almost surprisingly delicious.

EPICUREAN

SeedsOfChange.com

888-762-7333

The greatest thing about this site is that all of its products are ecologically sound, promoting the preservation of genetic diversity in all manner of plants. Primarily seeds are for sale here. But these seeds are the result of natural, open-pollinated plants, grown without chemical or genetic manipulation. The result is a selection of healthy, natural seeds for plants, flowers and herbs that will reproduce once mature (most commercially sold seeds don't). There's a lot of environmentally-conscious gear here as well, like watering timers and composting equipment. If you want your garden to be earth-friendly, this is the first place you should look.

GARDENING

SeelectTea.com

714-771- 3317

With an extensive assortment of teas, 100% fruit juice concentrates, noni juices, essential oils and seemingly out of place ingredients like citric acid, xylitol and food coloring, this site is borderline baffling with its selection. However, if you head straight to Premium Teas and Sante Oils, you'll find organic categories to serve you well. Surprisingly, you won't find these if you follow the Organic link from the home page; that is reserved for the likes of nondairy creamer, malted barley grits, snow cone syrups and vanilla beans. We'll take the oddities, though, because there's also a delectable assortment of organic smoothies to be found.

EPICUREAN

SelfIndulgence.net
800-982-0088

Shop the Organic section of this confectioner site to find a small but delicious-
and absolutely indulgent looking selection of truffles. The hardest part about
shopping here will be avoiding the temptation of the rest of the selection, which
may not be entirely necessary being as it's sometimes vegan, sometimes includes
organic nuts and always makes you hope there's something green about it to
justify the packaging, which is beautiful but begging to be recycled.

EPICUREAN	STATIONERY & GIFTS	

ShelburneFarms.org
802-985-8686

Combining humane treatment of animals with ecologically sound agricultural
practices, this Vermont farm network aims to "cultivate a conservation ethic,"
even going so far as to offer educational programs to promote its methods. The
principal results of their labor? Maple syrup, cheddar cheese and ham. Though
limited in scope, the all-around earth-friendly nature of these products makes
them seem all the more delectable, and supporting such regional devotion to
sustainability is something we'd all definitely love to see catch on, even as it
makes our meals taste better.

EPICUREAN		

ShiftYourGift.com
917-232-8952

Easy to rely on as a source of forward-thinking, eco-friendly gifts, this shop's
selection may vary, but its principles remain the same: promote recycling,
sustainability and conservation. Of course, here, this goes hand in hand with
offering a terrific, mid-to-high-end range of gifts and gift baskets, including
some executive toys, spa products and assorted housewares. A thoughtful gift
caters to a person's likes and interests. These do you one better—they also show
you think about the planet.

STATIONERY & GIFTS		

877-597-5678 **ShirtsOfBamboo.c**

Lately, there's a good chance you've heard a lot of bamboo fibers turnir in clothes. This is no accident; the hard grass can be woven into a surpris soft material that, properly cared for (you can find instructions on this should endure as a light and flirty component of your wardrobe. This shop exclusively with the stuff, at times blended with other sustainable fabrics as organic cotton. Offering casual basics for men and women, along with choice scarves and jewelry pieces, it's a decent place to look when you people start to talk.

ACCESSORIES WOMEN	APPAREL	MEN

510-332-7056 **Shoji-Designs.c**

Finding itself a nice little sustainable niche, this site's focus is on "nat elegant embroidered table and kitchen linens" that will reduce the ar of trash you produce. Using hemp and organic cotton blends along with based dyes, the San Francisco Bay Area company offers sustainably pro cloth napkins, hand towels and lunch bags, each bearing a quaintly embroi herb or vegetable. With these on hand you'll' never need paper napkins, t or lunchbags again, and once you see how lovely cloth alternatives can be won't want to.

FURNISHINGS		

888-551-0225 **ShopAccaKappa.com**

As difficult a name as this is to say, the site operates fairly simply, guiding you to the fine-quality personal care lines by Italy's most prominent beauty brand. The line of toiletries, hair, skin, bath and spa products is "dedicated to respecting and maintaining environmental consciousness," meaning you can count on nontoxic and cruelty-free production, and hair-brushes made using reforested wood. Every little thing might not yet be verdi, but this lovy assortment of beauty products is definitely getting close.

HEALTH & BEAUTY		

ShopBlueHouse.com   877-276-1180

Taking green commerce in a bluer direction, this Baltimore store offers a wide variety of eco-friendly finds for your home and everyday use. For online shopping purposes, it acts more as a gift shop than a true lifestyle retailer, even if you decide to keep some of these gifts for yourself. With a smattering of products ranging from towels and bamboo serviceware to recycled desk accessories and LED light bulbs, you shouldn't have any trouble finding products you can get behind as an environmentalist, and it's a safe bet everything you see will also live up to you're your standards of good taste as well.

ACCESSORIES	SERVICE		STATIONERY & GIFTS

ShopEnvi.com   617-764-0771

Rejecting the notion that "all eco-friendly clothing [is] made from recycled potato sacks," the founders of this small online boutique used the internet (of all things) to find a spate of lesser known designers who mesh forward fashion with forward thinking. The result is a very small but refreshingly quirky selection of clothes and accessories—so small, in fact, that you might want to skip browsing the product categories altogether and just focus on those designers, some of which are bound to be better known in no time, with or without Google's help

APPAREL	WOMEN	

ShopEquita.com   412-353-0109

"Bridging the gap between hippie ethics and hip aesthetics," this homegrown family enterprise proves as ethically sound as it is clever. Primarily a good source of popular eco-apparel labels, the site also features a smattering of food and drink items, bath products and accessories for the forward-looking fashionista. They tell us that Pittsburgh is one of the more environmentally progressive cities in the country, and with shops like this to represent it, we have little doubt.

ACCESSORIES WOMEN	APPAREL	EPICUREAN

ShopNatural.com
520-884-0745

As "your trusted online source for natural and organic products," this web shop offers more than 6,000 products for those sensitive to the ecological problems caused by chemicals and mass production. Most of these items will be found in the Grocery section, where a simple layout doesn't immediately reveal the fact that each product page includes a written description, ingredients list and nutritional information, so shoppers can rest easy knowing their orders satisfy their own ethical and dietary restrictions, whether buying in small proportions or in bulk.

EPICUREAN | **HEALTH & BEAUTY**

SierraSolar.com
888-667-6527

Literally putting the power of sustainable living in your hands, this fascinating clean energy site makes it easy for you to turn your abode into the self-sufficient household of the future. Simpler, everyday options include long-lasting light bulbs, energy-efficient appliances and solar water heaters, while the more adventurous homeowner might opt for a not-as-bad-as-it-sounds composting toilet. However, the shop's greatest (and priciest) products actually generate electricity, making solar, wind and hydroelectric technologies available on a residential level. Say goodbye to utility bills.

APPLIANCES | **BUILDING SUPPLY**

SiliconSolar.com
800-653-8540

Making the most out of sunlight is this national company, which has been exploring solar energy solutions for the better part of a decade. Thoroughly knowledgeable about the technology behind harnessing power from the sun, these guys have assembled a valuable and varied assortment of photovoltaic products, including power sources for the home, RV's, mobile electronics and appliances. You'll even find a few more fun items like solar fountains, Christmas lights and remote control cars. Buy something here, or just learn a lot; either way it's worth a visit.

APPLIANCES | **HOUSEHOLD**

SimpleShoes.com   866-896-3708

The Simple brand of shoes will be familiar to anyone partial to comfortable, casual footwear. What you might not know is the company's Green Toe imprint, which incorporates sustainable materials into their classic, signature sandal and shoe models. Also relatively new is a small collection of bags and backpacks that utilize similar design concepts, all comprised of recycled materials and minimal packaging. There's obviously nothing flashy here, but it's easy to see this as a good thing.

ACCESSORIES	MEN	WOMEN

SimplyWoodRings.com   773-936-3936

If it's possible to pack more meaning into the great symbol of a wedding band, this unique shop has succeeded. Rather than fashion rings out of gold, this "eco-conscious wood jewelry" specialist uses a variety of responsibly sourced lumbers. The most interesting wedding band sets are made from reclaimed logs of ancient kauri trees, which grew for well over a thousand years before being preserved for 50,000. The beautifully rendered rings could be considered precious wood, occasionally threaded with precious metals, and expresses one planet size love.

ACCESSORIES WOMEN	MEN	WEDDINGS

SlingFings.com.au   61-2-6680-8633

Cited as the point where "eco meets retro," this Australian manufacturer relies on solar power, composting toilets and, for the most part, "recycled or reclaimed materials." Down Under may seem like a long way to go for fashion items, but this unique assortment of vintage style dresses, tops and handbags is at least worth a look. The company's original sling design is still among its best, and the funky patterns make for a particularly great baby sling. Finding your preferred color and pattern could be tough in this recycled-fabric-reliant brand, but the options are numerous, so a little patience goes a long way too.

ACCESSORIES	APPAREL	WOMEN

SmallFlower.com
800-252-0275

While this Chicago apothecary has only been online for less than a decade, it's been in business for more than a century. Though the site is by no means technologically advanced, its selection has kept up with an ever-changing world of beauty and hygiene, without losing sight of the time-tested, all-natural toiletries, dental health, makeup, bath, skin and hair products that have helped the store flourish for so long. We're particularly glad to find them online as, frankly, we're not sure if their aging building can safely house the huge amount of health and personal care products we found here. It could be all you need.

BABIES MEN	HEALTH & BEAUTY WOMEN	MATERNITY

SmartHome.com
800-762-7846

Home automation isn't the first thing that leaps to mind when you think of the environment, but making your home a little smarter can help you conserve energy and better control your household's passive heating/cooling capabilities. You can program your curtains to open or close with the sun, lights to turn off when no one's around or simply add dimmers to reduce energy consumption. If you're not convinced, just check out the shop's Solar & Energy Savers section to see what water-and-power efficient products turn up.

APPLIANCES	BUILDING SUPPLY	

Solardyne.com
503-830-8739

Whether you're focused on solar energy, wind power, energy efficiency, water conservation or all of the above, this small Oregon-based company can help. The name makes it sound as if it came right out of science fiction, and products like UV water sterilizers, tankless water heaters and solar freezers would seem to back up the idea. However, these products are quite real, and can help make your home efficient and even self-sufficient. Don't go into the future without them.

APPLIANCES		

Speesees.com 415-552-5808

Though limited in product selection, this small baby brand out of San Francisco is so dedicated to the concepts of sustainability and fair trade that you won't want to miss it. Um, it helps that the layette, toddler attire and bonnets are adorable as well. The organic cotton items are grown, colored with herbal dyes and manufactured in small Indian villages, where employees receive a living wage and health benefits, with a portion of the profits donated to support local schools. However, you'll probably remember it most as a lovely place to shop for baby gifts.

ACCESSORIES	APPAREL	BABIES

Spinnery.com 800-321-9665

For the past twenty-five years, this Vermont spinnery has been exploring "environmentally sound ways to process natural fibers." The result is the lovely little "worker-owned operative" behind this simple but very worthwhile web shop. The sustainably produced, vegetable-dyed and chemical-free yarns here may green, but you'll actually a great variety of colors and textures, most of them soft and luxurious to the touch. Eco-conscious knitting enthusiasts will rarely do better.

CRAFTS & HOBBIES		

SpiritOfNature.co.uk 44-870-725-9885

This well-stocked planet-friendly UK shop might overwhelm you from time to time as you try to navigate its many pages and widely varied selection, so we'll tell you the best products here, which might warrant looking across the Atlantic to order. First off, they have organic maternity clothes—not a lot, but they are hard to find elsewhere yet. You'll also find some bamboo lingerie, organic cosmetics, green grooming tools and some great biodegradable disposable nappies, also known as diapers.

APPAREL HOUSEHOLD	BABIES MATERNITY	HEALTH & BEAUTY WOMEN

888-775-3555 **SqueakyMonroe.com**

If you want to switch to natural and nontoxic personal care products, but don't trust yourself to choose brands that are both safe for the environment and effective for your body, do yourself the favor of checking out this earnest small business. Its handpicked selection is entirely "plant-based, renewable, and free of petroleum or synthetic preservatives." When you're talking about such relaxing stuff as massage items, hair treatments, skin care, bath additives and all manner of fragrant soaps, it's only tough to be disappointed.

HEALTH & BEAUTY

805-641-3286 **StewartBrown.com**

Wearing premium knits is always a pleasure, but somehow Mongolian cashmeres and Peruvian merino wools feel all the softer when you know they come from gently-raised livestock. This eco-aware brand offers just such beautiful knits, as well as a great assortment of organic cotton garments made using low-impact techniques. Any way you look at it, you'll find guilt-free, luxury shopping from this mom-and-pop company store that directs a small percentage of its profits to an environmental advocacy charity.

APPAREL **WOMEN**

402-435-5176 **StrawSticksAndBricks.com**

Named for the straw bale house that inspired it, this Midwestern store was created in response to the difficulty its founders had finding green building materials. Now, seven years later, their diligent research has uncovered a wealth of partly and fully-eco alternatives to flooring, plumbing, roofing and walls, as well as a few better than conventional plywoods. Mostly comprised of sustainable or recycled materials, with some pretty great water conserving toilets thrown in, this could prove an invaluable asset to your green home, sticks, stones or otherwise, even if a few of the young site's best products require a complicated phone order.

BUILDING SUPPLY

SuiteSleep.com

866-753-3337

A comfortable night's sleep comes easier when the mattress you lie upon hasn't created a lot of pollution or waste. A sustainable ethos makes the products of this high-end sleep specialist all the sweeter, beginning with a variety of natural rubber-based mattresses and including some of the more opulent organic bed linens we've seen. If all this weren't really enough (and it is) copious amounts of information on the science of bed rest and the ecology of materials will brush you up on the ins and outs of why this is such a great shop, and at the very least will give you just the right kind of reading material to help you doze off.

FURNISHINGS

SukisNaturals.com

888-858-7854

With only a handful of products for the offering, we're enamored with this beauty line more for what it doesn't carry. In particular, a long list of unnatural, toxic and/ or pollutant ingredients listed under the Standards link, ingredients that "you will never find in suki pure skin care products." On top of being natural, many of the ingredients they do use happen to be organic, and the results are not only earth-safe, but appropriate to those suffering chemical sensitivity, eczema or other skin responses to conventional treatments. Of course, you don't need to wait for your skin to revolt to enjoy this beautiful, natural brand; you can always start now.

HEALTH & BEAUTY | **WOMEN**

SunburstTrout.com

800-673-3051

Most of us associate trout with river fishing expeditions, cooked fresh over an open campfire. Of course, the truth is many streams and rivers must now be artificially stocked with trout, as overfishing and other environmental impacts have taken their toll on the freshwater fish. Fortunately, you can get sustainable trout without need for a fish license, hooks or lures. This family business out of North Carolina operates a streamlined, low-impact fish farm of clear, unpolluted waters and they intend it to stay that way. The fresh or smoked trout and caviar might not taste as good as that you've caught yourself, but nothing ever does.

EPICUREAN

603-456-2020　　　　　　**SundanceSolar.com**

Searching for sustainable and functional solutions to your energy needs might sound like a drag, but pay a little attention to this site and you'll see how fun harnessing the sun's power can be. Along with the requisite voltaic panels, rechargeable batteries and one of the web's better assortment of long-lasting light bulbs, the solar-centric shop offers gifts, gadgets, backpacks and portable electronics accessories, saving the earth and stirring the imagination in the process.

APPLIANCES	HOUSEHOLD	TRANSPORTATION

888-269-9888　　　　　　**SunOrganicFarm.com**

This San Diego area organic foods specialist will not be winning any awards for web design any time soon. However, as a source for organic nuts, grains, dried produce, flours, oils, spices and other essential pantry items, it's pretty good. Sure, you can't find out much about any given product, let alone what it might look like, but the bare-bones approach is the result of a small business with loads to offer, competing online with limited resources, decent prices and an obvious devotion to pure, sustainable agriculture.

EPICUREAN		

800-924-5304　　　　　　**SunriseCyclery.com**

Check the Shop By Category link of this bicycle shop and you'll find triathlon models, track bikes, BMX styles and cruisers. You'll also see a great selection of road bikes, and a very interesting assortment of folding bikes. The latter offer all the urban accessibility of a road bike with the important distinction that you can easily fold them up for travel or storage. This helps solve the problem of a cramped apartment or mixed commute. It should also make carrying your bicycle upstairs less of a hazard to yourself and your neighbors. Whatever your biking need, this family-owned New York area shop has all the choices you'll need.

TRANSPORTATION		

SwedX.se

46-8-441-8444

A surprising twist to the notion of sustainable manufacture, this Swedish niche electronics manufacturer disdains the plastic casing of televisions and computer monitors in favor of wood remnants reclaimed from a cabinet factory. Obviously, a TV doesn't exist that is truly low impact, but this high-end affairs come pretty close. Their true value lies in aesthetic appeal, though, because wood grains just about always look better than molded plastic or even buffed metal.

 APPLIANCES

SweetEarthChocolates.com

805-544-7759

Ironically, these fair trade, organic, vegan and gluten-free chocolates aren't always entirely sweet—the California brand offers 65 and 72% pure cocoa "bittersweet" options for the connoisseur. Don't fret your sweet tooth, though, there are still plenty of bars, hot cocoa mixes and confections that will thoroughly satisfy your choco-lust. The small company only sources from countries offering organic and fair trade certification, and contributes a portion of profits to establish similar programs in other developing nations. In other words, they are doing something good, which, which makes their entire inventory all the sweeter.

 EPICUREAN

SweetgrassFibers.com

877-391-8936

Boasting men's and women's attire made from hemp, organic cotton and the occasional bamboo, this site's lack of variety is more than accommodated by the garments' neat and clean appeal. A particularly good spot to find skirts, shorts and trousers, you might also stumble across the likes a very nice, affordable empire waist dress or utility pants. Whichever you choose, you will have to expressly mention the eco-friendliness of this garb for anybody to notice; otherwise, nobody will be able to tell the difference.

 APPAREL   MEN   WOMEN

800-582-5122   TakuStore.com

It's amazing how something so simple as buying salmon can create a complicated ethical crisis; on the one hand, wild salmon most assuredly grew by natural means, on the other, buying salmon from fish farms ensure your purchase is not depleting an over-fished species. This site offers a happy medium: troll-caught, wild Alaskan salmon. It's genuine, unmanipulated fish caught using managed fishing methods and taken from a thriving population. At this shop, the only question that remains is whether you want it Hot Smoked, Cold Smoked or Fresh Frozen.

EPICUREAN		

13-0-73-83-86   TaneOnline.com

Do businessmen wear eco-friendly attire? Well, they can if they start shopping from this Australian manufacturer that produces quality neckwear with minimal environmental impact. A small but elegant assortment of ties are achieved by sourcing organically produced silk, which would, one presumes, involved feeding organic mulberry leaves to the silkworm. The results may not always be jaw-dropping, but remember, we're talking about ties here. They are beautiful, in their own way, and interesting without ever getting unprofessional.

ACCESSORIES	MEN	

877-325-9129   TaraLuna.com

In many ways, this Northern California "Fair Trade, Organic & Green" family business is representative of your old school environmentally-friendly shop; it's even named in part for the "Goddess of peace and protection, the Mother Creator." Many of the home accents, apparel and accessories even betray the store's hippy/bohemian roots, which in this case is a great thing, because the stuff is beautiful. You'll also find a healthy assortment of wonderful gifts for people of all ages and political leanings, and even a few for pets, proving that eco-conscious retail, as well as those of us who love it, have come a long way.

ACCESSORIES FURNISHINGS	APPAREL STATIONERY & GIFTS	BABIES WOMEN

TerraFirmaBotanicals.com   800-837-3476

Fans of herbal tinctures and tonics (and we know you're out there) will relish this homegrown Oregon business, which uses only organic and wildcrafted herbs in its healing products. Even skeptics may want to check out the small shop to get a first taste of the natural health alternative. If nothing else, you might enjoy the rich variety of massage oils. Get used to these and you may just be back for sore muscles salves, then eventually immunity bolsters, then before you know it your medicine cabinet could be completely refurnished.

HEALTH & BEAUTY

TerraPlana.com   44-207-379-5959

If you really wish to tread lightly upon this earth, take a look at this UK footwear company that "aims to be the most innovative and sustainable designer shoe brand in the world." Employing vegetable tanned leather and recycles materials taken from (among other things) blue jeans, car seats, coffee bags and foam bed, the brand delivers sneakers, pumps, flats, slip-ons and sandals that come pretty close to meeting its goals. Stylish as well as activist, there may not be a lot of designs to choose from, but the fact we have to look across the Atlantic to find them speaks volumes.

ACCESSORIES   **MEN**   **WOMEN**

ThanksgivingCoffee.com   800-648-6491

Two simple categories are available for perusal on this coffee site: Organic and Fair Trade. Truth is, you'll find a hefty overlap, with even the occasional Kosher selection. Featuring a variety of global sources, coffee fanatics may delight in trying the dozens of available roasts, and environmentalists will take pleasure in the knowledge they're supporting a business operating on low impact principles that includes the use of energy efficient roasters, biodiesel transport trucks, diverse recycling policies and conversion to solar power.

EPICUREAN

877-876-8247   # TheBetterHealthStore.com

The name of this site illuminates a truth slowly dawning upon the American public: what's good for the earth is often better for your health. Natural, organic and nontoxic ingredients go into a wide variety of products found here, including nutritional supplements, household cleaners, health foods, over-the-counter remedies, dietary aids, toiletries, cookbooks and more. Low prices and free shipping incentives make this a great site to visit when you want to stock up on your sustainable living essentials.

EPICUREAN PETS	HEALTH & BEAUTY	HOUSEHOLD

760-340-3731   # TheBodyDeli.com

Perhaps the only line of bath and skin care that's almost good enough to eat, this stuff is not just made of all-natural products, but organic products at that. For proof, we refer you to the Ingredient Glossary. Though it includes a few off-putting names, like Ascorbyl Palmitate and Azulene, it explains how these substances are extracted from more comforting sources, like citrus fruit, chamomile, plums, roses and cacti. Thanks to this spa-quality fare, you no longer have to put anything on your skin that you wouldn't put in your stomach.

HEALTH & BEAUTY		

866-433-6426   # TheGoodDogCompany.com

Don't expect to find a huge variety when you visit this somehow incredibly complicated web site. Find your way through its bungling pages and you'll pretty much come across three things: collars, leashes and dog toys. However, these are comprised of hemp and organic cotton, as the company is committed to environmental stewardship. The real reason you'll want to check it out, though, is that this line of collars and leads offers a bit more variety than similar hemp products we're used to seeing, and thus should exclusively be the destination for dog owners who want to add a little fun to your pooch's basic look.

PETS		

The-Green-Apple.co.uk   44-2476-511056

Promising "ethical shopping at its most stylish," this UK green e-tailer isn't far off the mark. Though its overseas shipping policy gets a little tricky for anything much bigger than a shirt, this leaves just about enough room to take advantage of the site's hip apparel options, including some organic cotton t-shirts and jeans. Anything beyond that and you'll want to email customer service before committing to an order—but take a look around and you might consider doing it anyway.

APPAREL STATIONERY & GIFTS	BABIES	FAMILY

TheGreenLoop.com   866-898-5483

All the products you'll find on this forward thinking site "are made by conscientious companies who are committed to environmental stewardship and social responsibility," and we're here to tell you that this turns out way better than it sounds. More closely resembling a Hollywood fashion boutique than an eco-shop, this store (actually based in Oregon) features upscale and designer apparel and accessories for men, women and children, as well as cosmetics, body and skin care products. Activism's never looks so good.

ACCESSORIES MEN	APPAREL WOMEN	HEALTH & BEAUTY

TheGreenOffice.com   800-909-9750

Although this altruistic office supply store makes an earnest effort to feature sustainable products and a host of green online resources, we hesitate to call it an entirely earth-friendly shop due to the sheer volume of conventional products it also sells. However, the site does make it perfectly clear which of its wares are biodegradable, energy efficient or made from recycled materials, and which are not, and when eco-products are simply not available it encourages buying items made by companies that have made a commitment to the environment. In other words: to make a statement.

APPLIANCES	HOUSEHOLD	OFFICE

631-477-3671   **TheGroovyMind.com**

"Trading in higher consciousness," this organic and fair trade gift shop may not be easy on the eyes, and it won't give you a comprehensive variety of gifting options. However, it does offer some eco-friendly gift baskets that will work in a pinch. These usually include some combination of organic chocolates, coffees and cookies and choosing between them should be a quick matter, so you can get that nagging gift order out of the way and turn your mind to other things, or back to nothing at all.

EPICUREAN	STATIONERY & GIFTS		

866-437-9729   **TheHonestKitchen.com**

If your dog or cat has been giving you "the look" every time you fill its food dish, maybe it's time to upgrade to something healthy, natural and delicious. This brand, for example, which uses only "organic grains, hormone/antibiotic-free meats and non-GMO produce." In other words, real food that any animal would crazy not to wolf down—in fact, since "all ingredients are guaranteed 100% Human Food Grade," it might be a good idea not to feed this to your pets on an empty stomach.

PETS			

888-986-6676   **TheMonsoonGroup.com**

Put together by "Two Gals in a Hot Pink Woodshed in Vermont," this small business shows us exactly what can be accomplished when people commit themselves to using recycled materials in manufacturing. Comprised of discarded packaging from products such as laundry detergent and toothpaste, this small line of bags, trash cans, umbrellas and slippers also makes a statement about the intrinsic wastefulness of our consumer culture. Here you can take a first step in being part of the solution.

ACCESSORIES	HOUSEHOLD		

TheNaturalStore.co.uk   44-1273-746-781

If you ever get the feeling you're seeing the same eco-fashions over and over, make a bee-line for this UK site that offers something a bit different. Actually, it offers a lot of things, and all the little differences add up to something great. It begins with a fantastic array of lingerie, as such playful, yet elegant green designs are hard to come by this side of the Atlantic. But the same certainly holds true with the whole range of womens' apparel and accessories, and also with truly adorable children's attire, men's shoes or shirts, and some distinctly European cleaning tools.

ACCESSORIES FAMILY	APPAREL HEALTH & BEAUTY	BABIES HOUSEHOLD

TheOrganicBistro.com   480-664-8729

"Organic ingredients, thoughtfully combined with optimal nutrition in mind." These words kind of sum up what most of us are looking for in a healthy, sustainable meal. It's also exactly what this small company provides, along with the convenience of a prepared dinner. Six delectable meals include Ginger Chicken, Savory Turkey and Wild Salmon, with hopefully more varieties to come. Each are flash frozen and sent in bulk orders to your door, ready to stock your freezer and satisfy any time you desire a balanced dinner but don't have time to make it yourself.

EPICUREAN		

TheOrganicWineCompany.com   888-326-9463

Intending to take the morning-after headaches out of wine, the French-born siblings behind this site picked up the organic tradition begun on their grandfather's vineyard and have expanded it, decades later, with this San Francisco-based wine specialist. Proclaiming, "we can only sell what we actually enjoy drinking ourselves," the two have personally tasted wines from all over the planet, selecting only the best from "France, Italy, Spain, Portugal, New Zealand and even California!" The result is a well-regarded variety of minimally preserved organic wines that will please your palate—without any unpleasant side-effects!

EPICUREAN		

541-388-3637   **TheSolarStore.com**

The next time you find yourself sweating and burning in the summer sun, take it as a reminder that you could be using this light and heat to improve the efficiency of your home, save a little on energy costs and reduce your carbon footprint. Then check out this terrific solar power web shop. While similar sites focus on large, pricey solar panels to lay on your rooftop, this store also includes more modest applications of the technology, including solar powered fans and vents, outdoor lighting, garden fountains and water heaters. At least something positive can come from global warming.

APPLIANCES TRANSPORTATION	BUILDING SUPPLY	GARDENING

888-653-7883   **TIAS.com**

This site houses an enormous conglomeration of shops from all over the western hemisphere, each offering its own, unique selection of antiques and collectibles. The result is an original and extensive, although very convoluted, design. The only real problem is that while all stores reside on the TIAS server, you can only purchase from them one by one. So, if you want to buy a Kiss lunchbox and a vintage doorknob all at once, you're out of luck. If, on the other hand, you're open to buying trinkets from these shops, one at a time, it's great to know somebody's keeping them out of the landfill.

FURNISHINGS	STATIONERY & GIFTS	

202-832-4000   **TibetCollection.com**

Few places on Earth inspire as much consciousness and imagination as Tibet, and as it's usually thought of as a Buddhist spiritual center or as a cause for human sovereignty, we rarely see it as a source of consumer items. However, this certified fair trade dealer offers a rare glimpse at the country's beautiful cultural artifacts while actually supporting Tibetan refugees in India and Nepal. While the products include handmade incense boxes, massage stones and ceremonial chimes, foremost are the journals, stationery, gift wrap and other paper items made from lokta, a sustainably harvested natural fiber. You'll rarely see better.

STATIONERY & GIFTS		

TingLondon.com   44-20-7734

"Crafted using salvaged materials," it may not sound like the belts, bags, wallets and luggage of this upscale UK manufacturer are of a better quality than their conventional counterparts, but one glance at these items is all it takes to convince you otherwise. Using vegetable-tanned leather, reclaimed leather belts and seatbelts, for starters, these guys craft a strikingly beautiful collection of wares with high style in mind. Even if you don't buy something right away, the memory of these ultra-stylish accessories will be enough to bring you back for a second look.

ACCESSORIES WOMEN	MEN	TRANSPORTATION

TinyBirdOrganics.com   512-535-0514

What might be the least inspiring home page in all of e-commerce welcomes you to this deceptively boring site. It's simply a menu; a text list of product categories ranging from cloth diaper selections to natural toys and baby bedding. Don't be fooled. Follow these links and you will find a stellar selection of adorable, mostly organic products for infants and toddlers, bolstered by great pictures and detailed descriptions written by the shop's devoted "work at home mom" proprietors. Log on, and support a delightful small business.

ACCESSORIES FURNISHINGS	APPAREL	BABIES

TotallyBamboo.com   818-765-9000

Lighter and more durable than porcelain, bamboo seems in many ways a superior material when it comes to making plates and service accessories. Add the fact that the fast growing grass is highly sustainable, continuing to grow from the roots when it's cut, one begins to wonder why ceramics and plastics are still more common. Cutting boards, bowls, trays, chopsticks, sushi plates and a variety of kitchen tools make this a shop not to be missed. Bamboo: it's totally not just for eastern cooking anymore.

SERVICE		

877-258-0865   **ToteLeMonde.com**

Designer Tia Wou sites the "importance of versatility in fashion" as a motivating force behind a lot of her designs. Thus, you will find handbags that turn into backpacks, which can be converted into totes, which may be worn as a shoulder bag and etc. Whether convertible or not, these great designer bags are constructed of a propriety recycled plastic weave. If quality breeds success, success should be close behind this selection.

ACCESSORIES	MEN	WOMEN

805-798-0299   **ToyMobile.com**

With a variety of fun toys, dolls and games made from sustainably forested wood, organic fabrics, vegetable dyes and paints and avowedly nontoxic, this European toy distributor based in central California does it right. Children of all ages will delight in this selection, which is always on par with fair trade and safety standards and in most cases charming as can be. We love to promote an earnest, family-run business such as this, and truly think shopping here will become a habit you won't want to break.

BABIES	CHILDREN	

800-873-4960   **TreeBlocks.com**

Balancing "nature's elegance and the ingenuity of humankind," this small, unique manufacturer out of Santa Barbara, California, offers building blocks and educational toys you won't likely forget. Made from the discarded bits and branches of managed forest lumber, theses toys are so sustainably produced that they still look like the bits and branches. However, they have been intricately cut and polished so that the unusual shapes will stack up against any traditional geometric blocks. Earth-friendly and highly educational, they promise to be the kind of toys "you'll be playing with long after the kids have gone to bed."

CHILDREN		

TreeGivers.com   800-862-8733

Finally a gift for the person who has everything: a tree. Not a tree for the yard or garden, but a tree planted somewhere on the planet, in a place that needs it. Basically, by shopping here you are supporting reforestation efforts and helping to plant trees around the globe where deforestation has left microclimates reeling. If you know somebody who is concerned about the depletion of our natural resources, you may buy a tree in their name, and they will receive a certificate in the mail letting them know that you get it, that their interest has been acted upon and quite literally taken root. Hopefully, it's a gift that will outlive us all.

| STATIONERY & GIFTS | | |

TreeInABox.com   800-343-2313

One way to counter deforestation is to plant a tree. This sounds great, but how many people actually get around to it? Savvy use of this clunky, narrowly focused web shop could actually make a difference, as it offers just what it says: a tree in a box. Actually, what it offers is a tree seed, packaged with necessary nutrients in a biodegradable pot. This affordable gift and/or party favor will grow, with minimal attention, into one of a variety of trees, and must eventually be planted in the ground. Plant one on a newborn's birthday, or have your wedding guests celebrate the growth of your marriage while giving back to the earth and its atmosphere.

| BABIES WEDDINGS | GARDENING | STATIONERY & GIFTS |

TsarNicoulai.com   800-952-2842

Enjoying caviar is the key to enjoying this gourmet specialist and, to the uninitiated, the beautiful little pyramids of roe pictured on the site may not seem appetizing. To those of us who know, however, they could not seem more delicious. Despite what the company's name might suggest, most of this caviar does not hail from Russia, rather from a sustainable sturgeon farm in California. You may find some imported Sevruga caviar, along with the high prices you might expect; then again, if you're hooked on the stuff, chances are you can afford it.

| EPICUREAN | | |

800-366-3800   # Tupperware.com

Once cause for a party, Tupperware still has a place in American culture—even in the green lifestyle. Granted, the food storage containers here are made of plastic. However, this is durable, reusable plastic, which makes it a good alternative to using disposable plastic bags for the same purpose. So take it to lunch, put your leftovers in the fridge or bring it to a restaurant so you won't have to ask for a doggy bag; if it can reduce the amount of garbage you produce, it's helping you go green.

HOUSEHOLD		

812-876-9352   # TwistedLimbPaper.com

This one's easy enough to straighten out: it sells handmade invitations and other stationery made from 100% recycled cardstock. The beautiful, artistically rendered paper goods often include the option of wildflower seed inserts, but the cards and envelopes will make a beautiful statement regardless. If you'd rather not endure the long wait time for the invites, do-it-yourself kits and reams of paper are also available, but if your wedding's still a ways off, customizing these gorgeously eco-friendly invites will definitely pay off.

STATIONERY & GIFTS	WEDDINGS	

800-426-4336   # UncommonScents.com

For more than thirty years this Oregon retailer has been offering natural bath and body products including its own diverse line of fragrant oils, lotions and soaps. A long list of other brands range both in popularity and green appeal, but most generally provide safe alternatives to the synthetic, excessively packaged products typically found in your local drugstore. Whether its incense, cosmetics, massage oils, sun treatments or shaving products, this personal care superstore with modest roots knows its stuff, and has been satisfying customers for almost as long as there's been an Earth Day.

HEALTH & BEAUTY		

UnderTheCanopy.com   888-226-6799

Just how good can organic clothing look? Log on to this site to find out. "Sown and grown without the use of these chemicals," sustainably produced denim, cotton angora and soy-based fabrics contribute to its way-too-small assortment of eminently fashionable women's apparel. With luck, the company will grow, and with it the smattering of products for men, babies and the home. In the meantime, you'll definitely want to keep an eye on these stylish seasonal selections.

APPAREL WOMEN	BABIES	FURNISHINGS

UnderTheNile.com   800-710-1264

Bringing a bit of altruism into the manufacture of baby apparel, this green company offers 100-percent cotton clothing and accessories that promise to be all-natural and organic, as well as supportive of free trade practices. Does this mean these wares lack in quality? Definitely not. If you're looking for such basics as cloth diapers, layette, baby blankets, hats and bibs this site will prove a welcome sight on your internet horizon. It even offers a few similarly responsible plush toys that you can trust in your child's mouth.

ACCESSORIES	APPAREL	BABIES

UnderwoodGardens.com   815-338-6279

Representing "a rich heritage of plants which have produced tried and true results, without chemicals, for generations," this certified-organic, family-owned seed business is devoted to salvaging the lineages of the world's purest flowers, best tasting herbs, most succulent vegetables and a fourth grouping referred to only as "curiosities." We hope your interest is piqued, as ours certainly is. Shopping from this site doesn't merely endorse the concept of organic gardening; when you plant these seeds you actively nourish the earth's hard-won evolutionary splendor, which will feel as good as it smells and tastes.

GARDENING		

800-234-8327   **UptonTea.com**

With one hundred varieties of organic teas among its more than more than four hundred loose tea offerings, we wish this site made it a little easier to browse. Fortunately, there is, if you look toward the bottom of the left frame of the home page, an Organic Teas link that will send you the right direction. At that point you will have to browse meticulously to find the green, white, black, pu-erh and oolong teas you prefer. The good news is, you may opt for small samples of each tea, or select huge bags of those you know you like.

EPICUREAN

877-287-8732   **Upurea.com**

Making an effort to deliver "unique all-natural and organic products from around the world," this skin and hair care specialist actually offers a few popular brands to go with the rare ones, formulating a complete selection without inundating you with endless options. Brands like Ole Henriksen, Juice Beauty and Kimberly Sayer demonstrate a commitment to natural, nontoxic beauty care, often incorporating organic ingredients—not because it's cool but because it's safer and it works. Men, women and even expecting mothers will benefit from these cleansing, toning and moisturizing regimes, whether or not the world has yet heard of them.

HEALTH & BEAUTY

800-603-3431   **USA.EnviroSax.com**

With cities around the world restricting or outright forbidding use of the ubiquitous plastic grocery sack, now is the time to outfit yourself with a reuseable shopping bag. This shop might be a good place to start, with a wide variety of patterns covering durable, lightweight bags that carry twice the load of a paper grocery bag and fold up to fit into a tiny space, say your glove compartment. You can go one further by sticking to the Organic Series, which offers bags that are less colorful, but made from hemp and with soy-based inks.

ACCESSORIES

UsedCardboardBoxes.com   888-269-3788

Product packaging is a major source of consumption when you shop, which is why we've highlighted those sites listed in this book that make an effort to use recycled boxes to ship your orders. This unique company offers you a chance to do the same in your life. Of course, reusing boxes you receive through your online orders is a start. But if you have a greater need for packaging supply (if you're moving, for example) this site will set you up with a hefty supply of previously used cardboard boxes that represent the most efficient method of recycling: direct. The next step in these products' life cycle is up to you.

HOUSEHOLD	OFFICE	

UsedWeddingDresses.com   972-365-7603

Whether you are a budget or eco-conscious bride, it's going to be tough to overlook this jewel of a site. A gorgeous selection of used gowns, veils and tiaras makes elegance and glamour affordable to everyone, without using up any raw materials. After all, seeing as your typical bride wears this dress only once in her life, it's not like you're buying a used gown that has a lot of wear and tear. For under two hundred dollars you can have the beautiful vintage or designer wedding dress of your dreams and spend the leftover money on the honeymoon attire.

ACCESSORIES WOMEN	APPAREL	WEDDINGS

VereGoods.com   866-410-8373

Claiming to have "created a truly evolved chocolate," this Manhattan chocolatier incorporates organic ingredients, low sugar content, no artificial additives and fair labor policies into beautiful dark bars, brownies and confections that "could stand up to the world's best chocolates." Truffles, chocolate-almond clusters and wafers are promised to be rich in shade-grown cocoa, made available with assorted Vegan and Gluten-free options to make this a terrific tasty gift for even the pickiest of sweet-tooths.

EPICUREAN	STATIONERY & GIFTS	

VermontSoap.com
866-762-7482

As you might imagine, soap heads up the list of items available from this site; specifically, organic, vegetable-based soaps scented with essential oils. They are available in simple cut bars, or in bulk as large bricks you may cut yourself. However, there are plenty of other, more interesting products to be found, including a fruit and veggie wash, a yoga mat wash, incense and a nontoxic air freshener. None of these products contain artificial preservatives, foaming agents or any other questionable ingredients, making it healthy on top of smelling pretty. Oh, and you'll never guess which state this homegrown business calls home.

HEALTH & BEAUTY		

Vickerey.com
800-963-1050

Devoted to "the art of living," the proprietors of this small active lifestyle shop out of Colorado don't stock their shelves exclusively with environmentally-friendly products, but they definitely do recognize the effect sustainability can have on quality of life. Hence, among the fantastic selections of yoga apparel you will find dedicated Eco Boutiques, which feature soy, bamboo, hemp, organic and recycled fabrics. The handpicked selection also includes some particularly special journals, sketchbooks and stationery that allow your self-expression to be tree-free.

APPAREL SPORTING GOODS	HEALTH & BEAUTY STATIONERY & GIFTS	MEN WOMEN

VintageTrends.com
323-562-0065

Finally, a site willing to explain the semantic and price discrepancies between *thrift store* and *vintage* clothing. While both are used, vintage garments are "hand picked... for their quality, desirability and historical significance." In other words, only the rarest, most fashionable secondhand clothes are elevated to *vintage* status, which is why you'll like these shirts, jeans, trousers, jackets and robes. The clothes are extensively organized so browsing the dozens of subcategories may turn you off even if the prices don't, but if you can patiently appreciate this outstanding array of old garb, you'll almost certainly leave happy.

APPAREL	MEN	

VitalChoice.com   800-608-4825

Promising to sell "only sustainably harvested seafood products," this fresh and frozen fish retailer delivers with flavor, nutrition and awareness, a terrific combination. Though it can be hard to determine what constitutes sustainability when it comes to plucking fish from the ocean, here it seems to refer to fish raised in "pristine habitat and well-managed commercial fisheries" of Alaska, including scallops, crab, sashimi quality tuna and, of course, all the salmon you could want.

EPICUREAN

VivaTerra.com   800-233-6011

Driven by a "dedication to living in harmony with nature," this eco-friendly lifestyle shop manages to offer environmentally sound home products, gifts and beauty products without seeming to sacrifice anything in terms of quality or appeal. By the looks of it, this could be any small department store, except you may shop here without a twinge of liberal guilt that you're contributing to the slow degradation of the world around us, which means it's just a little bit better than any department stores we're used to.

ACCESSORIES   **EPICUREAN**   **FURNISHINGS**
SERVICE   **STATIONERY & GIFTS**   **WOMEN**

Vivavi.com   866-848-2840

With "contemporary, sustainable furniture and home furnishings for the environment-minded modern lifestyle," this Brooklyn shop takes a love of designer furniture into the new millennium, ensuring that it suits the burgeoning demand for eco-friendly products. As of this writing, the broad assortment of household items was still pretty limited, but as great as it all looks, you're bound to fall in love with something. Maybe the three-dimensional wallpaper, the cat cocoon, a nontoxic cleaning solution or one of the many inspired, highly conceptual benches. You won't know until you pay a visit.

FURNISHINGS

800-966-6546 **WalMart.com**

In a world where we are quick to condemn Wal-Mart for the destruction of all things good, we must acknowledge their efforts to change the way mass market looks at the environment and applud them for their commitment to incorporate more sustainable practices. On their site they have a section dedicated to eco-friendly products including energy efficient appliances, clothing, bedding, lighting and more. We have found a silver lining in a most unexpected place.

APPAREL FURNISHINGS	APPLIANCES HOUSEHOLD	FAMILY

888-272-8775 **WellnessGrocer.com**

All over the country, alternative grocery chains are catering to the growing demand for bulk grains, organic vegetables, chemical-free cleaners and natural supplements. However, their terrific selections aren't available online. That's where this super online market comes in. Offering "premium brands that are found in Whole Foods, Wild Oats and many independent health food stores," the site offers recycled paper goods, personal care items and basic household necessities in addition to a wealth of food. Be sure to read up on its perishable items policies, though, as the packaging may warrant special consideration.

EPICUREAN	HEALTH & BEAUTY	

707-822-7307 **WhitMcLeod.com**

Standing behind the claim that "no standing trees have been harvested for our furniture," this Northern California furniture crafter salvages old growth redwood and oak from the likes of water tanks, wine casks and the occasional demolition site. It then uses natural upholstery and finishing processes to create gorgeous (and pricey) tables and chairs that establish new standards of taste for wood furniture. As nice as the leather looks, opting for hemp canvas will boost the eco-value of these pieces, but either way you will find yourself with elegant furnishings without contributing to continued deforestation.

FURNISHINGS		

WholeLifeEssentials.com 612-408-8227

We're all used to hearing the words "natural," "pure" and "aromatherapy"—so used to it, in fact, that the founder of this small Massachusetts company claims they "have come to really mean nothing anymore." She's out to change that, though, by offering only organic and wildcrafted essential oils that have been extracted in optimal conditions by a single type of plant. The ensuing oils and blends may therefore be trusted all the way back to the roots, which is saying a lot these days.

HEALTH & BEAUTY

WildflowerOrganics.com 512-320-0449

Straight out of Austin, Texas, comes this local retailer that's long had an eye toward sustainability. The greatest selection you'll find here happens to be furniture, most of which is comprised of sustainable and nontoxic materials, whether you're shopping for your baby's nursery or the general household. However, you'll also spot some lovely bedding options, a few pretty comfy looking robes and even the odd piece of recycled jewelry. It's great to know you can buy something from the Lone Star state that has nothing to do with oil.

ACCESSORIES FURNISHINGS | **BABIES WOMEN** | **FAMILY**

WildlifeWorks.com 888-934-9453

It's pretty tough to protect the planet's wildlife by making a purchase, but that can be what you accomplish here. Promoting the concept of "Consumer Powered Conservation," this nature advocate puts proceeds from its sales towards protection of animals and their habitats. The products? Organic cotton and hemp graphic t-shirts, mostly, with a smattering of yoga wear besides. This is actually some pretty quality casual apparel, often items found on other sites we've featured. If you're going to own this stuff anyway, you might as well hope it's making a difference.

APPAREL | **MEN** | **WOMEN**

888-966-2489   WooCity.com

Though not without its problems, this Ohio company does offer one thing: certified organic ice cream. Obviously, having ice cream shipped across the country is not the best, most expedient way to enjoy the sweet dairy treat, especially when you realize that you must order a minimum of six containers in a single flavor to complete your online purchase here. On the other hand, this brand promises to raise your ice cream standards, not just in terms of sustainable production, but in taste as well, so if you have absolutely no other natural, organic ice cream recourse, now you know where to find it.

EPICUREAN		

800-776-6853   WoodSpoons.com

If you're wondering whether this e-tailer sells nothing but wooden spoons, the answer is no: it also has small selections of wood tongs and cutting boards available. You may ask yourself why Jonathan, the proprietor of this small Pennsylvania-based company, has such a deep-rooted obsession with the dullest of utensils (in relative sharpness to knives and forks, of course), but ultimately the important thing worth knowing is that these are great-looking service wares comprised of locally-sourced, managed-forest cherry wood.

SERVICE		

800-995-0154   WorldwideChild.com

It's natural for parents to want to buy their children the world, but once you realize how plastic that world is, you might change your mind. This retailer of non-synthetic toys and furniture finds most of it's wares in Europe, where stricter manufacturing standards prohibit use of potentially harmful chemicals in children's products. It sounds like common sense to us. And so does the realization that some of these brands incorporate sustainable materials and production into their creative, educational and/or simply fun toys. Happy shopping with this lovely alternative store for toddlers.

BABIES STATIONERY & GIFTS	CHILDREN	FURNISHINGS

XtraCycle.com 888-537-1401

"When it's a hassle, chore, major brain job, or just plain no-fun to use your bike for a trip or errand, it's not bicycle lifestyle." This is the message imparted by this small company based in California's Sierra Nevada foothills. It's also the reason they manufacture what they call Sport Utility Bicycles and Hitchless Trailers. The bikes feature an extended frame, which pushes back the rear wheel, making room for greater storage capacity so you can cart around food, sporting goods, a change of clothes or briefcase. The trailer kit allows you to "retrofit" your existing bicycle to this purpose, facilitating your car-free lifestyle.

TRANSPORTATION

YoloColorHouse.com 503-493-8275

With zero volatile organic compounds, this interior paint and primer brand allows you to go ahead and paint the baby's nursery without fear of toxic fumes or lingering odors. It sounds almost too good to be true, but really we can't think of a single reason why paint should require toxic elements in the first place. With forty colors to choose from, you should have no trouble finding what may be the safest, most environmentally safe paints out there. It might to be time to consider repainting the rest of the house.

BUILDING SUPPLY

YummyEarth.com 201-857-8489

Seeing as organic candy can be hard to come by, you might enjoy this small company, which focuses exclusively on lollypops and hard candy drops. With bulk orders available for children's parties, you'll have your choice of flavors, including Wet-Face Watermelon, Cheeky Lemon, Mango Tango and the ever-enticing Pomegranate Pucker. Or, you may order the simple treats in smaller quantities and try to limit access to the kids and yourself, or the sugary snacks will quickly disappear.

CHILDREN | **EPICUREAN**

727-789-4084 — Zanisa.com

Whether they exist online or in the real world, gift boutiques are meant to make it easier for you to browse for presents. Why? So we don't have to waste any time finding interesting, memorable and thoughtful items for our loved ones, of course. This beautiful site succeeds with aplomb, even when you're determined to procure a socially responsible gift. Simple iconography delineates each item among the jewelry, housewares, accessories, gourmet sweets, spa products and pet stuff as Organic, Natural, Fair Trade, Recycled and/or Sustainable, making it virtually impossible to go wrong.

ACCESSORIES HEALTH & BEAUTY	EPICUREAN STATIONERY & GIFTS	FURNISHINGS

800-251-4555 — ZapWorld.com

This last name in transportation alternatives might be the first on your lips when you're ready to switch to an electric vehicle. The first thing you notice may be the assortment of electric cars, including a pickup truck, that can travel up to 60mph. Although these may not be available online for awhile, you find a small selection of scooters that are ready to ship, and will efficiently transport you around the neighborhood on a minimal charge. Or, if your commuting needs are met, check out the electric dirt bikes and four-wheelers that might just be the future of off-road recreation.

TRANSPORTATION		

866-450-1457 — ZolaFurnishings.com

When a Washington husband-and-wife bought a handcrafted furniture company, they discovered many toxic and non-sustainable materials involved in their new business. Though it couldn't have been easy, they shifted focus to "environmentally friendly, non-petroleum based, chemical free home furnishings." The result is beautiful, low-VOC upholstered seating utilizing wood from managed forests, organic cotton, hemp and organic wool. The great looking selection is supplemented by green fabrics, and handful of eco children's furnishings, towels and the great Indika line of bedding. Change can be good.

FURNISHINGS		

product index

a

accents (for the home)

bathroom

recycled

accessories

designer

hemp

recycled

Africa products

air filters

alternative energy

alternative health

antiques

t

y

NOTES:

_____

_____

_____

_____

_____

_____

_____

_____

_____

_____

_____

_____

_____

_____

_____

_____

_____

_____

_____

_____

key word index

Use this section as a quick reference guide to help you fidn the right green selections.

ACCESSORIES: Accessories may be functional, like wallets and reusable grocery bags, or fashionable, like shoes, jewelry and scarves.

APPAREL: This mostly constitutes clothes made from sustainable fabrics, including casual, athletic, designer and even some formal garb.

APPLIANCES: This key word refers to appliances, electronics and gadgets, most of which are energy efficient, if not energy producing.

BABIES: If you're shopping for anybody under the age of three, you'll want to keep an eye out for this key word, in combination with others.

BUILDING SUPPLY: Whether you're engaging in simple home improvements or some pretty serious rebuilding, these sites will help.

CHILDREN: Sadly, there is not a huge amount of green gear for kids these days, but you will find it all with this, or the *Family* key word.

CRAFTS & HOBBIES: Ranging from sustainable yarns and fabrics to nontoxic art supplies, if you prefer your creativity to have a natural bent, look here.

EPICUREAN: Earth-friendly food and drink is ably covered by this key word, as you will find a lot of tantalizing fare, including wine and coffee.

FAMILY: When a site offers apparel, accessories, furnishings or bath products for someone of every age, we'll note it with this key word.

FURNISHINGS: Looking for furniture, home accents, bedding or bath towels? This would be the key word to watch out for.

HEALTH & BEAUTY: Beauty products make up most of the goods you'll find with this key word, with the occasional alternative health site.

HOUSEHOLD: Keeping house can be a dirty job, so we've noted all the clean, efficient, nontoxic and otherwise eco-friendly household utility products you may find with this key word.

MATERNITY: We didn't find a whole lot of green maternity apparel, so this usually refers to maternity health products and nursing apparel.

MEN: Guys might have the least trouble switching to green accessories and apparel, but some of the beauty products may be a nice surprise.

OFFICE: Your office can get greener all the time, and there are plenty of sites like these that will help at work or at home.

PETS: They may be the most earth-loving members of your household, so shop where you see this key word to let them join the movement.

SERVICE: Dinnerware, glassware, napkins and other service accessories are important to every household. Shop here to keep it green.

SPORT & OUTDOOR: Most green sports and outdoor options involve fitness apparel, but it's some darn good apparel, often using recycled synthetics.

STATIONERY & GIFTS: Whether it's sending a gift or thanking someone with a card, there's no reason our cultural customs can't be eco-friendly.

TRANSPORTATION: Getting around without burning a lot of gas might be a little easier when you shop from stores marked by this key word.

WEDDINGS: Of course your weeding can be greener! But check out **thepurplebook wedding** for more great shopping suggestions.

WOMEN: Women will not find anything lacking when they shop these clothing, accessories and beauty sites.

ACCESSORIES

APPAREL

APPAREL (CONT.)

APPLIANCES

BABIES

BUILDING SUPPLY

CHILDREN

CRAFTS & HOBBIES

EPICUREAN

FAMILY

FURNISHINGS

GARDENING

HEALTH & BEAUTY

HOUSEHOLD

HOUSEHOLD (CONT.)

MATERNITY

MEN

OFFICE

PETS

SERVICE

SPORTING GOODS

STATIONERY & GIFTS

TRANSPORTATION

WEDDINGS

WOMEN

NOTES:

_____

_____

_____

_____

_____

_____

_____

_____

_____

_____

_____

_____

_____

_____

_____

_____

_____

_____

_____

_____

company index

NOTES:

_____
_____
_____
_____
_____
_____
_____
_____
_____
_____
_____
_____
_____
_____
_____
_____
_____
_____
_____
_____
_____

NOTES:

NOTES:

_____

_____

_____

_____

_____

_____

_____

_____

_____

_____

_____

_____

_____

_____

_____

_____

_____

_____

_____

_____

thepurplebook

submissions & feedback

Submission Guidelines

Here at **thepurplebook**, we've viewed over 35,000 online retailers, and we're just getting warmed up. If you know of a site you think we haven't seen, or that may have undergone improvements since our last visit, please follow the Submissions link of our web site:

www.thepurplebook.com

Additionally, you may email us at:

submissions@thepurplebook.com

Please be sure to include the site URL in the subject line.

[NOTE: We will only consider sites operating with secure, functional online ordering capabilities. If a site has been recently updated or redesigned, please indicate the launch date of its current incarnation, so that we may be sure to re-evaluate it].

Feedback

If you have any additional comments, questions or suggestions, please or visit our site or send an email to:

feedback@thepurplebook.com

To learn how to use **thepurplebook** for corporate gifts or promotions, email us at:

editor@thepurplebook.com

Thanks in advance for your input!

www.thepurplebook.com